GENDER GAP

Gender Gap

BELLA ABZUG'S GUIDE
TO POLITICAL POWER
FOR AMERICAN WOMEN

BELLA ABZUG
WITH MIM KELBER

HOUGHTON MIFFLIN COMPANY BOSTON 1984

Library of Congress Cataloging in Publication Data

Abzug, Bella S.
    Gender gap.

    1. Women in politics—United States. 2. Political
participation—United States. 3. Voting—United States.
4. Electioneering—United States. I. Kelber, Mim.
II. Title.
HQ1236.A29   1984   324.7′088042   83-22854
ISBN 0-395-36181-8
ISBN 0-395-35484-6 (pbk.)

Printed in the United States of America

P 10 9 8 7 6 5 4 3 2 1

TO OUR DAUGHTERS
and to young women everywhere,
the future leaders of our nation

Acknowledgments

This book could not have been written without the assistance of Carol Casey, a highly experienced political scientist. She assisted us in the research on the gender-gap and electoral data, and helped to analyze the material and construct the 1984 projections. She shared with us her great fund of political information and worked closely with us throughout the many months we spent gathering material and writing this work.

Kathy Wilson, Pam Curtis, and Demetra Lambros of the National Women's Political Caucus were extremely cooperative in providing us with information about the caucus, and Wilson and Curtis kept us briefed on the activities of Republican women. Mildred Jeffrey, Koryne Horbal, Peggy Spector, Midge Costanza, and Joanne Howes helped reconstruct the history of women's efforts in the 1972, 1976, and 1980 presidential campaigns. Women members of Congress and women candidates kindly took the time to answer a detailed questionnaire about their political experiences, which we sent to them. Dr. Ruth Mandel and Kathy Stanwick at the Center for the American Woman and Politics were also very helpful in providing information about women candidates.

David Huckabee, Joseph Cantor, Leslie Gladstone, and Michael Kolakowski of the Congressional Research Service, Library of Congress, provided us with data on elections, campaign financing, members of Congress, and public opinion polls. Our thanks, too, to Dr. Barbara Farah of the University of Michigan, Dr. Ethel Klein of Harvard University, and Dr. Marjorie Lansing of the University of Michigan for providing us with information and interpretations of difficult material. Curtis Gans, head of the Center for the Study of the American Electorate, was a valuable consultant, even though he did not share our optimism about the power of the women's vote.

Kathleen Frankovic, Martin Plissner, and Elda Vale of CBS graciously provided us with polling data and analyses, as did Jeffrey Alderman and Peter Begans at ABC. Polling consultant Dotty Lynch also helped with public opinion data.

Special appreciation goes to Jack Newfield, who first suggested this book about the gender gap, and to Frances Lear, Shirley MacLaine, and Brownie Ledbetter, who encouraged the project. Our agent, Esther Newberg of International Creative Management, and our editor, Frances Tenenbaum, were endlessly patient and supportive. We also acknowledge the help of copy editor Gerry Morse, Martha Baker, Saul Rudes, Harold Holzer, Maggie Peyton, Lee Novick, Howard Brock, volunteers Chris Hodge and Leepe Joseph, who typed parts of the book, Louise Cooper, and Joan Nixon.

Finally, thanks to Martin Abzug and Harry Kelber, who fetched and carried, photocopied material, gave us moral support, and were role-model feminist husbands.

Contents

GENDER GAP

Introduction

ON NOVEMBER 9, 1982, top aides to President Ronald Reagan held an emergency session in the White House. The topic was an alarming trend that had been confirmed in the congressional and gubernatorial elections a week earlier: women were voting differently than men, and they were voting *against* the President's policies and candidates.

The phenomenon had a name: the Gender Gap.

It had been observed in the 1980 election, in which Reagan had won the presidency with eight percentage points' less support from women than from men. After two years of Reagan rule, public opinion polls and electoral results both showed that, if anything, the gap was widening. Women were becoming more opposed to Reagan's handling of the economy, foreign policy, environmental protection, and issues touching on equality of the sexes.

In the 1982 elections, more women than men voted Democratic in thirty-three of forty-four U.S. Senate and gubernatorial races. They provided the winning difference in the election of three governors and turned some Democratic victories into landslide mandates for progressive change.

Women's political power had arrived on the national scene, and the Reagan administration was worried.

Those who attended the postelection meeting in the Roosevelt Room of the White House discussed a fourteen-page analysis of the gender gap that had been hastily prepared by Ronald H. Hinckley, a poll analyst in the White House Office of Planning Evaluation. Although it was specifically addressed to two Reagan advisers, it was of urgent interest to all those concerned with the political fortunes of the President and his party.

The memo was blunt. The women's vote, it warned, "can and has been translated into electoral behavior that is not good for Republicans." In other words, the women's vote could turn the President out of the White House in 1984 and end GOP control of the U.S. Senate.

As polls continued to show eroding support, the White House clean-up squad began to work on changing the President's fading image among women voters. Female staff members were shuffled about, and some cosmetic reshaping of the Reagan persona was evident when he appointed two women to his cabinet and went so far as to devote a whole paragraph to women in his State of the Union message. Reagan's quick-change act turned out to be one of his most unconvincing performances. Every time he spoke to or about women, he got an *F* rating. By the late summer of 1983 the scenario was turning into farce, as Barbara Honegger, a Justice Department woman official who had resigned after exposing as a sham the administration's program to eliminate legal discrimination against women, was promptly derided by White House aides as an "Easter bunny" and a "munchkin."

In apparent desperation, the President turned to his daughter Maureen Reagan as a consultant, but there was no evidence that he would listen to her. Surely he knew that she was an ardent supporter of the Equal Rights Amendment, and the best piece of advice she could give him was to stop opposing constitutional equality for women?

Of course, Democratic and independent women could be expected to criticize the President, but the problem was that more and more Republican women were speaking out publicly against White House policies. Six of the nine Republican women in Congress wrote to Reagan, reminding him that "our first priority is the prompt passage of the Equal Rights Amendment." A June 1983 CBS/*New York Times* poll reported a 24 percent gap between Republican men and women on the issue of whether the President deserved a second term.

The next month, in San Antonio, Texas, Kathy Wilson, the young Republican head of the multipartisan National Women's Political Caucus, created a political sensation when she called Reagan "a dangerous man." She went further. "There is one thing President Reagan can do to help women and clean up his name with us," she said. "And that's what I ask him to do today. Mr. President, one term is enough. For the sake of American women — Republicans, Democrats, and independents — please step down. Do not seek the Republican nomination. Four years is enough. As a matter of fact, it's entirely too much."

In alarmed tones, Edward J. Rollins, the President's chief political adviser, told a meeting of the Republican Women's Leadership Forum, "The gender gap is part of an enormous wave of demographic change sweeping the country that threatens to swamp the Republican Party." He warned that "the political party that gets the women's vote will be the majority party, while the party of men will be the minority."

Meanwhile, Democratic Party officials were celebrating — perhaps prematurely — the new electoral development. Analyses of the gender gap showed that the Democrats could not take the women's vote for granted, even though women were now a majority of the party's supporters. The new women's vote is thoughtful, reflecting the values of the organized women's movement that has become a permanent part of the American landscape. It is based largely on a candidate's position on important public policy matters, not on party affiliation or whether the candidate has charm or smiles a lot.

Being a Democrat is no guarantee of election for a candidate who is a war hawk or a big military spender, or who favors cutting such domestic programs as job training, equal employment opportunities, family planning, Social Security, and pollu-

tion control, or who opposes the ERA and the right to reproductive freedom. Increasingly, these are the issues women voters care about.

For the moment, the female vote has been favoring Democrats. In 1981 pollster Louis Harris asserted that the entire
margin of the Democratic Party's popular support depended on
women. Shortly before the 1982 midterm elections Patrick Caddell, a polling analyst for the Democrats, remarked jokingly
that the best guarantee of victory for the party would be if all
the men stayed home and only women voted. He called the
gender gap "the greatest political upheaval of the century."

Ann Lewis, political director of the Democratic National
Committee, was more cautious. "The gender gap does not mean
that American women have given this party their proxy," she
said. "It means they have given us an opportunity."

The scope of that opportunity was demonstrated in a November 1983 poll by the *New York Times,* which showed that only
38 percent of women, compared with 53 percent of men, favored President Reagan's reelection, a fifteen-point gender gap,
while 52 percent of women, compared with 41 percent of men,
thought it was time "to give a new person a chance to do
better."

As Republican and Democratic political strategists ponder
the long-term meaning of the newly emerging electoral gender
gap, another gender gap remains firmly entrenched in the political structure of our nation. It is, in fact, more than a gap. It is
a wide and deep chasm that separates two contradictory realities. Women are a majority of the population, yet they hold only
a pathetically small percentage of elective and appointive
offices. Women may vote for what they hope will be compassionate and peaceful government policies, but they do not oc-
cupy the seats of power where the real decisions — about how
we are to live, and how we may die — are made.

There is, too, yet another entrenched gender gap, one that
keeps women locked up in an economic ghetto and enriches
American industry and business by billions of dollars a year.
For almost thirty years, working women have averaged only
fifty-nine cents an hour in pay for every dollar men earn. Despite all the efforts of the women's movement to achieve equal

pay for work of comparable value, that wage gap remains unchanged. True, more women are breaking past age-old barriers into male job territory, earning higher salaries, and winning pay-discrimination lawsuits, but women as a whole are a majority of the poor, and their numbers are multiplying. The widely noted "feminization of poverty" development means that the poor increasingly consist of white women, black, Hispanic, and other minority women, single women heads of households, and elderly women. The one hopeful sign is that thanks to rising feminist consciousness, women are organizing to demand their economic rights. Their new voting behavior is a product of their desire to win equality in the pay envelope as well as in the Constitution.

Whether or not the differences in voting patterns show up strongly in the 1984 or succeeding elections, whether or not Ronald Reagan or a Republican replacement runs for President, the gender-gap issues will not go away, and the distinctive political voice of women will continue to be heard, louder and stronger.

Women are a majority of Americans, and for the first time in our history they are at odds with their government on almost every important issue of foreign and domestic policy. They are constantly confronted with government actions that ignore their needs, deny their aspirations, and threaten the peace of their families and the entire world. Each day's scary headlines make them more worried and angry about the enormous gulf between what they believe should be done and what an unrepresentative government of white upper-middle-class and rich men is doing in the name of all Americans.

At this writing (fall 1983), Reagan had taken the preliminary steps toward announcing his candidacy for reelection, a move that came as opposition of women to his macho foreign policy was rising. In the national revulsion against the terrorist slaughter of young U.S. marines who had been sent by the President into the thick of the fierce, intractable tribal warfare of Lebanon, all the fears women had expressed in 1980 that Reagan would get us involved in war were being confirmed. Against the backdrop of an out-of-control nuclear arms race, U.S. military intervention in Lebanon, Grenada, Central America, and other areas raised the specter of more Vietnams and perhaps even that abiding nightmare, a nuclear calamity.

In a time of great anxiety, women have become the moral leaders of our nation, pointing an alternative direction in which we should go to assure the peace and security of our nation. In this book, I report on the significance for all Americans of the new and old gender gaps, and describe the ways women can use their newfound power at the polls to change the nation's course, and in doing so win political leadership in their own right. It is a quiet but powerful revolution, and its arena is not the battlefield but electoral politics.

I hope male and female politicians will recognize that the days of conformity and subservience by women are over, but I hope even more that the 87 million women who are eligible to vote will realize that they have at their disposal a peaceful weapon of enormous significance, if only they will use it.

Nineteen eighty-four is not yet the year of Big Brother in our land. It can be the year of Big Sister — not an Orwellian counterimage of totalitarian menace, but an ordinary woman with a democratic vision and a sense of her own political potential — holding an olive branch in one hand and pulling down a lever in a green-curtained voting booth with the other.

1

The Possible Dream

LAST NIGHT I dreamed I was back on Capitol Hill. The Senate and House had been called into special joint session to hear the President make an important speech. It was 8 P.M., prime television time, and the atmosphere in the huge old chamber was crackling. Every seat was filled, the crowd a mosaic of white, honey-toned, and dark faces and brightly colored dresses, flecked here and there with a somber oxford gray suit. The heavy paneled doors to the center aisle opened and on the threshold appeared the doorkeeper, a tiny creature with a booming voice. "The President of the United States," she announced.

Smiling her famous winsome smile, the white-haired chief executive walked down the aisle with a light, firm step, pausing along the way to clasp hands with legislators who reached out to touch her. While we applauded and cheered, the President, elegant and almost regal in her purple silk dress, stood on the podium, surveying with pride her cabinet and the Supreme Court justices — eight women and one man — who were seated in the front row, and then she glanced up and waved to the crowded balcony, where her husband and children, along with the diplomatic corps and the husbands of her cabinet officers, stood in tribute. She shrugged in mock helplessness as the ovation continued and turned to exchange a few laughing remarks with the Vice President and the Speaker. Finally, she motioned the crowd to silence and began to read from the TelePrompTer: "Ms. Speaker, Ms. [Vice] President, distinguished members of the Congress, honored guests, and my sister Americans. . . ."

I woke up. It was impossible — an absurd, impossible dream. A bit like the times, at feminist sessions, when we played the "if women ruled the world" game and acted like power brokers, deciding who could be President, who would be in the cabinet, and wondered ironically when our women-ruled nation would be ready to consider a *male* Vice President.

It would be justice at last, the first time in recorded history that a country was run almost exclusively by women. Even if some turned out not to be geniuses or great leaders, they could hardly do worse than our male leaders had done — and they would probably do better, if only because they would come into political power without a sizable vested interest in the institutions and forces that are turning the American dream into a nightmare.

So why not, for an about-time change, try a female President, a female cabinet, a female Congress, and, eventually, a female Supreme Court? Finding women to fill those positions would not be as difficult as the male establishment would have us think. (When President Richard Nixon had four separate opportunities to name a woman to the U.S. Supreme Court and didn't, he implied that he couldn't find one good enough. I said then the problem was that he couldn't find a woman bad enough. President Ronald Reagan had to settle for appointing a conservative woman who disagreed with him on the ERA.)

From time to time national polls ask Americans whether they would vote for a woman for President if she were qualified, and a majority says yes. That word *qualified* provides the escape hatch for bigots. The pollsters never bother to ask voters whether they would support a male candidate if he were qualified. Maybe that's because history would give them the horse laugh. We have had some truly great Presidents, who are memorable only because there were so few of them, but we have also had chief executives who were ignorant, slow-witted, coarse, boring, lecherous, emotionally unstable, corrupt, and certified liars. Politics, not high qualifications, put them in the White House.

The same characteristics have been noted among Congressmen, only there are more of them. To be fair, I must say that many of these men are intelligent, hard-working, and dedicated legislators, and some of my male colleagues in the House were extraordinarily so. I admire them. But I have never known any elected official whose job could not have been performed as well or better by any number of the women — ranging in ability from average to sensational — whom I have met in my years of public life and travels around our country.

Even though a world or nation run by women would be an interesting and perhaps successful experiment, candor compels me to admit that my dream is not only impossible but unfair. Men constitute almost half the world's population — 47 percent in the United States — and it would be undemocratic, stupid, and really criminal to exclude them, with all their skills, creativity, ideas, energy, talent, and occasional genius, from a share in running our government and political institutions.

No need to worry about fairness, however. The dream is impossible for one reason alone: men simply would not stand for it. If by some miracle they were to awake one morning and find that Washington, D.C., the White House, and Capitol Hill had been taken over by women, they would grab their guns and start a counterrevolution — with the assistance of the men in the Pentagon, who no doubt would call them freedom fighters. You can imagine all the impassioned, learned, sarcastic, and rebellious speeches they would make and the newspaper editorial outcries about the outrageousness of excluding virtually an entire sex from governing the greatest democracy in the world.

And they would be right.

But that, of course, is exactly what men have done, and women have allowed it to happen. Aside from the minor roles played by a tiny percentage of women in government, men run our country and its political institutions. They like it that way, and they will keep it that way, fair or no fair, as long as women let them get away with it.

Let's replay that opening dream scene and see where women are in real life: mostly up in the balcony, as spectators. The President and Vice President are male; so has it been since the founding of our Republic. When the President addresses the Congress and the nation, his opening greetings are directed to his "fellow" Americans. He is introduced by a male doorkeeper, surrounded by male officials, and speaks to an audience that is predominantly male and white. There are at present only 2 women among the 100 members of the Senate, and only 22 among the 435 members of the House of Representatives. In all, about 4½ percent of our national lawmaking body represents the 53 percent of our population who are female. (Blacks don't do very well, either. There are none in the Senate and only 21 in the House, 2 of them women. There are 10 Hispanic Representatives, all men.) Three of the 13 Reagan cabinet members — including the United Nations ambassador, who has cabinet rank — are women, and that's the most any President has had. The U.S. Supreme Court is composed of 8 male justices and newcomer Sandra Day O'Connor, the first woman named to the highest court in our land, which for almost two hundred years has interpreted and been the final authority on the constitutional rights of all Americans.

A few women employed by the legislators have enough clout to get standing room in the back of the chamber, and some also sit in the balcony with the political wives. Whether Republican or Democratic, the First Lady customarily appears to follow the advice contained in a 1972 GOP campaign memo to candidates' wives: Look adoringly and attentively at your husband while he is speaking and keep your knees covered.

That is the picture of women's presence in the top ranks of our federal government, and it is no consolation to say that it has been even worse in the past. It is still a national disgrace.

I do not intend to suggest, however, that American women today are powerless or submerged in a stagnating political system. To the contrary, women now stand on the threshold of achieving more political power than they have ever had before. A *possible* dream can become real if women translate their beliefs and votes into an organized electoral and political force. That bloc is already shaping up with the appearance of the gender gap in the 1980 and 1982 elections. Pollster Louis Harris agrees, saying, "One of the major developments of the 1980s will be the full-blown emergence of women as a powerful new force in American politics."

As a result of the profound and continuing changes in women's roles in our society and the consciousness-raising of the women's movement that has affected their lives and self-perceptions, American women are more ready than ever before to express their attitudes, not just in the privacy of their homes, but in programs and action in their communities, organizations, workplaces, and public affairs. Author Nora Ephron wrote sardonically, "The major concrete achievement of the women's movement in the 1970s was the Dutch treat." That's nothing new for women, who have been paying, one way or another, throughout history. What is new is the self-respect and self-confidence the movement has brought to women of all ages and backgrounds, whether or not they call themselves feminists. There are, too, the improvements in their legal and economic status that women have won through their own efforts.

Most American men and women have no cohesive political ideologies other than general designations of themselves as liberal, conservative, or middle-of-the-road. Yet, in the process of liberating themselves, women, of necessity, have had to learn how to fight against institutionalized discrimination, violence, and oppression, and it has been a transfiguring experience.

Today, women are both leaders and rank-and-filers in the movements for change, and they significantly outnumber men as a progressive force in our society. They are in the antinuclear peace movement. They are among the groups seeking security and better quality of life for senior citizens, a majority of whom are women. They are organizing to save their communities from the perils of Love Canal and other chemical death pits. They are unionizing office workers and spotlighting new technological dangers in the workplace. They are exposing the profiteering behind the degradation of women in the flourishing male-owned pornography businesses. They are associating their own struggle for equality and economic justice with similar aims of minorities and the poor. They are pioneering new kinds of family and personal relationships, defying traditional sex roles, working and succeeding at jobs that had been barred to them for generations, and everywhere proposing changes and policies that would make our nation a healthier, saner, and more secure place in which to live — for men, women, and children alike.

This all involves political action, and American women are terrific at it. They have a wealth of experience in organizing, demonstrating, lobbying, and turning on the pressure to accomplish their goals. They have been politically active for years, beginning with Elizabeth Cady Stanton, Susan B. Anthony, and other suffragists who conducted an almost century-long campaign to win the right to vote.

But they have not won political recognition commensurate with their efforts, and one reason is that until recently they did not take the next crucial step of expressing their political goals in electoral terms. Trying to achieve political power without electoral power is like unlocking a door and then failing to open it. Feminists organized a superb campaign for adoption of the Equal Rights Amendment. They succeeded in winning the support of a majority of American women and men, but they lost partly because that widespread support was not embodied in enough elected officials in a couple of holdout state legislatures. The absence of a small number of key votes blocked ratification of a constitutional guarantee of equal rights for women under the law, and when the ERA was reintroduced in Congress, it was defeated in the House largely by Republican members.

Electoral power involves using the organized strength of women to elect men *and* women, from local office to the highest national positions. Even more important, it means making certain these elected officials know that their victories were a result of women's efforts and women's votes and that they must represent women's interests if they expect to be reelected. When black voters turned out in record numbers to elect Chicago's first black mayor, the whole country sat up and took notice. There probably wasn't a politician around who didn't start researching the number of potential black votes in his or her area. Politicians don't have to research women. We are everywhere, and we come in all colors.

Now let's go back to the *possible* dream. The one I said we can make a reality. It is a dream in which women share political authority equally with men — in the political parties, the city councils and state legislatures, the judiciary, the governors' mansions, the Congress, and the White House. Let's not quibble about exact numbers. In some places and at certain times there may be more men or more women in power. Some years, there may be a male President and a female Vice President, or the reverse, or two women, or two men, but whoever conducts our government will have to recognize this is not a "for men only" nation.

Never again will we have a chief executive who reports to his "fellow" Americans on the State of the Union and refers to the state of women only once in a half-sentence or not at all. Nor will we have the insulting spectacle of a President choosing, in time of crisis, a committee of Wise Men — usually the same men who got us into the crisis in the first place — to advise him and ignoring the wisdom and recommendations of women. Nor will we have an all-male Senate debating and voting on women's right to abortion. (I can recall House discussions on abortion in which it was clear that some of my male colleagues knew less about the uterus than about a U-Haul, but that did not stop them from deciding the fate of women.) Nor will we have budget planners who insist that an MX missile is more important than jobs for the unemployed, that low-priced meals for Pentagon generals are more necessary than nutrition supplements for mothers and infants, that tax breaks for multinational corporations are more desirable than cost-of-living adjustments for Social Security recipients, that nuclear power plants are more essential than protection of our soil, air, and water.

The overall gains made by some groups of women in recent years have come about because of their growing collective female consciousness that they have common experiences, problems, and unmet needs, but they have a long way to go before those needs can be met. While the nations of the world squander more than $600 billion annually on armaments, the economic gulf between rich and poor nations — and between men and women — gets wider. According to a 1980 United Nations report, women represent 75 percent of the world's illiterates, receive only 10 percent of its income, and own less than 1 percent of private property! They make up one third of the world's official labor forces, but work twice as many hours as men — for much less pay. That's not counting the additional hours they spend in unpaid labor, doing housework and taking care of the children.

In the United States, where women make up almost half the labor force, they still earn, on average, only 59 percent of what men do. Minority women earn less. Although our poverty and deprivation of basic human services do not compare with the abysmal conditions endured in many Third World nations, American women, too, are a majority of the poor. In 1980, in our great and rich nation, two out of the three adults who lived below the poverty line were women.

Women — together with their families — are faced with other kinds of insecurity. Like the rest of the world, the United States is in deep trouble. It is caught in an international economic crisis that its own policies have helped to create. Unemployment hurts women as well as men, and as the auto and steel industries — once the anchors of our economy — operate far below capacity, millions wonder if they will ever work again. Corporations are turning our land into one big garbage dump of poisonous chemical wastes. Our leaders are littering space with military metal junk and debris from their space shots and planning to orbit the earth with nuclear weapons. (Star light, star bright, how many millions will be killed tonight?)

Even though our male militarists have enough nuclear hot stuff to blow up every living creature and our planet itself twenty times over, they insist that they must have still more weapons to "protect" us. That kind of protection racket is not cheap, especially when it comes wrapped in the flag.

In the United States alone, the arms race has cost us more than $2 *trillion* (that's more than $2000 billion!) in the last three decades. And about the time I was having my dream, President Reagan was calling for an additional $1.8 trillion expenditure on the military in the 1980s because it appears that what we bought for the previous trillions was something called a "window of vulnerability."

I know a dozen more sensible and productive ways to spend — or even not to spend — that money. So do other women who have analyzed and been horrified at our Pentagon-burdened national budgets that slash the domestic programs needed to help women and their children cope better with their enormous problems of everyday survival.

American women are realizing that the way to begin solving these problems is to force their male political leaders to pay attention to them. To ensure that concern, women must become leaders and activists themselves because progressive change for women comes only at the initiative of women. It is not enough to ask men what they can do for us. We must ask what we can do for ourselves. Men may become allies or followers in the struggle for women's equality, but I doubt that they lose much sleep worrying about how to achieve justice for the female sex.

I believe that government of, by, and for women and men will prove to be better than any government we have had so far. I know it will happen only if women get together first to make it happen. And when it does happen, men will find that they, too, have benefited. Progressive change for men as well as for women (see, I don't discriminate) will come only when men accept the idea and the practice of both sexes working together, each bringing its full strength, unique insights, abilities, and participation to the task.

Women face continuing obstacles and new opportunities as we seek our share of political power. The struggle has been going on for a long time, but the big change has come only in the very recent past as a result of the changing status of women and the growth of the organized women's movement.

2

A New Kind of Political Woman

"I BELIEVE WOMEN (bless their hearts) vote as individuals. They are probably the most independent group of voters in the nation."

That was Ronald Reagan, then governor of California, as quoted in the January 1972 issue of *Harper's Bazaar*. In the cloying manner he usually adopted when speaking of women, he was answering a query to possible presidential candidates and other political leaders about whether women's rights groups would succeed in creating a women's bloc vote.

Reagan was not the only male politician who believed, or perhaps hoped, that women would vote without any consciousness of sex roles. Vice President Hubert Humphrey, Governors George Wallace of Alabama and Nelson Rockefeller of New York, Mayor John V. Lindsay of New York City, Democratic National Committee Chairman Larry O'Brien, and his Republican counterpart, Robert Dole, offered similar sentiments. As reported by *Harper's Bazaar*, the only political leaders who thought women would become a cohesive political force were presidential aspirant George McGovern — and Congresswoman Bella Abzug.

"Women have had the vote since 1920," I said, "but they have been using it almost exclusively to elect men to office. They haven't had much choice. Now they're ready to come out of the back rooms and to demand equality in the political arena."

In its heroic battle for the right to vote, the American suffrage movement had involved millions of women in political activity. Once women won the vote, however, the electoral power structure remained virtually an all-male preserve, with women consigned to the drudgery of inner party chores, the "housework" of politics. But beginning in the 1960s, the time of the civil rights and anti–Vietnam War demonstrations, and the renascence of the women's liberation movement, the political awareness of women also grew, and a new kind of political woman began to emerge. What followed was a long seeding process, which eventually bore fruit in the distinctive voting pattern that we call the electoral gender gap.

Feminists sounded the rallying cry, "The personal is political," bringing a different perspective to what women had been brainwashed by the dominant culture into believing were individual, personal, or unique family problems. They saw many of their problems as reflections of the values and practices imposed by a male power structure that controlled both the economy and the government, and they contended that these were legitimate matters for national concern and government action.

With more women — married, single, divorced, and widowed — streaming into the labor market and coming smack up against the sexist barriers of occupational segregation, pervasive discrimination, and the continuing wage gap, it became evident that they would have to seek to change both the political and economic practices of the nation. Political power of, by, and for women became part of the feminist agenda.

As the born-again women's movement probed into every aspect of American life, women unloosed an explosion of needs, self-discovery, and new insights into personal and social relationships. They recognized that what we required on the legal front were the repeal of thousands of old repressive laws, passage of new laws and programs, and wrapping it all up, adoption of the Equal Rights Amendment to give women a constitutional guarantee of equality. Just as the "votes for women" demand mobilized women of earlier generations, ERA became the heart and soul of the contemporary women's peaceful revolution, with its quest for equality and economic justice. It was the legal bedrock on which all other changes were to be inscribed.

The working mother needed quality child care for her preschoolers and income tax deductions for child-care and household services. The middle-class housewife who had stifled her own abilities and ambitions to wait on her husband needed educational opportunities to start her own career. The poor woman who had to go on welfare to support her children also needed low-cost or free child-care centers and job training as her escape route to self-respect and independence. The young woman who had suffered the painful indignity of a back-alley abortion, as well as the Native American woman on a reservation and the black woman in a slum who had been forcibly sterilized, wanted the removal of laws that prevented them from choosing when and if to have a child. The minority woman at the bottom of the economic ladder, the underpaid factory worker drudging away at a dead-end job, and the junior executive or college instructor who had been passed over for a deserved promotion that went to a less-qualified male colleague wanted affirmative action programs and other legal remedies against job and pay discrimination. The student who, in the old days, had to choose between being a secretary, nurse, or teacher wanted the legal opportunity to become an electrician, truck driver, engineer, doctor, lawyer, or astronaut. The aging woman whose husband had divorced her for a younger woman wanted guaranteed Social Security in her own name, and the struggling businesswoman wanted access to credit and loans. The victim of wife-beating wanted a place where she and her children could take shelter. The lesbian wanted the repeal of laws that threatened her with arrest for her private sexual preferences and an end to discriminatory practices that threatened her with loss of her job, apartment, or child custody. The raped woman wanted the right to a trial of her assailant in which she was not made to feel like a criminal. And the loyal political volunteer who had always helped elect men to office felt it was time to get herself and other women elected to positions of power and responsibility.

From the founding of the National Organization for Women (NOW) in 1966 through the 1970s, the women's movement spread out in many directions, growing rapidly in strength and influence, involving its adherents in political struggle, and working inside and outside the system to change women's lives. As an active feminist, lawyer, social reformer, wife, mother, and independent woman who, happily, was born the year that suffrage was approved, I have spent much of my life working outside the establishment, organizing and helping to create pressures for constructive change. As a three-term Congresswoman and as a presidential appointee, I have also worked inside the establishment, and I am convinced of the necessity for doing both. Demonstrations, public meetings, grassroots lobbies and citizens' actions, political strategizing to get legislation enacted or changed — all these are the ABC's of the democratic process — but the end of the line is what happens inside the halls of power when the votes are counted and the decisions made.

I have been an instinctive feminist all my life, but I came to political feminism by way of my activities in the women's peace movement and my involvement in Democratic Party reform politics. One of my abiding passions has been to break through the existing electoral bottlenecks that prevent grassroots Americans, men and women, from getting the leadership that really represents their best interests and desires. Over and over, I have seen our government leaders and political parties obstruct and operate in ways contrary to what the people want: President Lyndon Johnson, elected in 1964 on a pledge of "no wider war," escalating the war in Indochina to horrendous dimensions; Chicago Mayor Richard Daley's police viciously beating up hundreds of men, women, and young people who were trying to make the 1968 Democratic Party convention respond to their peace demands; President Richard Nixon ordering the secret bombing of Cambodia and covering up his Watergate scandal, and President Gerald Ford, in turn, covering up for Nixon and pardoning him; President Jimmy Carter backing out on his commitments to women and arms reductions; the Republican Party abandoning its historic support for the ERA; President Ronald Reagan giving still more to the rich, taking from women, children, and the poor and declaring that he was prepared to send U.S. troops "anywhere on earth"; members of Congress cravenly going along with big budget slashes in necessary social programs; male-controlled state legislatures blocking debate and votes on the ERA.

Witnessing this continual process of misrepresentation, many of us have felt it essential to change the process — to open up the political parties to inner reforms and rules changes that would make their structures and presidential nominating conventions more democratic, and to open up government by electing more women, minorities, and other underrepresented groups. These two concerns became the major thrusts of the political wing of the women's movement in the 1970s, and feeding our insurgent movement were thousands of women who had been politicized in the nationwide campaigns for the ERA, abortion rights, and other legislation.

My experiences in Congress further convinced me that women had to be organized to gain an equal share of political power if they were to improve their economic and social status. One of my first acts as a newly elected Representative in 1971 was to hold informal hearings with Congresswoman Shirley Chisholm, a sister New Yorker, on the child-care needs of working women and others. Chisholm and I introduced a model comprehensive child-care act and succeeded in getting key sections attached to a bill sponsored by Senator Walter Mondale, the Minnesota Democrat. Congress passed the measure, only to have it vetoed by President Nixon, who sanctimoniously denounced government-sponsored child care as communistic subversion of the traditional family.

Since I considered Nixon, with his saturation bombings of Indochina in an illegal, undeclared war, as no better than a mass murderer of men, women, and children (I introduced a motion to censure him for this deed), I wasn't impressed by his pretense of concern for families. Although Nixon and the Republican Party were then on record as being in favor of the

ERA, that was a statement of legal principles, not a money program in the immediate sense. His hypocritical posture as a moralist was really just another kind of cover-up: he was against spending the $2 billion proposed for an adequate child-care system. (Three Presidents later, we still don't have the kinds or numbers of child-care facilities desperately needed by working parents or welfare mothers who are trying to break out of the poverty trap.) Nixon later impounded funds appropriated by Congress for social programs, and here, too, women were the big losers.

Founding the National Women's Political Caucus

The continuing evidence of the disregard for women's economic and social needs and my disgust with the type of men perpetrated on us as Presidents and political leaders made me feel the urgency of electing more women to Congress. At that time there were only twelve of us in the House and one in the Senate. True, some sympathetic male colleagues introduced or cosponsored legislation beneficial to women, but the main impetus and ideas came from the women members. We needed more of them.

In the spring of 1971 I began sounding out friends and co-workers on the notion of forming an independent women's political organization, and got a quick response of interest. I discovered that Betty Friedan, author of *The Feminine Mystique,* had been thinking along somewhat similar lines, though we disagreed on the approach to take. She seemed to feel we should support women for political office within fairly minimal guidelines, while I was not prepared to spend time getting just any woman elected. I felt our main goal should be to build a political movement of women for social change that would simultaneously help elect more women, minorities, and other underrepresented groups and build an electoral bloc strong enough to influence male politicians to support our programs.

I reserved a committee room on Capitol Hill, and on June 9 we held our first big planning session with a fairly good cross section of women. Shirley Chisholm and Patsy Takemoto Mink, a Congresswoman from Hawaii, were on hand to give the women a pep talk on the need for an independent political force, but most were already convinced. There was a large turnout of Washington women from NOW, black organizations, government agencies, religious and social action groups, and students from local colleges. Jane Galvin Lewis of the National Council of Negro Women and Edith Van Horn of the United Auto Workers were there; Republicans included several women from Governor Nelson Rockefeller's staff, and the New York contingent included Gloria Steinem, the eloquent feminist, Friedan, Ronnie Feit of NOW, Mim Kelber, my close friend and longtime associate, and other feminists. Liz Carpenter, Lady Bird Johnson's former White House press secretary, came with her young daughter, explaining that she didn't want her to face the kind of discrimination she had encountered in her own career. We gave ourselves a month to organize a national conference, and we met our deadline.

On July 10, 1971, when our founding conference of the National Women's Political Caucus (NWPC) opened at the Washington Hilton, some three hundred women from all over the country — a mix of elected officials, community activists, feminists, Democrats, Republicans, radicals, union women, homemakers, students, blacks, Hispanics, and lesbians — were on hand.

One of the putdowns that has continually plagued the women's movement is the charge that it speaks only for white middle-class women. To the contrary, there has always been an acute sensitivity to the need for representing the interests of all women. As one of the keynote speakers at that first NWPC meeting, I said the hope of building an effective women's political movement lay in "reaching out to include those who have been doubly and triply disenfranchised — reaching out to working women, to young women, to black women, to women on welfare — and joining their strength with that of millions of other American women who are on the move all over this country, demanding an end to discrimination and fighting for their rights as full and equal citizens."

There were cheers and applause when I said, "I don't think any of us intend to replace the *male* white middle-class elite that runs this country with a *female* white middle-class elite."

I also took on the issue of whether we should commit ourselves to supporting any woman candidate over any male candidate. "I am not elevating women to sainthood," I said, "nor am I suggesting that all women share the same views, or that all women are good and all men bad. Women have screamed for war. Women, like men, have stoned black children going to integrated schools. Women have been and are prejudiced, narrow-minded, reactionary, even violent. *Some* women. They, of course, have a right to vote and a right to run for office. I will defend that right, but I will not support them or vote for them."

Fannie Lou Hamer, a black woman who had been involved in the struggle to get Mississippi's Freedom Delegation of blacks officially seated at the 1964 Democratic convention, was pointed in her remarks to us: "America is sick," she said. "Something has got to change in this country, and we can't stand around waiting for the white man to change it."

The women approved a "statement of purposes" to oppose sexism, racism, institutional violence, and poverty through the election and appointment of women to political office, reform of party structures to give women an equal voice in decision making and selection of candidates, and support of women's issues and feminist candidates across party lines, and pledged to work in coalition with "other oppressed groups."

The statement made clear that we would support only women candidates "who declare themselves ready to fight for the rights and needs of women, and of all underrepresented groups." It said we would register new women voters and encourage women to vote for women's priorities, and "raise women's issues in every election and publicize the records on such issues of all male and female candidates, so that they shall be made to rise or fall on their position and action for human equality."

Our statement of purposes concluded by calling for "sweeping social change" and urging a reordering of the nation's resources "to pay for life instead of death." A list of issues was offered as "guidelines to the kinds of concerns . . . women must have *as women,* not as imitators of the traditional male style and male politics." The list included, of course, ERA, abortion rights, economic equity issues, and child care, but it also cited comprehensive health care, welfare reform, elimination of tax inequities, fair-housing laws, preservation of the natural environment, and withdrawal of U.S. troops from Indochina. It proposed "an end to war, and support for international agreements to end the arms race; an end to the use of physical violence as a traditional 'masculine' way of resolving conflict." No one could say we were parochial or limited in our goals. Righteous as our tone was, we were speaking for a vision of America that would benefit men as well as women, and, indeed, the world. The concerns we spoke of as far back as 1971 are the concerns that have surfaced in women's recent electoral voting patterns.

The conference ended with the election of a national policy council,* which was cochaired for the next nineteen months by a Republican, Virginia Allen, former chair of President Nixon's Task Force on Women's Rights and Responsibilities, and by me. (The first women's task force in the executive branch had been set up in 1961 by President John F. Kennedy at the urging of Eleanor Roosevelt, who became its head.)

In the next twelve years, the caucus grew to a membership of more than seventy thousand women, with a professional staff headquartered in Washington, local caucuses in all the states and major cities, and a very active caucus of women who work on Capitol Hill, which I organized. (These savvy women play an important behind-the-scenes role in briefing their bosses on women's rights issues, writing their speeches aimed at female audiences, and narrowing the wage gap between what congressional women and men staffers earn. Since those early days, female administrative aides in Congress have doubled their

---

*Among those elected to the council were Chisholm, Steinem, Friedan, Carpenter, and Hamer; Myrlie Evers, widow of slain civil rights leader Medgar Evers; Wilma Scott Heide, NOW chair; Nikki Beare, a Florida NOW leader; Olga Madar, a UAW vice president; LaDonna Harris, an Indian rights leader; Dorothy Height and Vivian Carter Mason of the National Council of Negro Women; Beulah Sanders, a welfare rights leader; Mary Clarke of the Los Angeles Women Strike for Peace; Midge Miller, a Democratic member of the Wisconsin legislature; Elly Peterson, Jill Ruckelshaus, and JoAnne Evans Gardner — three prominent Republicans; Shana Alexander, then chief editor of *McCall's* magazine; Joan Cashin of Alabama and Elinor Guggenheimer of New York, both active in the Democratic Party. Seven members were blacks, and four seats on the council were reserved for Hispanic women and women under thirty, to assure a more representative mix.

average annual pay to $34,825, which is within sight of the $39,000 averaged by male aides. Although more women are being hired for top policy posts on the Hill, men still hold 76 percent of those jobs.)

The NWPC has concentrated on three action areas — issues and legislation, party reform, and election and appointment of more women to political office. Electing more women has proved among the most difficult of its tasks, for reasons that I will describe in chapter 9, but slowly and persistently, the work of the caucus and other groups has raised the number of women in government. While there are almost twice as many women in Congress in 1983 as when I entered the House in 1971, twenty-four women out of a total of 535 Representatives and Senators remains a scandalously low figure. Women have been more successful in getting elected to state legislatures; their number has tripled since 1969, but they still hold only 13 percent of all state legislature seats. These gains, modest as they are, could not have been accomplished without the caucus and the atmosphere we created, which encouraged more women to run for office.

In 1971, when the NWPC was just getting started, we had no paid staff and no money — just enthusiastic volunteers and a vision of what had to be done. Most of the women who attended the conference went home and began to organize state and local caucuses. Some had already started doing that *before* the Washington meeting. In a speech to the National Press Club a week later, I was able to report that caucuses were being formed in fifteen states.

Our founding conference was reported as major news in the media, but the response from some male political big shots was to treat us like cheesecake served up at a stag party. The newspapers had carried a wire service photo of Chisholm, Steinem, Friedan, and me at a July 12 press session announcing the decisions of our meeting. We looked serious, as we were. Several days later the press described the White House reaction.

The subject was brought up by Secretary of State William Rogers, while he and Nixon were having their pictures taken with Henry Kissinger. Smiling broadly, Kissinger said he had heard Gloria Steinem was at the women's caucus meeting.

"Who's that?" asked our know-nothing President.
"That's Henry's old girlfriend," Rogers joked. Then he mentioned our photo.
"What did it look like?" Nixon asked.
"Like a burlesque," said Rogers.
"What's wrong with that?" Nixon replied.
This witty exchange was duly recorded in the press. "Obviously," I commented at the time, "the President and his advisers are accustomed to viewing women only in terms of flesh shows." Gloria issued a statement saying she was not then and had never been a girlfriend of Kissinger, nor, in fact, was she a woman friend.

A few months earlier, Vice President Spiro Agnew, speaking at a fund-raiser in Maryland, had delivered what he thought was a crowd-pleaser by exhorting Republicans "to keep Bella Abzug from showing up in Congress in hot pants." My response, which proved to be accurate on both counts, was that "hot pants will disappear from the national scene, along with Mr. Agnew and Mr. Nixon."

Although an extraordinary number of the men who ran Washington were ill prepared to treat women as equals either on a political or personal basis, the growing popularity of the women's movement and its effective lobbying was forcing them to face the new political realities. The emergence of the caucus, the increasing membership of NOW — the major feminist group — and the special-interest and single-issue women's organizations springing up in Washington and in towns, communities, and campuses everywhere made it impossible for Congress to avoid considering our issues. Congresswoman Martha Griffiths, a veteran Michigan Democrat, had been leading the fight in the House for approval of the Equal Rights Amendment and was known as the mother of the ERA. She succeeded in winning House approval in 1970, but the measure was lost in the U.S. Senate. When she brought it up again in 1972, the climate was more favorable. National polls showed that a majority of Americans favored ERA, the ranks of women in Congress had been strengthened by the arrival of some strong women's rights advocates, and the grassroots pressure was rising. This time the amendment was approved by both the House and Senate and referred to the states for ratification. All the women members, Democrats and Republicans, took a prominent part in the debate and voted for the amendment, with the single exception of Congresswoman Leonor Sullivan, a Missouri Democrat. She voted against it, explaining, "ERA says you are my equal . . . I think I'm a whole lot better."

Some of the arguments against ERA used by the male Representatives were the same ones that had been used against suffrage — it would destroy the family and religion, expose women (all of us presumably living atop pedestals) to sordid realities with which only men were fit to cope, and other lofty sentiments usually trotted out by the privileged when they're trying to keep the rest of us down. One reactionary Representative from California wound up his opposition remarks by saying that his wife had told him to vote against the ERA. When it came my turn to speak, I said, "My husband, Martin, didn't tell me how to vote."

Other important legislation was approved at that time, a reflection of the increasing political power of women. The Equal Employment Opportunity Act of 1972 gave the federal enforcement commission greater powers and wider scope in acting against job discrimination. Title 9 of the Education Amendments of 1972 banned discrimination on account of sex in most federally assisted educational institutions. The Equal Pay Act, which had been passed in 1963 during the Kennedy administration, was extended to cover administrative, professional, and executive employees. These measures had a potential impact on millions of women.

The new laws, of course, did not simply glide through the complex machinery of Congress and the White House. Their passage took hard work and skillful negotiations by a bloc of women and men Representatives and Senators, backed up with intensive lobbying by women's groups. Liberal members could usually be counted on to support so-called bread-and-butter women's legislation, but many defected on the emotionally charged issue of abortion rights. Here, too, the national polls showed majority support for a range of reproductive freedom options. The many separate local women's groups that had been working for repeal of state antiabortion laws since the mid-

1960s coalesced into a national organization, and I introduced an Abortion Rights Act. It was still in committee when the U.S. Supreme Court, in its landmark January 1973 decision, affirmed women's constitutional right to abortion.

That victory touched off a struggle between pro and antiabortion rights forces that has been even fiercer than the division over ERA. At this writing, the increasingly effective political organization of the reproductive freedom advocates has defeated attempts in the Senate to approve an antiabortion constitutional amendment. On the issues of a woman's right to control her own body and family planning, Congress has lagged far behind public opinion. Many Senators and Representatives who don't blink an eye at voting billions of dollars for weapons of mass destruction or cutting funds for maternal and infant-care programs deliver hypocritical lectures to women about the sanctity of the unborn fetus, and still others vote cowardly against their personal convictions and own practices for fear of reprisals from the Right to Life and Moral Majority movements. During my six years in Congress, I never felt the absence of significant numbers of women members as acutely as during the debates on the withdrawal of Medicaid funding for abortions and the other restrictions voted by the House. It was exasperating to see one man after another rise to proclaim piously that he was against abortion ("Then don't have one," I felt like saying) while women whose bodies and futures were on the line were absent from the debate.

It is particularly ironic that many of the proposed antiabortion constitutional amendments would declare that the fetus is a person under the Fourteenth Amendment, yet women are not considered "persons" under that amendment, by reason of disparate court decisions. It is because the courts have not uniformly extended the protection of the Fourteenth Amendment to women as persons that it has become necessary for us to amend the Constitution with an equal rights guarantee. Some of the same individuals who would turn the unborn embryo or fetus into a legal person are opposed to constitutional personhood for women. Federal Trade Commissioner Patricia Bailey speculated about this contradiction in a June 1983 speech to the NWPC convention, asking, "Would all unborn beings be constitutional persons until the moment of birth, after which point only those who were male would continue to be 'persons' while those that were female would not?"

An Inside View of Party Reform

Reproductive freedom, the ERA, and women's growing demand for economic equity were among the many feminist issues that had become matters of public policy. They had to be confronted in the Congress, the White House, and the courts, and also in the political parties. Immediately after organizing the National Women's Political Caucus, we launched major campaigns for reform of the Democratic and Republican parties' rules and procedures. Our aim was to make the process more democratic, opening up the conventions to women and other underrepresented groups and giving them a bigger role in nominating the presidential ticket and formulating the platforms. We were to achieve a notable victory in making the Democratic Party more representative of women and minorities, accomplishing what political scientist Byron Shafer called an institutional change of major significance in a remarkably short time. He gave women full credit for this achievement. The secret of our success lay in organization, persistence, a mastery of intricate rules, and a passionate commitment to equality for women. Initially, with just one year of hard work, we succeeded in tripling the number of women delegates to the Democratic convention, from 13 percent of the total in 1968 to 40 percent in 1972, and we doubled the number of Republican women delegates, from 17 percent to 35 percent. By 1980 we were to win equal numerical representation of women at the Democratic convention and in all structures of the party, a fundamental reform that has an important bearing on the genesis of the gender gap.

Our campaign for equal representation had historic roots. In the first few years after the suffrage amendment was adopted in 1920, male politicians were quite responsive to women's demands. The 1920 Democratic platform included twelve of fifteen provisions advocated by the newly formed League of Women Voters, and Warren Harding, the successful Republican candidate for President, endorsed the concept of equal pay for women, an eight-hour day, protective maternity and infant-care laws, and creation of a federal department of social welfare. Both parties named an equal number of men and women to their national committees, a largely ceremonial move that did not give women any real power within the inner circles of party bosses. By the mid-1920s, male politicians had stopped trying to curry favor with women, and their representation in the parties also lagged. For one thing, women were not voting in the large percentages that had been expected, and they appeared to vote the same way the men in their families did. Another reason for the backlash against women was a growing national conservative trend, which was marked by isolationism, the corrupt practices of Harding's Teapot Dome administration, and the anti-reform, pro–big business policies of the Coolidge administration.

Until recent times the high point of women's political influence and participation in party affairs came during the New Deal, owing largely to the intervention of Eleanor Roosevelt. She and Molly Dewson, a leader of the National Consumers League and a close family friend, had done a spectacular job of organizing women to vote for Franklin Roosevelt in his two gubernatorial campaigns and his presidential race in 1932. They created a nationwide network of women to mobilize the Roosevelt vote and were rewarded with the creation of a Women's Division in the Democratic National Committee. Dewson was appointed to head the new division, and after Roosevelt's victory she reportedly arrived in Washington with a list of sixty women whom she recommended for top positions in the new administration. By 1935 more than fifty women, including Secretary of Labor Frances Perkins, had been appointed, a record number. The First Lady believed that "the new order of things should reflect the understanding hearts of women," and many women flocked into government, attracted by the social welfare reforms of the New Deal. The female influence was reflected, too, in Democratic Party structures and programs. Seven of the eight planks proposed by the Women's Division were included in the 1936 platform, women were granted parity on the Platform Committee, and they received a guarantee of equal representation with men on the national committee. Mrs. Roosevelt was a firm believer in equal division, or fifty-fifty, as she called it.

The 1972 Conventions

The equal-division goal was just as important to us new-style feminists, and one week after the National Women's Political Caucus was founded, I raised the issue in a letter to Minnesota Congressman Donald M. Fraser. He and Senator George McGovern headed a Democratic Party commission set up in the wake of the disastrous 1968 convention in Chicago, and after extensive hearings the commission had issued guidelines requiring the state parties to take affirmative action to assure that the delegations to the 1972 convention would have "reasonable representation" of women, minorities, and youth that would fairly reflect their numbers in the population. (According to the 1970 census, women composed 52.2 percent of the adult population.)

Writing on behalf of the NWPC policy council, I informed Fraser that we intended to monitor the delegate selection process and would support challenges to the seating of delegations in which women of all races, ages, and socioeconomic levels were not reasonably represented.

"As standards for reasonable representation," I continued, "the caucus voted that each state delegation should be composed of no less than 50 percent women. It voted that racial minorities and young people should be present in each delegation in percentages at least as great as their percentage of the total state population."

It was our belief, based on hard experience, that unless the guidelines were pinned down with a numerical commitment, we would lose out. It was already evident, I told Fraser, that his commission's guidelines were not being vigorously enforced by the state parties. My letter concluded by urging the commission to provide the states with guidance as to what was meant by "reasonable" representation "in terms of acceptable percentages" and to "explicitly define the responsibility of each state party for living up to these standards."

Two things happened. Within a very short time, after a few of us met with Fraser and Patricia Roberts Harris, temporary chair of the convention credentials committee, Harris ruled that the presence of fewer than 50 percent women in a state delegation would constitute prima facie evidence of noncompliance, and the burden of proving nondiscrimination would be on the state committee. In just a few months we had succeeded in transforming fairly general language about affirmative action and reasonable representation into an explicit requirement of numerical standards.

Next, to make sure that women got to the 1972 convention in large numbers, I set up a Women's Education for Delegate Selection project, with the assistance of Sandy Kramer, a southern feminist, and Ken Bode, former research director of the McGovern-Fraser Commission and now a TV commentator. The project taught women how to run for election as delegates to both major party conventions. Women from all over the country reacted eagerly and enthusiastically; this kind of political assistance was just what they had been waiting for.

The NWPC used the Harris ruling to file a substantial number of challenges of delegations, particularly those from areas that had traditionally excluded women and minorities. In all, eighty-two challenges of thirty states and one territory were filed by various groups and individuals, and half were still under consideration when the Democrats assembled in Miami in July 1972. A record-breaking number of women, 40 percent, were delegates, and they included whites, blacks, Hispanics, and other minorities, as well as women from all income levels.

We estimated that only about 10 percent of the more than eighteen hundred women delegates and alternates were NWPC members, but it was clear right from the beginning that a majority of the women delegates were with us on the issues, regardless of which presidential candidate they were nominally committed to support. To get elected as delegates, some women chose to run on slates committed to the presidential candidate most likely to carry their states, even if they were not enthusiastic about the man. One of our strongest feminists and civil rights activists, Brownie Ledbetter of Arkansas, turned up as a delegate for Wilbur Mills, an old antagonist of hers. She later became state manager of the George McGovern campaign in Arkansas. Other women came as delegates for Edmund Muskie, Hubert Humphrey, or other candidates, but most of the NWPC women were committed to McGovern, and a smaller number supported Shirley Chisholm, who was running an independent campaign for the presidential nomination. (She received 152 votes on the first ballot.) As a delegate from New York who had been committed to support McGovern before Chisholm decided to run, I — and other women delegates in my situation — was not free to give Chisholm my undivided support, but we all recognized the importance of her challenge to the white-male presidential image. In my preconvention speeches around the country I urged women to become Chisholm delegates in those selected states in which she was running.

When we arrived in Miami and set up NWPC headquarters, appropriately enough, at the Betsy Ross Hotel, a modest establishment that reflected our poverty but not our aspirations, we had visible evidence of our role in shaping the convention. Although some party establishment figures and media pundits badmouthed the delegates as a collection of kooks, we were elated at the sight of so many women, minorities, and young people — proof that the party was indeed being democratized. There were other firsts. The convention cochair was Yvonne Brathwaite Burke of California, the first black woman to hold that post, and women were also liberally represented on the convention committees. A convention eve rally held by the caucus was jammed with a huge standing-room-only crowd, which had come to hear what the presidential candidates would say on women's issues. Indicative of the changing times, the candidates had requested invitations to appear before us. The biggest applause went to Chisholm and McGovern, who pledged support to a fifteen-point women's rights program for which I had successfully led the fight in the party platform committee. His one disagreement with us was on abortion rights, but he pledged "unequivocal" support to our challenge of the South Carolina delegation, in which men outnumbered women almost three to one. We had decided to make that a floor-fight test of the 50 percent representation issue.

The caucus ran a round-the-clock operation of meetings, strategy sessions, and education of both female and male delegates on our substantive issues. The response was enthusiastic, and I sensed a feeling of pride and excitement among the women that at last our concerns were receiving national attention. A majority of the women delegates came together across candidate lines to support our positions, and large numbers of men also agreed to vote with us.

What happened on the convention floor was another episode in the continuing political saga of men in power ignoring or underestimating women and abandoning their commitments to them, with, I regret to say, help from some women. When our challenge to seating the South Carolina delegation came to a vote, we had already rounded up enough support to assure a victory. All the McGovern delegates, and many others, were pledged to us. Within the previous hour, I had personally worked the floor to win us an additional two hundred votes. A voice vote was held and ruled indecisive. As floor coordinator for the women's caucus, I moved for a roll-call vote, and as it progressed, it appeared that we were going to win as expected. Suddenly, some states began to switch, casting their votes against us and leading a bewildered Walter Cronkite to tell his national TV audience, "The McGovern forces are losing ground. This is a serious setback. I don't understand what's going on." We lost our challenge by the small margin of 126¾ votes. The mystery was cleared up when McGovern representative Anne Wexler admitted to a CBS reporter that Rick Stearns, McGovern's chief floor strategist, had signaled his floor captains to switch some delegate votes to the forces who were against the principle of equal representation for women.

It was not that the McGovern people were opposed to the principle — in the abstract, anyway — but our challenge ran afoul of a complicated tactical problem, which involved whether a subsequent California challenge would be decided by a majority of the votes (1509) of the total convention or a majority (1433) of the delegates who would be eligible to vote on the challenge. The McGovern strategists feared that if the vote on South Carolina fell between 1497 (the number eligible to vote on that particular challenge) and 1509, the chair would rule that 1509 votes were needed, and this number would then be applied to the California challenge — a threat to their belief that they needed to win the California vote to guarantee McGovern the nomination. Rather than jeopardize that, they dumped us. The whole maneuver was unnecessary. We had the 1509 votes to sustain our challenge, but the McGovern strategists lacked confidence in our ability either to get votes or count them. Moreover, Patricia Harris was prepared to rule in favor of the McGovern camp, but as one of his strategists later explained, they were too paranoid even to ask for an advance ruling on how a majority vote would be determined.

My close friend Shirley MacLaine, a California delegate who had taken a year off from her movie career to campaign for McGovern, argued with me about it on the floor as I shouted that the women had been sold down the river. Writing about it later in the *New York Times,* Shirley admitted that I was right and that the McGovern strategists "had gotten nervous too soon" but said I "hadn't realized how hard it had been for them to sacrifice idealism on the altar of pragmatism." What Shirley did not realize was that it hadn't been at all hard for them to sacrifice a women's issue to the cop-out plea of political pragmatism, expediency, or what I would call opportunism. We had had too much experience with being made sacrificial victims, from friends and foes alike.

There was some question as to whether McGovern even knew that Stearns and Wexler had decided to abandon his commitment to support our South Carolina challenge, but there was no doubt that he opposed our efforts to get a statement of support for abortion rights into the party platform. As a member of the Platform Committee, I advised him that it would be better to include a plank on abortion than to have an all-out floor fight on the issue. The McGovern strategists feared that it was too controversial a subject for them, even though national opinion polls showed majority support for freedom of choice, and they refused to have it mentioned in the platform. Because this point was of such overriding importance to many women, a delegate introduced for a floor vote a minority plank stating that "in matters relating to human reproduction, each person's right to privacy, freedom of choice, and individual conscience shall be fully respected, consistent with relevant Supreme Court decisions." We lost, by a vote of 1569 to 1103.

Washington Post writer Myra McPherson reported on July 13 that McGovern used "his enormous leverage and tough staff to defeat" the minority plank and added this sidelight: "It was a fight that divided husband and wife. NWPC member Phyllis Segal and Massachusetts McGovern delegate Tony (Antonia) Chayes were battling for the plank, while Eli Segal and Abe Chayes were caucusing for 'no' votes. Mrs. Chayes said some operatives told her husband to 'get to' his wife and pull her off. 'That only made me work all the harder,' she said."

Another NWPC member was quoted as saying, "We got everything we asked for except abortion, so I suppose people will say, 'See, those women aren't effective; they lost on abortion.'"

In fact, we had won more than had ever before been included in a Democratic Party platform: our fifteen-point Rights of Women plank, which included commitments to "a priority effort to ratify the Equal Rights Amendment," strict enforcement of laws banning job discrimination and other sexist practices, maternity and pregnancy benefits, child care, revision of the Equal Pay Act to provide "equal pay for comparable work," and other proposals to widen educational and economic opportunities for women. Also, the plank promised that women would be appointed to positions of top responsibility in all branches of the federal government, "to achieve an equitable ratio of women and men," stating that these positions would include "Cabinet members, agency and division heads, and Supreme Court Justices" as well as "women advisers in equitable ratios on all government studies, commissions, and hearings." We had received a full commitment to our equity demand, and even though its implementation depended on the election of McGovern, we had succeeded in deepening and extending the party's position on women's rights. Also, we had made an independent showing of our political strength by nominating Frances "Sissy" Farenthold, a Texas attorney and legislator, for the vice presidency. It was a spur-of-the-moment decision, which came after Chisholm turned down a proposal that she run for the post. We succeeded in winning enough votes to have Farenthold place second to Senator Thomas Eagleton, McGovern's vice presidential choice.

Despite my differences with McGovern on the abortion issue and my anger at the way our South Carolina challenge had been sabotaged, I later agreed to serve with Shirley MacLaine as the cochair of his campaign's Women's Division. Along with many other women, I greatly admired McGovern's performance and record as a Senator and his leadership in opposing the war in Indochina and the ever-escalating nuclear arms race. He was by far the best candidate we could realistically hope for, and I worked hard for him, in the vain hope that he could defeat Nixon.

McGovern met with women leaders after the convention and pledged that we would have coequal status throughout his campaign. He made another conciliatory move. At his urging, Jean Westwood, a Utah Mormon and women's rights supporter, was selected as chair of the Democratic National Committee. One month after McGovern's massive defeat in the 1972 election, she was forced to resign in a contest with old-style politician Robert Strauss. In the battle for control of the committee, he defeated Westwood by only four and one-half votes.

Although the NWPC's major effort was focused on the Democratic convention, reflecting the fact that most caucus members were pro-Democratic, a small, informal group of Republican feminists and legislators made some minor gains at the GOP's August convention in Miami, which had all the regal trappings of a coronation of King Richard and Queen Pat.

The Republican women won approval of Rule 32, which said that each state should "endeavor" to have equal representation of men and women in its state delegations to future conventions. The Republican National Committee did not endeavor very hard, angering party feminists into creating a formal task force that affiliated with the NWPC and worked more effectively at the 1976 convention. The Republican women did not oppose Nixon's renomination, and no one could have predicted then the open revolt that broke out when Ronald Reagan won the presidency eight years later.

The only real fight over issues that occurred at the Republican 1972 convention in Miami was the successful effort by

Congresswoman Margaret Heckler of Massachusetts to win agreement for a platform plank advocating federally sponsored child-care centers, even though it was opposed by Nixon. She had to redraft the plank ninety-six times and, at one point, argued for two hours in favor of using the word *quality* to describe the kind of child-care centers parents wanted.

For a first effort, our accomplishments at the two conventions were promising, but our resources remained pitifully small in comparison to the funds necessary to achieve our goals. We had managed to raise $120,000 in the first year of the NWPC's existence, most of which was used for the convention operations. Our money did not stretch to letting us get formally involved in the Nixon-McGovern contest. Nevertheless, the 1972 campaign brought five new women members into the House, four of them feminists.

Two new political organizations came into being — the Women's Campaign Fund, created with help from liberal millionaire Stewart Mott and others to provide seed money for women candidates, and the Women's Education Fund (an outgrowth of our Women's Education for Delegate Selection project), which, supplementing the work of the venerable League of Women Voters and other organizations, held training workshops for women interested in politics.

McGovern was swamped by the Nixon-Agnew juggernaut campaign, with its huge resources of laundered money, its endless bag of dirty tricks, and its propaganda apparatus that kept the Democratic candidate on the defensive. In retrospect, it is clear that McGovern's indecision about whether to drop his proposed running mate, Thomas Eagleton, was less significant than the Republicans' burglary at Democratic headquarters in Watergate, but that was not the way the press saw it back then. Political commentators were more derisive of the grassroots, seemingly disorderly flavor of the Democratic convention, with all those women, blacks, and antiwar delegates, than they were of the almost totalitarian control over the delegates to the Republican event, which actually had a script that directed the main players where to stand and what to say.

Although McGovern received only about a third of the popular vote, he did better among women than among men. According to figures cited by Dr. Ethel Klein, a political scientist at Harvard University, McGovern received 38 percent of women's votes, compared with 32 percent from men. Nixon received about 1 percent fewer votes from women than from men, according to the Gallup pollsters. Our women campaigners for McGovern worked hard, but we were always hampered by insufficient funds and other resources. Moreover, McGovern did not make the issue of women's rights and inferior economic status a central part of his campaign, even though he said the right things when he spoke exclusively to women. Dr. Klein believes that even though McGovern could not have won the election on the basis of a feminist vote, "had he campaigned on women's rights, McGovern might have been saved from such a monumental defeat."

The first month of 1973 saw Nixon start his second term of office and the U.S. Supreme Court's historic affirmation of the constitutional right to abortion. (I spoke at a counterinaugural mass rally that was held at the Washington Monument to protest Nixon's war policies and the unraveling Watergate conspiracy.)

In February 1973, when the NWPC held its first major convention at Houston, Texas, a few Republican women attempted to whip up an attack on me because I had criticized Nixon as "the nation's chief resident male chauvinist" and denounced his budget cuts and impoundment of funds for education, job training, health services, and other programs that particularly affected women. Helen Bentley, one of the few high-ranking Nixon female appointees, claimed that the President had a "higher regard for women's rights than any other chief executive we ever had," which wasn't saying much, and rebuked me for being partisan. I replied that I wasn't criticizing our Republican caucus members but was sending to them and other women a cry from the heart "not to stand aside while the social legislation that is the best part of America is destroyed."

Later, at their separate caucus, some Republican women proposed that the members vote to admonish me for my anti-Nixon remarks. Instead, they approved a statement of concern about the severity of Nixon's budget cuts. A year and a half later, reporting on a July 1974 NWPC meeting in Wichita,

Kansas, the *New York Times* said that "sentiment for the impeachment of President Nixon was so strong among caucus members — about one-third of whom are Republicans — that Mrs. Abzug received a standing ovation when she made a mere reference to 'the necessary business of impeachment.' "

Within a month Nixon was out of the White House, in disgrace over the Watergate affair. His speedy pardon by President Gerald Ford and his recent reincarnation as adviser to both Democratic and Republican Presidents are symptomatic of the way the old-boys network of American corporate political power operates to protect and advance its own men. Even after his downfall, Nixon retained the support of leading male politicians, ideologues, publishers, and media magnates and is back among us in the persona of the wise elder statesman. During the unfolding of the Watergate scandal, I pointed out that it was a tale without any significant female characters in it, aside from poor, loyal Rosemary Wood, Nixon's secretary. Whether this was because there were no women of significant authority in the Nixon administration or the inner circles of the Republican Party, and thus none available to be corrupted, or because women in leadership would have had different values can be argued, but one thing is clear: the caliber of Nixon and other Presidents we have endured should strip away any pretense that intrinsic merit, ability, character, or emotional strength has anything to do with being in the White House. None of the alleged weaknesses for which women as a sex have been declared unfit for political leadership have stood in the way of men.

Winning with Women

In 1974 the women's movement was making new gains, reaching out to broader sections of the population and working on the economic equity issues that were later to surface as among the important concerns that motivated the electoral gender gap. The NWPC mapped its first "Win with Women" campaign, targeting increases in the number of women officeholders in local and state government as well as in Congress. NOW focused increasingly on ratification of the ERA, the unifying force in our free-wheeling, diverse movement. The Coalition of Labor Union Women was organized in Chicago by more than three thousand working women who came together from all parts of the country, and Mexican-American women founded their own national group. Black women had long had their own organizations, like the National Council of Negro Women, but they, too, developed a myriad of ad hoc groups in their communities and around particular issues.

Mindful of the unwarranted charge that feminists didn't care about housewives, the Wisconsin Commission on the Status of Women, chaired by Dr. Kathryn Clarenbach, sponsored a series of regional conferences that examined the problems and needs of homemakers. (I find it interesting that with all the alleged concern about the family emanating from the Moral Majority, every single proposal to improve the status of married women and homemakers has come from the women's movement.) Congress approved the inclusion of 1.5 million domestic service workers under the minimum wage, which was raised to $1.90 an hour, the result of a special effort organized and led by Shirley Chisholm. Another legislative triumph was adoption of the Equal Credit Opportunity Act, an amalgam of bills introduced by Congresswomen Sullivan, Heckler, and me. The new law was intended to eliminate the flagrant discrimination women encountered when they tried to get a home mortgage, bank loan, or credit card. I later led a delegation from our informal Congresswomen's caucus to a meeting with Chairman Arthur Burns of the Federal Reserve Board, at which we protested the weak federal regulations that had been issued to implement the law. We succeeded in getting the "regs" strengthened.

International Women's Year

While right-wingers continued to organize against the ERA and abortion rights and talked with hope about a backlash against women's expanding roles, a 1975 Harris poll showed a deepening national trend in support of our goals: 59 percent favored the improved status of women, 54 percent approved of legalized abortion, and 67 percent thought we needed more child-care centers. That year had been designated International Women's Year by the United Nations, and in January 1975 President Ford appointed a thirty-five-member national commission to observe IWY and "promote equality between men and women." He named Jill Ruckelshaus, a leading Republican feminist and wife of Environmental Protection Administrator William Ruckelshaus, to head the commission, and I was selected as one of four congressional members. In June I flew directly from the NWPC's convention in Boston to Mexico City to attend the official UN-sponsored IWY conference as a congressional adviser to the U.S. delegation.

It was an impressive gathering of women and men from almost every nation in the world, the first such meeting ever held — vibrant, colorful, turbulent, and in its own frustrating way symbolic of the ambiguous position of women. Inside the formal conference hall many of the official delegations of the UN member nations were headed by men, and women delegates were not free to vote against the official lines of their governments. Representatives of the Arab nations and other Third World delegations used the occasion to heat up their conflict with Israel and succeeded in adopting a Declaration of Mexico that included a condemnation of Israel as "racist," the first, but unfortunately not the last time that the UN equated Zionism with racism.

I advised the American delegation to vote against the declaration, which it did. The anti-Israel atmosphere injected into a conference about women dismayed many of us, and we were especially disheartened when Jihan Sadat, wife of Egyptian President Anwar Sadat, led a walkout from the hall as Leah Rabin, wife of Israeli Prime Minister Yitzhak Rabin, rose to speak. That was not our idea of the way to demonstrate the international solidarity of women, and later I and other American feminists issued a statement deploring the linkage of Zionism with racism. (Sadly, the 1980 UN Mid-Decade Conference on Women, held in Copenhagen, was marred by PLO supporters who tried to make Israel, rather than the conditions of women, the major issue. Betty Friedan and I led a protest against this tactic.)

The real sense of sisterhood came from outside, from a simultaneously held nongovernmental IWY tribune on the other side of Mexico City, which was attended by thousands of women of many different nationalities. They spoke of dire poverty, dying babies, illiteracy, disease, and hunger; of overwork, underpay, and too much childbearing; of unjust laws, family customs, and barbaric sexual practices that victimized women and children; of the fact that even educated women had to struggle against the effects of pervasive male and class control of political, economic, and cultural life. But the women were also brimming over with eloquence and the hope that by coming together and organizing as women, internationally and in their homelands, they could improve their lives and those of their families. It was a profoundly moving experience, causing me to feel that our own American struggle was part of an international coming to political maturity by women and that perhaps our common problems could unite us across national barriers.

Back in Congress, I introduced a bill proposing that a federally financed national women's conference be held as part of what had now become the UN's International Decade of Women, projected for 1975 to 1985. The House Government Operations and Individual Rights subcommittee that I chaired held hearings and reported out my legislation, which also incorporated parts of bills introduced by Patsy Mink and Peggy Heckler. It was passed at the end of the year and approved by President Ford, but not without a fight on the House floor, where I managed the bill. One Congressman, apparently visualizing our project in the male image of conventions, objected, saying that we would be using federal funds for wild parties and drinking. I commented that in all my years of going to out-of-town women's meetings, I had never been aware of any demand for the services of "call boys." Congress authorized half the $10 million we had requested to hold state meetings and a national conference. The $5 million allocated for the first government-sponsored national women's meeting in our history amounted to less than a nickel for each female in the United States. The money was not actually appropriated until June 1976.

Changing the Guidelines

Meanwhile, a new problem was developing. Reacting to the 1972 McGovern defeat, old-line forces in the Democratic Party were seeking to weaken the McGovern-Fraser guidelines that had brought so many independent-minded delegates to the Miami convention. With chairman Robert Strauss in control, the party was positioning itself for a middle-of-the-road 1976 presidential campaign against Nixon's bland successor, Gerald Ford. But the democratization process was not easy to stop, and the Democrats were committed to holding a miniconvention in 1974.

The Kansas City gathering scored two historic firsts — it was the first time a major political party had held a national convention in a nonpresidential year, and it was the first time a major party had adopted a written charter firmly setting out its rules and structures. A commission headed by Barbara Mikulski, then a Baltimore city councilwoman, had the delicate task of trying to recommend new party rules that would be acceptable to both the new and old elements in the party, and Strauss was urging both sides to compromise. The commission adopted a rule requiring "full participation by all Democrats, with particular concern for minority groups, Native Americans, women, and youth in the delegate selection process and in all party affairs." It set an affirmative action goal of participation by these groups "as indicated by their presence in the Democratic electorate" but said the goal would not be accomplished by the "imposition of mandatory quotas."

This represented a step back from the McGovern-Fraser guidelines, which assured "reasonable representation" of women, minorities, and youth that would fairly reflect their numbers in the population, and the Harris equal-division ruling. Nevertheless, our women's caucus, working in close cooperation with the black caucus, felt that it was important to get the new language, which applied only to delegate selection for the 1976 convention, permanently included in the new charter to be approved at the Kansas City meeting.

By the time the proposed charter got to the miniconvention in December 1974, the phrase about "particular concern" for women, minorities, and youth had been eliminated, and another change brought strong objections from our women's caucus and the black caucus, which at one point threatened a walkout. Although we were willing to compromise on some items, we drew the line at a section which said that "composition alone shall not constitute prima facie evidence of discrimination, nor shall it shift the burden of proof to the challenged party." This was a direct reversal of the 1972 policy we had fought for and won and that had provided the basis for challenging unrepresentative delegations. We succeeded in getting this objectionable section deleted from the charter over the angry opposition of Al Barkan of the AFL-CIO and others. But we no longer had a guarantee that the burden of proof would be shifted to the challenged party because the charter remained silent on that point. We did not have a commitment to equal division, but we did negotiate a new section, which said that equal division between men and women would not be construed as a quota. This meant the state parties were free, but not required, to have equal representation of men and women.

Because of the more loosely constructed language and the weakening of our ability to challenge delegations as unrepresentative, the number of women delegates at the 1976 convention was down to 34 percent of the total, compared with 40 percent in 1972, and minority representation declined from 20 percent to about 9 percent. This slippage confirmed our belief that we needed an absolute guarantee of equal division at future conventions and enforcement of affirmative action for minorities.

Love and Promises from Jimmy

In 1976, after three terms in the House, I decided to seek the Democratic nomination for Senator from New York, a contest I was to lose by a margin of less than 1 percent. I was also deeply involved in the 1976 Democratic presidential campaign. I had endorsed Congressman Morris K. Udall of Arizona, the most liberal of the contenders, but by the time the convention opened in New York in mid-July, Jimmy Carter already had the nomination assured. As in the 1972 convention, the women delegates were committed to various candidates, but women's groups had been working on issues jointly for months in advance. In the preconvention skirmishing at the Rules and Platform committees, we were operating through the Democratic Women's Agenda '76, a coalition of the NWPC Democratic Task Force, headed by Mildred Jeffrey, and the Democratic National Committee's effective women's caucus, headed by Koryne Horbal of Minnesota and Patt Derian of Mississippi, both also NWPC members. As a southerner, Derian was supporting Carter, and she and Margaret "Midge" Costanza, then the vice mayor of Rochester, were our main links to the candidate. Together with coalition representatives and other women members of Congress, I testified at the Platform Committee hearings in favor of a women's plank. A DNC staff member later informed us that the platform would not have separate planks on issues of concern to special constituencies; rather, these concerns would be addressed throughout the document, and we were told that only two of our proposals — abortion rights and gay rights — would present a problem. Our other demands for continued ERA support, economic and educational opportunities, child care, and so forth, were included in the platform, though not in as specific detail as they had been in the 1972 platform. This was a more moderate platform, molded in the more moderate image of a southern governor who had been made a national figure almost overnight by clever packaging.

Our efforts to obtain recognition of the civil rights of gay men and lesbians ran into a stone wall; however, the coalition was able to negotiate language in support of the U.S. Supreme Court's abortion rights decision with DNC staff members, only to have them renege on the agreement later. An intense pressure campaign was mounted by the women's coalition and other groups, including the National Abortion Rights Action League, Planned Parenthood, and NOW, and a compromise was finally reached. We accepted the rather backhanded language drafted by Stuart Eizenstat and Joseph Duffy of the Carter campaign for inclusion in the platform: "We fully recognize the religious and ethical nature of the concerns which many Americans have on the subject of abortion. We feel, however, that it is undesirable to attempt to amend the U.S. Constitution to overturn the

Supreme Court decision in this area." It was progress of a sort, in view of Carter's strong opposition to abortion and the counterpressure from the U.S. Catholic Conference and the Right to Life movement.

Horbal later explained how the agreement had been reached: "We let the Carter organization know that their own women were supporting our position and that we had the votes to take this issue to the floor of the full convention for debate on prime time." Neither Carter nor the DNC wanted any evidence of disagreement within the party to blemish the coming campaign against the incumbent, President Gerald Ford.

There was a more prolonged battle over our key issue of equal division. It started with a letter to the Rules Committee chair, former Congresswoman Martha Griffiths, from our coalition leaders, requesting that the party adopt a rule requiring equal numbers of men and women delegates to the 1980 convention. When the committee met in Washington on June 19, our proposal had wide support from its members and appeared headed for approval. By the next day the Carter people had been persuaded by Strauss and Mark Siegel, executive director of the DNC, to oppose it. They came up with different language, proposed by W. Averell Harriman, substituting the word *promote* for *require* in the phrase "the call to future national conventions shall require equal division between delegate men and women." This passed the Rule Committee, and a rebellious Carter woman delegate immediately filed a minority report restoring our original language.

We were prepared to make a fight on the issue when the convention opened in New York on July 12, and this time we had a classy operation going, one that was more highly organized and visible than it had been at our debut in Miami. We set up headquarters — Women's Action Central — at the Penn Statler Hotel, across the street from the conventional hall. It was staffed by fifty women volunteers, who also ran a daily Women's Political News Service that kept the press corps briefed and gave them access to women delegates for interviews that would popularize our demands. Within a few days we held five separate briefing and strategy meetings of women delegates and conducted a successful fund-raising party at the glittering glass and marble Metropolitan Opera House in Lincoln Center, attracting more than twenty-five hundred paying guests.

I thought it would be a good idea for Carter to meet with women's rights advocates before the convention opened, and Patt and Midge set up a session for us at the Americana Hotel, Carter's headquarters, on the Saturday before the formal sessions started. About a hundred women, including key delegates, Congresswomen, other women leaders, and feminists, were invited. Many of us were meeting Carter and his wife, Rosalynn, for the first time. We made brief speeches at each other, he exuding general remarks about his belief in women's equality, which he said he had learned from his mother and wife, who had always been working women, and I, as spokeswoman for the group, stressing the specifics of our concerns.

Other women present also spoke strongly of the neglected needs of the female half of our population. At Carter's suggestion we set up a small group to meet with him the next day to work out the details of the commitments he was prepared to make. The understanding was that if these were satisfactory, we would consider accepting the compromise on equal division and avoid a floor fight at the convention. Among those of us who met with Carter and his aides were Patt Derian, Congresswoman Elizabeth Holtzman of New York, C. DeLores Tucker, Pennsylvania's secretary of state and the only black woman to hold that post, and New York Lieutenant Governor Mary Anne Krupsak.

The nine-point agreement we negotiated after two meetings provided, in addition to the "promote" equal division language, commitments to have "full representation" of women on all party commissions and committees and to give the Democratic Women's Division an independent role, "strengthened by adequate staff and funding, enabling it to promote and implement feminist objectives." Carter also pledged to consult personally with representatives of our caucus; if elected, to use his presidential office to secure ratification of the ERA, to appoint women to cabinet posts and throughout the judiciary, and to seriously consider a woman for the next Supreme Court opening. The caucus agreed to set up a talent bank of women whom he would consider for appointments to key posts. He also com-

mitted himself to compensátory action necessary for women, as
well as minorities, to overcome patterns of past discrimination
in employment. Finally, the pact stated that "a major portion
of Governor Carter's commitment to the nation will be the
elimination of the remaining legal barriers against women."
The language was general, but we believed that it was backed
up by the substantive programs described in the party platform.
We also felt that our negotiating session itself provided recognition of our strength as a political force, and also as good organizers. While we were negotiating, our caucus was making all the
preparations to conduct a floor fight on the equal-division issue,
but because the Carter forces had such a commanding lead, we
were not certain we had enough votes to put across our minority report.

The pros and cons were argued at a meeting of more than a
thousand women delegates, to whom we brought the proposed
agreement for approval. I presented it and argued for it
strongly; some prominent leaders, among them Karen DeCrow
of NOW, Sissy Farenthold, and Betty Friedan, believed that we
should hold out for an airtight requirement of equal division,
but when the vote came, the "promote" language was overwhelmingly approved.

Columnist Ellen Goodman later wrote:

> When the NWPC was founded, it consisted of some "names," a
> good press, and a grassroots feeling labeled sisterhood. Today, the
> Democratic women have learned the ropes, the Robert's Rules of
> Order, and the arts and crafts of political numbers.
>
> As new insiders they have the pressure to be "realistic," the
> possibility of future successes, and the necessity of present compro-
> mises . . . Carter negotiated with them personally and at great
> length because, while they didn't have enough power to win, they
> had too much power to be dismissed. The women decided to negoti-
> ate rather than fight, because they had something to gain.

At the 1976 convention we gained not only the agreement
with Carter but other visible tokens of the growing political
importance of women. Congresswoman Lindy Boggs of Louisiana chaired the convention, Congresswoman Barbara Jordan of
Texas, who had won national attention with her eloquence at

the Nixon impeachment hearings, delivered a rousing keynote address, and women were evident in leadership throughout the proceedings. Even more important, the persistent efforts of the women's caucus, with Millie Jeffrey and Joanne Howes, a leading feminist, plugging away steadily at the issue, won subsequent agreement to equal division from the DNC for the 1978 miniconvention in Memphis. The official party call to the 1980 convention also required that there be equal numbers of men and women delegates.

In October Carter made a highly effective personal appearance at a crowded U.S. Women's Agenda meeting in Washington, at which he described in greater and more satisfactory detail his support for economic and social programs needed by women and their families. He was applauded enthusiastically when he said he wanted to be known as the President who had achieved equal rights for women, just as President Johnson had won civil rights legislation for blacks. Ratification of the ERA, he assured us, would be one of his top priorities. "If I become President," he added, "I intend to tear down the walls that have kept you out of decision-making, policy-making participation in your government — and you can depend on that."

Later that afternoon, Mim Kelber and I flew to Atlanta, where we met at Carter campaign headquarters with two staff members, Landon Butler and Jan Oliver, a feminist and close friend. I laid out a plan for mobilizing more women to help elect Carter and other ways to organize support among Democrats in Congress. (As we talked, we were joined by Hamilton Jordan. It seemed odd to me that this restless young man, casually dressed in jeans, work shirt, and high leather boots, and fidgeting in a swivel chair, was considered the chief tactician of the Carter campaign, but he was friendly and apparently eager to have my help. After Jordan instructed the others to work with me on my plans, we left and flew back to New York that evening. That was my first encounter with Jordan. My last one came several years later, when he crudely fired me as head of President Carter's advisory committee on women.)

Although I had reservations about Carter, I spent much of my spare time, after losing the New York Democratic Senate primary, in campaigning and speaking for him around the country. I was pleased by his selection of the liberal Walter Mondale as his running mate, and he was clearly preferable to Gerald Ford, both on women's rights issues and foreign policy. Carter seemed to be sincerely interested in curbing military spending and limiting the arms race, and he was for federally funded child-care legislation, tougher enforcement of antidiscrimination laws, and other of our major concerns. Both men said they favored the ERA and were personally opposed to abortion rights, but Ford supported a constitutional ban on abortion, wanted to weaken enforcement regulations, and had also vetoed the Child Care Standard Act.

Reagan on the "Exotic Species"

At the GOP's 1976 nominating convention in Detroit, the NWPC Republican Women's Task Force was better organized than it had been four years earlier but found itself conducting mostly a holding operation, even though the number of women delegates was up slightly, to 31.4 percent. Although they made no endorsements, many privately preferred Ford to Ronald Reagan, whose campaign leaders had not even acknowledged repeated requests to meet with them. Peter Hannaford, spokesman for issues in the Reagan campaign, told the task force that his candidate believed in removing discrimination and increasing participation, but had no specific programs for achieving this goal. He said Reagan did not feel that women were some "exotic species" that should be specially treated. Unlike Ford, he was definitely against the ERA.

Most of the Republican feminists' energy went into achieving a narrow victory that prevented the GOP from dropping its traditional platform support of the ERA. The task force was not active in the platform abortion fight, though Congresswoman Millicent Fenwick of New Jersey and some others tried hard, but unavailingly, to prevent the Platform Committee from approving a constitutional ban. The feminists continued to press on the issue, however, and in a close voice vote on the convention floor, the antiabortion plank was defeated. (They were to lose on that point when Reagan won the nomination at the 1980 convention.)

In a later report on the 1976 convention, the NWPC task force spoke of the Republican Party's "distressing inclination to turn its back on a history of consistent advances for women. Women held fewer important posts at the 1976 convention than they had in some past conventions; only a letter from task force chair Patricia Goldman, shortly before the convention, resulted in the inclusion of a few more women speakers in the program. Any hope of strengthening Rule 32 [on delegate selection] was abandoned as task force members fought to avoid diluting what had proved to be an already leaky commitment to expanding women's participation in the conventions."

The contrast between the roles and achievements of the Republican and Democratic women at their respective conventions was striking, but although Carter squeaked out a narrow victory over Ford, he got about 1.4 million fewer votes from women than from men. The explanations were varied. Folk wisdom credited Betty Ford, the outspoken, independent, and pro-ERA First Lady, with being her husband's biggest asset among women.

3

The Spirit of Houston

JIMMY CARTER published *Keeping Faith: Memories of a President* almost two years after he left the White House on January 20, 1981. Alone with his word processor in his Plains, Georgia, home, far away from pressure groups and pesty feminists, he wrote of the crises he had faced during his four-year term, selecting those he considered most important, and of how he had kept faith with the American people on his campaign commitments.

Our former President is reputed to have an excellent memory, but he drew a blank on women. They are not in the book. Nowhere. Not a word about his accomplishments in behalf of women, nor his failures, nor what happened to his stirring commitment to make ERA ratification the hallmark of his administration. One photo caption identifies Rosalynn Carter as being present at the National Women's Conference. Nothing is said about why the conference was held or what it did.

Left to their own devices, Presidents and lesser male political leaders find it easy to forget about women. To them, women are a side issue, a mere afterthought, a constituency to be dealt with at voting time and placated only in proportion to the urgency with which they press their demands.

In the early days of 1977, however, the climate for women was very favorable in Washington. Taking the new president at his word, the National Women's Political Caucus put together the Coalition for Women's Appointments, a network of more than sixty national women's organizations, and supplied the administration with the résumés of women professionals well qualified for appointment to the executive branch, which (like the Congress) was predominantly male at the upper policy levels. The caucus also set up a Judicial Appointment Project: there were, at the time, only five women judges in the entire federal court system. (When similar lists of highly qualified women were submitted to the White House after Ronald Reagan's election in 1980, there was no response. Finally, an administration spokesman claimed that the names had been lost or misplaced.)

By the end of his single term in office, Carter claimed to have appointed more than nineteen hundred women to top policy jobs, which accounted for 22 percent of his major appointments. According to a National Organization for Women analysis, however, about a thousand of his women appointees were named to honorary, unpaid, per diem, or temporary posts in the many commissions and committees that Presidents set up from time to time. That left about nine hundred women or about 12 percent of his appointments assigned to full-time, high-level "plum" jobs. Fourteen percent of his appointments were minorities, men and women. Not a great record, but better than that of previous White House occupants.

In his 1980 campaign literature, it was asserted that Carter had appointed "half of all women Cabinet Secretaries in our history." Translated, the statement meant that three earlier Presidents each had one woman department head in his cabinet, starting with Franklin D. Roosevelt's appointment of Frances Perkins in 1933 as his Secretary of Labor. Carter appointed three women to his cabinet: Patricia Harris, who was moved from the Housing Department to the Health and Human Services Department, and Shirley Hufstedler, who was named to head the Education Department after Juanita Kreps, his other appointee, resigned as Secretary of Commerce. He also appointed forty women federal judges, raising their presence in the federal judiciary to more than 5 percent. Some 152 new federal judgeships had been created under recently enacted legislation, and the women's organizations felt that even though Carter had done more than preceding Presidents, he could have done better. He was always careful to avoid making a commitment to fill the next Supreme Court vacancy with a woman, though, as it happened, the occasion did not arise during his term. One of the few specific commitments Reagan was to make to women in his 1980 campaign was a pledge to name a woman to the high court. After he made that promise, public opinion polls registered increased support for him among women voters.

Many of Carter's women appointees were liberals and feminists who performed admirably as inside advocates sensitive to the needs of women and their work and family problems. They brought a new and necessary dimension to the development of policy and the administration of laws and regulations. One of the most outstanding was caucus member Patt Derian, who as Assistant Secretary of State in charge of human rights literally saved the lives of hundreds of political prisoners in Argentina and Brazil. Department heads Harris, Kreps, and Hufstedler hired large numbers of women, and Harris issued orders that all advisory committees were to have adequate representation of women, minorities, and disabled individuals. Other excellent appointments included Alexis Herman as head of the U.S. Labor Department Women's Bureau and Eleanor Holmes Norton, a black attorney who had headed the New York City Human Rights Commission. She became chair of the Equal Employment Opportunity Commission, taking on the tough assignment of cleaning up a backlog of thousands of job and pay-discrimination complaints from women and minority workers.

Carter had offered me the EEOC post, telling me there was no one he could propose who would have greater support among women and blacks, but I declined because we had already reached a consensus among women's groups to support Norton for the post. Carter asked me to meet with him, and also with Hamilton Jordan, to canvass other positions I might fill in his administration. They variously offered me seats on the Federal Trade Commission, the Federal Communications Commission, and the chair of various agencies. I had been interested in becoming Secretary of Transportation because of my congressional expertise in mass-transportation problems, but he chose Brock Adams, another member of Congress, for that post, and the FTC chairmanship, which also interested me, went to Michael Pertschuk. House Speaker "Tip" O'Neill and other members of Congress wrote to Carter, urging him to name me to the FTC chair or another high post, but as I finally told the President, I wanted to help his administration in any way possible, but I wasn't really looking for a job.

The truth was that I had reservations about working in a subordinate position within the Carter administration, feeling that it would cramp my independent style. I wanted to be free to call the shots as I saw them and to run for electoral office again. I did accept the appointment as nonsalaried presiding officer of the National Commission on Observance of International Women's Year, whose membership Carter expanded to thirty-nine women and three men in an executive order issued on March 28, 1977. The commission had the task of holding public meetings on women in all fifty states and six territories, culminating in a National Women's Conference, as prescribed in my legislation. Naturally, I had to be there.

Mainstream Feminism

Later we called it the "rainbow of women" conference. Our official report to the President and the Congress was titled "The Spirit of Houston." Both phrases convey a sense of the historic uniqueness of this event — the first time American women had come together in a federally sponsored meeting as elected delegates from every state and territory to voice their needs and hopes for the future. The full meaning of what we had accomplished washed over me in a great tide of emotion that swept the vast meeting hall as Commissioner Gloria Scott, a black Houstonian who was also president of the Girl Scouts of America, rapped her gavel and declared the conference open. There was an explosion of sound, a visceral roar erupting from the guts of the thousands who had arrived from every part of the country and were standing and cheering in a moment of revelation and empowerment, a coming-of-age for American women. *Time* magazine reported afterward that the Houston conference showed American women had reached "some kind of watershed in their own history and in that of the nation." In a 1983 special anniversary issue, it identified the meeting as one of the most significant events of the past sixty years. A London newspaper, the *Evening Standard,* said, "Mainstream feminism has evolved into the most broadly based movement for egalitarianism that America possesses . . . The women's movement is now a truly national, unified engine of change which could conceivably become the cutting edge of the most important human issues America faces in the next decade."

We had traveled a long way from the first women's rights meeting at Seneca Falls in July 1848, when sixty-eight women and thirty-two men had come together to "discuss the social, civil, and religious rights of women." That was the beginning of the crusade for suffrage and equality. Suffrage had been won in 1920, but real equality was still far off, and the women at Houston knew it.

Before the conference opened on November 19, 1977, there had been hopeful predictions that it would be a disaster, a free-for-all cat fight. "Houston will finish off the women's movement," Phyllis Schlafly stated on television. Ultra-right-wing groups planned to hold their own "pro-God, pro-family" meeting in Houston at the same time, and Robert Shelton, Imperial Wizard of the United Klans of America, announced that he would be in the vicinity. "Some of our women members and sympathizers will be in the meetings to oppose what is going on," he said. "Our men also will be there to protect our women from all the militant lesbians. It's not safe for a decent woman to be there."

In fact, the Houston conference and the preceding state meetings were probably the most democratic ever held in our nation. More than one hundred fifty thousand women (and some men) had come to the state sessions, which had been widely publicized in advance. Although right-wing and religious groups had packed some state meetings with women who looked to male leaders for guidance, overall they commanded the support of only about 20 percent of the women. Those who attended the state meetings debated and passed more than four thousand resolutions on a wide variety of subjects, and the substance of any recommendations that had gained the approval of twelve or more state or territorial meetings was included in a proposed National Plan of Action. This twenty-six-plank program, comparable to a political party platform, was the product of an almost year-long democratic process. The participants in the meetings had also elected delegates and alternates to the Houston conference. Both in the states and in the elections for the national conference, intensive efforts had been made to assure that a true cross section of women would participate. Poor women and minority women who could not afford to go to Houston on their own were awarded financial "scholarships," special facilities were provided for the disabled, and child-care centers were made available. The commission also appointed several hundred delegates-at-large to make certain that the heads of every major national women's organization and religious, ethnic, and racial group would be included.

Besides the two thousand elected delegates, about eighteen thousand women and men came as guests, observers, and participants in workshops, and there was a large representation of women from other nations. A novel touch was the many young men who carried their babies while their wives went to meetings. To those of us who saw the great diversity of women at Houston, it was not surprising when analyses of the 1980 electoral gender gap showed that it included women of all ages, colors, and backgrounds.

We were also assured of political diversity: among the delegates were Mary Crisp of Arizona, cochair of the Republican National Committee, who later resigned from her post in protest against the Reagan takeover of the 1980 GOP convention; Jean Westwood of Utah, a former Democratic Party chair; women members of Congress from both parties; large numbers of elected women officials; and women who considered themselves independent or belonged to fringe parties. On the platform as the conference opened sat First Lady Rosalynn Carter and two former First Ladies, Lady Bird Johnson and Betty Ford, who spoke in their own names. (Mrs. Carter said later that Houston was the most important and exciting conference she had ever attended.) The large crowd contained women of every political description, including the approximately 20 percent of the delegates who opposed the National Plan of Action.

All twenty-six planks in the National Plan were open to debate. Seventeen were adopted by large majorities. One, on equal credit, was approved unanimously. Three amended resolutions and four substitute resolutions were also passed overwhelmingly, and one was rejected. One of the high moments of the conference came when a group of women — Maxine Waters, a young black assemblywoman from California; Billie Nave Masters, a Native American teacher; Mariko Tse, a Japanese-American; Sandy Serrano Sewell, president of the Comision Femenil Mexicana; and Coretta Scott King, the widow of Martin Luther King Jr. — took turns reading sections of a revised plank on minority women that they, with Gloria Steinem of the Resolutions Committee, had worked on for two days. It was another expression of the remarkable unity and sensitivity to one another's special concerns that made the conference unique. "Let the message go forth from Houston," Coretta King said, "and spread all over this land. There is a new force, a new understanding, a new sisterhood against all injustice that has been born here. We will not be divided and defeated again." The plan was approved by a large majority, and even some right-wingers stood in support.

At the heart of the National Plan of Action demands was approval of the Equal Rights Amendment, which had already been ratified by thirty-five states, where three fourths of the U.S. population live. Our other demands ran the gamut of issues that touch women's lives: equal opportunities for women in employment, education, business, politics, government, the arts and humanities, in sports and the media; extension of Social Security benefits to homemakers and programs to provide counseling and other services for displaced homemakers; assistance to battered women, disabled women, minority women, older women, rural women, and women in prison; an end to discrimination in the granting of credit and insurance and in divorce laws, inheritance laws, and our entire legal system; concern for women's health needs, a national health insurance plan, and the right to choose abortion, with federal and state Medicaid benefits for those unable to afford it; pregnancy disability benefits for employed women; civil rights for lesbians; protection against rape and child abuse; comprehensive childcare facilities; welfare reform and educational and job programs for poor women; an end to the institutionalized bias that has led to the double discrimination against minority women and to the conditions of poverty from which they suffer disproportionately.

Finally, maintaining that peace is a women's issue, the Plan proposed reduced military spending and sales of military weapons to foreign powers, called for peace education in the schools, and said that the United States should take the lead in urging all nuclear powers to start phasing out their nuclear arsenals and develop initiatives to advance world peace. Women, it stressed, should participate fully in formulating and executing all aspects of American foreign policy.

As Commissioner Alice Rossi, a leading sociologist, pointed out in a detailed study of the conference, the women at Houston were predominantly reformers seeking regulatory and legal changes in mainstream American life, not rebels trying to overthrow an entire system. They viewed government as a necessary instrument that should serve the practical needs of its people, and — in anticipatory contrast to Ronald Reagan's belief in less government — they wanted more direct government assistance and intervention to help women overcome the inferior position in which they had been kept by centuries of discrimination and prejudice. Clearly, there were differences — of class, social status, political loyalties, and ideological viewpoints — even among the eighty percent or more of the delegates who approved the National Plan of Action. But the spirit of Houston — a remarkably sensitive and mutually understanding approach — led them to meet on the middle ground of reform in support of what they saw as practical solutions to the economic, social, and political problems affecting millions of American women. The National Plan became the blueprint for action by women everywhere.

For many of the women Houston was also a time of coalition-building, networking, and organization of still more special-interest caucuses. Caucuses of black, Hispanic, and other minority women had already been established; to these were added groups of farm women, Asian-American women, American Indian and Eskimo women, Jewish women, young women, disabled women, women in the arts, and women peace workers, all of whom held first-time feminist caucus sessions at Houston and planned future cooperation. A continuing committee was authorized to work on implementing the National Plan on an interim basis.

Women eagerly swapped addresses and experiences, agreed to stay in touch, offered to help each other in particular causes and in ERA and election campaigns. The activist lines of communication that were then crisscrossing the country were deepened and extended. Representatives of the long-established national women's organizations and the feminist and activist groups born in the 1960s and 1970s came together at Houston, learning from each other and laying the foundation for coalition work in behalf of the ERA and other issues. In the 1980s, many of these old and new organizations joined in lobbies and actions to oppose Reagan budget cuts and plan mass voter-registration drives among women. Together, these organizations had an outreach to literally millions of women.

Political commentators saw broader implications in the Houston results. Echoing what had been my main political coalition theme in speeches I had been making throughout the country, *Newsday*'s David Behrens described the National Plan as "an egalitarian movement, an umbrella for the civil rights movement and the movement for economic equality, for the environmental and consumer movements and the movement for participatory democracy."

The paralysis of the conference threatened by right-wing opponents had not materialized. Clearly outnumbered and discouraged by the obvious unity of establishment and feminist groups, the small percentage of women and male delegates who opposed the National Plan in whole or in part engaged in only perfunctory debate and opposition on the floor. At one point I had to insist from the chair that anti–abortion rights speakers take the microphone and present their arguments. Many of these women, I knew, felt strongly that abortion was morally wrong, and although I disagreed with their views, I respected the depth of their feelings. Most of the right-wing rhetoric was reserved for an opposition meeting held in another part of Houston, at which Schlafly and a collection of male politicians and preachers lectured an audience of mostly women conscripts who had been bused into town in large numbers by their churches and "moral majority" organizations.

I find it significant that in contrast to the many women's rights leaders who have emerged in recent years, the right wing has produced hardly any nationally known women leaders, besides Schlafly and a few Right to Life spokeswomen, an indication that this reactionary movement does not care to encourage female leadership of any kind. Whenever the media want to present "both sides" of a women's issue, they almost invariably trot out Schlafly before the TV cameras, which may mean they are impressed by her charisma or simply that they can't find anyone else. I doubt, too, that the views of even conservative women who cling to traditional values and are uneasy at the new assertiveness of women are being represented when Schlafly calls for bigger military budgets and praises the nuclear bomb as "a marvelous gift that was given to our country by a wise God." And there can't be many who consider realistic her proposed remedy for the prevention of herpes. Both sexes, she says, should remain virginal until marriage.

Although the right-wing forces had little impact at Houston, they were gaining nationally in influence and political pressure on Congress and other institutions. The press interpreted their movement — wrongly, I believe — as proof that the American people were shifting to the right. Women were certainly not moving in that direction (Houston and national public opinion polls showed just the contrary), but male legislators and other politicians tended to be more responsive to right-wing pressures than to those of the women's organizations.

From the euphoric high of Houston, the women returned to their communities as 1977 ended and faced the hard political realities of male power: it would be no simple matter to get the National Plan, in part or in whole, enacted into legislation and executive policy. Alarmingly, the ratification process of ERA had stopped cold at thirty-five states, three short of the thirty-eight needed. In the first eight months after Congress approved the ERA in 1972, twenty-two states had voted to ratify the amendment, but after that the pace had slowed, with major campaigns, intensive strategy, and tough fights required to win passage in the other thirteen states over a four-year period. Indiana had become the thirty-fifth state to ratify the ERA in January 1977, a victory for which the brand-new Carter administration could take no credit, and since then not a single additional state had ratified it. In some instances the amendment was defeated by margins of one or two votes.

True, popular support for the measure was rising both nationally and in the states that had not ratified, and volunteers, new members, and even money were pouring into the headquarters of NOW, which had assumed major responsibility for the campaign.* But time after aggravating time, a hard core of male politicians who controlled the legislatures in those states, most of them in the South, blocked consideration or passage of the amendment. NOW's leaders began to feel, too, that the ERA was not getting enough practical help from the White House. Despite his vow to make ERA ratification an emblem of his administration, President Carter was confining himself to an occasional phone call to a recalcitrant or undecided Democratic state legislator, preferring to relegate ERA work to his wife and daughter-in-law, Judy Carter, and staff members. He called the women his "surrogates," as though campaigning for ERA was exclusively women's work.

The Friday Night Massacre

Our national IWY commission presented its official report on Houston to President Carter at a White House reception on March 22, 1978. The commission would be closing shop nine

---

*The ERA campaign has been among the biggest in American history, comparable in breadth to the suffrage movement. Among those actively involved are ERAmerica, a coalition of women's groups; the NWPC; the League of Women Voters; the Business and Professional Women of America; hundreds of other organizations; and hundreds of thousands of women volunteers and sympathetic men.

days later, as required by law, and he promised to replace us with a new committee on women's issues. (After Kennedy, each succeeding President had authorized a national commission on the status of women.) Carter dragged his feet on the matter for several months, creating a hiatus in our activities.

Midge Costanza, the first woman to be appointed a presidential assistant, was our advocate inside the White House. Midge had grown up in the Democratic machine politics of Rochester, New York, and was one of the first political leaders to endorse Carter when he ran for the presidency. Her White House post was a thank-you from Carter for her help in making him President, but by then she had become an ardent feminist and her independence did not sit well with Carter's male advisers. She lasted only twenty months at the White House.

Midge is a delightful woman with a wild, impish, irreverent sense of humor, and in her job as the President's liaison to the public — meaning women, minorities, and other groups — she was open and sympathetic to their concerns and an important asset to the administration. By August 1, 1978, however, she felt she had to resign. Most of her duties, and then her office, had been taken away, and she was demoted to a room in the White House basement. She had been too outspoken: she had been the first Carter top aide to call for Bert Lance's resignation, she had invited gay rights activists to meet with her, and she had criticized the President for his antiabortion statements. In a memorandum to Carter dated July 13, 1977, she informed him that she had received "an overwhelming number of phone calls from public interest groups, individuals, *and* White House staff members and Agency staff members expressing concern and even anger" over remarks he had made at his press conference the preceding day.

Replying to a question as to whether denial of Medicaid funding to poor women was not unfair, Carter, in a comment that was widely publicized, had said "there are many things in life that are not fair, that wealthy people can afford and poor people can't." He also called for very strict enforcement of the federal regulations allowing Medicaid funds for abortion only when a woman's life was in danger or when pregnancy was the result of rape or incest, and he had opened a hornet's nest by also opposing state funding of abortions, a service that some states were still providing. Carter returned the memo to Midge with a hand-written comment in the margin: "My opinion was well defined to U.S. during campaign. My statement is actually more liberal than I feel personally."

Carter's call for strict enforcement of the ban on Medicaid funding was interpreted so severely by Health and Human Resources Secretary Joseph Califano that Midge took aim at it in a speech to the National Press Club. "Sure," she said, "you do have a right to an abortion, but you have to report the pregnancy within forty-eight hours, then be examined by two doctors, two senators, and the Speaker of the House." In fact, under Califano's regime, Medicaid funding of abortion was cut by 98 percent.

But Midge did persuade Carter to keep his commitment on a replacement for the National IWY Commission, and on June 20, 1978, he announced the appointment of a forty-member National Advisory Committee for Women. What had been holding things up were Carter's opposition to spending any money on the committee and Rosalynn Carter's objections to my serving as its head. The First Lady told Midge that I did not represent the women of the country. "The women in Georgia wear pinafores and gloves," Midge recalls her saying, "and Bella doesn't wear a pinafore." If I had known about Mrs. Carter's views at the time, I could have pointed out that I usually wear a hat, but I had taken off my gloves a long time ago. White House staff members and adviser Patrick Caddell argued for me, however, and at my suggestion, Carter named two cochairs of the committee, Carmen Delgado Votaw, a former IWY commissioner and president of the National Conference of Puerto Rican Women, and me. We served without salaries. We were not given an independent budget, but were told we could borrow services and personnel from various departments and agencies. Alexis Herman found us three small rooms in the Labor Department building, and I spent weeks on the phone, cadging supplies, equipment, and staff workers from other government offices.

Although it was customary for a President to meet with a newly appointed advisory committee, no meeting took place. I would see Carter at various events, however, and we were always cordial and relaxed with each other. I rather liked him, even though I couldn't understand what made him tick, and, contrary to what was later reported, I never displayed my overcelebrated temper to him.

Over the summer we set up task forces to monitor implementation of the National Plan, and many of us on the committee were also busy working on the huge demonstration that NOW and other women's groups had called for August 26, 1978 — Women's Equality Day, commemorating the enfranchisement of women. A hundred thousand women, many dressed in the white and purple outfits favored by the suffragists, marched down Pennsylvania Avenue to the Capitol steps in support of a bill introduced by Congresswoman Elizabeth Holtzman, which proposed extending for another seven years the seven-year period allowed for ERA ratification. The time would run out in March 1979, and it was obvious that it would not be possible to get three additional states to ratify the amendment in the remaining seven months. After hearings and intensive lobbying, Congress voted a compromise, extending ratification time to June 30, 1982. (That second deadline, which occurred midway in the Reagan administration, elapsed without the ERA campaign being able to break through the anti-ERA blockade in the remaining holdout state legislatures. Signaling their determination not to give up, ERA supporters promptly reintroduced the amendment in Congress, starting the ratification process anew. The reintroduced ERA was defeated in the House in November 1983 when it fell six votes short of the required two-thirds vote, with 68 percent of Republicans and 16 percent of Democrats opposing it. Although some opponents as well as seven Republicans and seven Democrats who reneged on their cosponsorship of ERA claimed they voted against the amendment because it had been brought up under a rule limiting debate, I believe they opposed it because they were unable to attach an irrelevant antiabortion amendment and other crippling riders.)

Somewhat later than required by law, Carter sent a message to Congress on September 17, 1978, in which he praised the National Plan as a "national agenda to achieve women's full rights and equality" and reported on what he was doing to carry out the Houston recommendations. Our committee task forces analyzed the message and commended Carter for some of his actions, but they found others inadequate and, in some instances, disturbing.

In the face of rising unemployment and inflation, the President was proposing $15 billion in major domestic budget cuts at the same time he was seeking a significant increase in military spending, contrary to his earlier pledge to keep a lid on the arms race. The domestic cuts would seriously hurt jobs programs, welfare reform demonstration projects, preventive health services, vocational and sex equity education programs, family planning services, and other programs of importance to women. Once again, women's needs were to be sacrificed to the bottomless pit of the Pentagon. Moreover, Carter was proposing a 7 percent wage increase guideline that would lock women into discriminatory wage patterns and prevent them from closing that notorious wage gender gap.

Carmen and I, on behalf of the advisory committee, formally asked for a meeting with the President and members of his cabinet to present our views. In any case, as we were his advisers, we thought such a meeting was long overdue. On November 16 Sarah Weddington, a Texas attorney who had taken over Midge's work as liaison to women's groups, called to say that Carter would meet with our full committee for fifteen minutes on the afternoon of November 22, the day before Thanksgiving. No cabinet members would be present. Carmen and I were both disturbed at this short notice for so brief a meeting, but we nevertheless agreed to the appointment and alerted the committee members to the date. Some of the women would be flying in from such distant places as Hawaii, California, Texas, and Colorado, and they would have to scramble for plane reservations to get to Washington and back home on Thanksgiving eve in time for holiday preparations.

When about thirty of the committee members assembled on November 21, the realization sank in that they had come a long way at great personal inconvenience for what was going to be largely a ceremonial first meeting with the President. In the political trade, it is known as a "photo opportunity" session.

The smiling President would be photographed with a group of women smiling back at him, and by the time we had shaken hands and exchanged some chitchat, our fifteen minutes would be up.

"I don't think we should go at all," said Addie Wyatt, a vice president of the United Food and Commercial Workers union based in Chicago. Maxine Waters, the dynamic young Democratic legislator from Watts, California, agreed, and it soon became apparent that most of the other committee members felt they were being insulted. The serious issues they wanted to discuss were getting the usual offhand treatment from the male power structure. They grew even angrier when they later learned that the President was taking the time to fly to Utah the following week to receive an award from the Mormon Church, a leading source of opposition to the ERA and abortion rights.

With Carmen presiding over the meeting, Wyatt and Waters introduced a resolution to send a letter to the President, canceling the next afternoon's appointment and requesting a full-scale meeting at a later date. The resolution passed without visible opposition, and with only a few women abstaining. I had been away during this part of the meeting; when I returned and was told of the decision, I reopened the debate and argued strongly against it. I was worried that it would create needless animosity at the White House and cut us off from access there; also, I had a hunch that because of my reputation as a hard negotiator, I would be blamed. "I'll be the one to pay for it," I said. "They'll think I put you up to it." The committee went into executive session, argued it out again, and decided to stick with the cancellation.

We sent off the letter, which was conciliatory in tone, and Carmen and I followed up with a phone call to Carter, trying to soften the effect of our refusal to meet with him. He apologized for the brevity of the scheduled meeting, sounded very friendly and understanding, and agreed to a longer session at a future date.

The meeting with the President was finally set for January 12, 1979, on a week's notice, seven months after our committee had been appointed. A statement of the views we wanted to present to Carter was drafted, and it was reviewed by the committee when it convened in Washington on January 11 to plan who would say what when we met with the President. I was away for the day to fulfill a long-scheduled speaking engagement, but the official minutes of the committee meeting showed that many of the members thought the statement was not strong enough. NOW president Eleanor Smeal, with all the others agreeing, felt it had to reflect more of our concern for the fate of the ERA and that its ratification should be the President's number-one priority. She thought the statement should be less "thanking." *Redbook* editor Sey Chassler objected to its tone of supplication. "We should think of ourselves as a committee that represents the public interest, not as employees of the President," he said. The other male member of the committee, Richard Rossie of Georgia, who was generally regarded as the President's man, objected to the statement's including talk about inflation and its impact on women, discussing the minimum wage, and opposing the proposed increase in military spending, which was linked in our language to cuts in women's programs. All these subjects, he indicated, were outside our jurisdiction and expertise. He was alone in that view.

When I arrived the following morning, the statement had been rewritten to give more emphasis to the ERA. I agreed completely with its content and also with the wording of a press release, which had been approved by Carmen a day earlier and sent to the White House press office for public release after the meeting with Carter. Its heading read, "President Carter Challenged on Social Priorities by National Advisory Committee for Women." At our Friday morning committee session, we agreed that Carmen and I would make opening remarks to the President and that nine other committee members would talk about the ERA, employment, education, health, the disabled, appointment of more women judges, and a pending UN conference on women.

Our meeting with Carter was set for 2:30 P.M., and the whole committee arrived at the White House in total ignorance of a White House scenario that Gloria Steinem later dubbed "the Friday night massacre." Afterward, we found out that a decision to fire me had been made by Hamilton Jordan and Jody Powell the night before, when they had seen the committee press release. According to the *Washington Post,* Jordan and Powell met the next morning with Carter's media adviser, Gerald Rafshoon, Sarah Weddington, Stuart Eizenstat, Anne Wexler, and other staff members to decide whether I should be fired immediately and the meeting canceled, whether I should be told by the President during the meeting, or whether I should be told privately after the meeting, without the other committee members being informed. They decided on the last option and then met with Carter, who agreed to their plan. The White House had been going through a bad time with the press that week, with Billy Carter's Libyan connections making headlines and the President saying there was nothing he could do to restrain his brother. They couldn't fire Billy, so they decided to fire me. Jordan and Powell, reportedly in high humor, alerted the White House press corps that a "fun" front-page story would be breaking late that afternoon.

(After the event, a White House staffer explained to the *Washington Post,* "It's very frustrating around here. You get kicked from all sides and there's not much you can do to get back. But suddenly this was something that could be done — swiftly, decisively — to take care of someone who was really sticking it to us." At our post-firing press conference, Nancy Neuman of the League of Women Voters, one of the committee members who resigned to protest my dismissal, said, "When you have a tough day at the office you come home and kick your dog. They think women are vulnerable, like dogs." (My husband had a different view. "You're the only one I know," he said, "who can get fired from a nonpaying job.")

As we walked into the cowardly lion's den we met AFL-CIO president George Meany and other union officials coming out. Like the leaders of many other national organizations, they had been highly critical of the specific budget cuts Carter was proposing to reduce inflation, and there was also widespread disagreement within the Democratic Party about the President's policies. Meany told the press his meeting with the President had been very productive.

Our committee members sat around the very long Cabinet Room table and I introduced them to the President. He blew kisses to Millie Jeffrey, head of the National Women's Political

Caucus, and other women he knew personally. He apologized for the brevity of the scheduled meeting that we had canceled in November and told us our agenda was his agenda, but said he had become discouraged about our working relationship. He hoped it would be better in the future. I told him that we were strongly for the ERA because women had been left out of the Constitution, and that now we felt women were being left out of the formulation of public policy. We felt that it was important to consider the impact of all public programs on women and our major role in the economy.

Carmen spoke of the specific effect of the proposed cuts, mentioning that the reduction of CETA (Comprehensive Employment and Training Act) jobs would seriously affect minority women and the poor. I noticed that Carter seemed to wince when I said his commitment to NATO to increase the military budget should be balanced against the prior promises he had made to the electorate to reduce spending for armaments. I said that in view of his recognition of China, his Camp David initiative, and the pending SALT agreement, it should be possible to slow down the arms race and provide more funds for human needs. Then Ellie Smeal talked urgently about the ERA and asked him to speak about it in his forthcoming State of the Union address. (He gave it one sentence.) Addie Wyatt discussed rising unemployment among women and minorities; Marjorie Bell Chambers, president of the American Association of University Women, discussed proposed cuts in vocational and sex equity education programs; Jeffrey talked about the slow rate at which women were being appointed to federal judgeships; and Billie Nave Masters described the plight of Native American women.

When Carter replied, he seemed despondent, almost listless. He said he had been very disappointed in our committee. He did not object to criticism — "I'm not weeping," he said — but he had expected the women to be his allies and more supportive. (Weddington later told the committee which replaced us that they should be "loving critics" of the President.) Instead of cooperating with him, he said, we were giving the public the impression that we were in conflict with him; we had canceled our Thanksgiving eve meeting and issued a press release that was "95 percent" critical of him. There was, he said, an irreparable breach between us. Then, however, he perked up and said he wanted to develop a more harmonious and regular working relationship with us. He proposed that we set up small committees to meet with cabinet members and other administration officials on specific issues.

I replied that our statement was not intended as a personal attack on him nor was it meant to be disrespectful. We cherished our independence as a committee but wanted to be partners with him. I said our views represented "feminine anguish" about policies that affected women and on which we had not been heard. I pointed out that the committee wanted to give its advice to his administration — that was our role — but no cabinet official had ever consulted with us or sought our opinions. We, too, wanted harmonious relations, I said, and were pleased at his suggestion that we have regular meetings with department heads. I spoke with feeling, but at no time did I shout or get angry, as his aides later told the press. Indeed, I was not angry. I thought we had made our point and that our working relationship with the White House would be greatly improved. Our session with the President had lasted ninety minutes, and we all stood and applauded him when he departed. Like Meany, I thought our meeting had gone well, ending on a favorable note even though Carter had appeared to be very ambivalent in his attitude toward us. Carmen and I went out to the White House lawn and told the press and TV people waiting there that we had held a very positive meeting with the President and were pleased.

After our impromptu press conference, we returned to the White House. Both Carmen and I had been handed notes from Hamilton Jordan before the meeting. He wanted to see us separately, and Carmen went into Jordan's office first. He told her abruptly that I was being dismissed and asked her to suggest a replacement. She was stunned, and after she had protested the decision, she left, too upset even to talk to me. Then it was my turn. Jordan had the President's counsel, Robert Lipshutz, with him. Without any preliminaries, Jordan handed me the letter of dismissal he had signed and said, "The President has decided to replace you." I was shocked. "Why?" I demanded. "For heaven's sake, why?" Jordan replied that the committee had done some terrible things, like canceling the November meeting and issuing a critical press release. I protested and said that I felt I was being made a scapegoat. Lipshutz bridled, called me a liar, and said he hated the word *scapegoat.* He added, "Next you'll be saying we fired you because you're Jewish."

I protested that my being fired without cause was a mistake that would hurt Carter with women. They were adamant. I then said I was willing to resign and asked for time to discuss with the committee how it should be done. I said I wanted my departure arranged quietly because I had personal problems (my husband had been ill) and didn't want any fuss. Jordan said if I had personal problems, I shouldn't be the head of a committee. The two men continued to press me, and I walked out, saying I needed time to think it over.

When I reached the committee office, in tears at the shabby way I had been treated, the phone was ringing. It was Jordan. He said he had to know right away whether I was resigning because the press already knew about it. I told him to do whatever he pleased, and hung up. We then had the job of informing the others on the committee. About half a dozen were still in Washington, Millie Jeffrey, Ellie Smeal, and Brownie Ledbetter of Arkansas among them, and they rushed to the office. We spent what was left of the evening calling committee members at their homes. Carmen had already decided to resign to show solidarity with me. (According to an item in *U.S. News & World Report,* White House aides said they were sorry they hadn't fired her, too.) By the following morning a majority of the committee had also resigned. They agreed on a joint statement, which expressed full support for Carmen and me. It read:

> At the White House meeting on January 12th, we expressed our concern about the President's anti-inflation program because many of his economic savings are at a cost to women and their families, who are already at the bottom of the economic ladder and suffer greatly from continuing discrimination. Although we have repeatedly expressed our appreciation for his efforts in behalf of the Equal Rights Amendment, we also urged him to take more vigorous action to make ERA a reality.

The President's response was not to the issues we brought to him, but rather to use our co-chair, Bella Abzug, as a scapegoat in an effort to suppress our independence. We are especially shocked that at our 90-minute meeting with the President yesterday he did not tell our committee he was planning to ask our co-chair to resign.

We had great hopes for this committee, which attempted to cooperate fully with the Carter Administration in advancing the status of women. We regret the necessity to resign, but we see no alternative. We believe that all women and men of like mind will refuse to participate in an advisory committee in which disagreement with the President and legitimate criticism are not acceptable.

Among those who resigned were Smeal, Jeffrey, Chassler, Horbal, Ledbetter, Wyatt, Waters, Crisp, Ruckelshaus, Neuman, Marlo Thomas; Piilani Desha, head of the National Federation of Business and Professional Women; Joyce Miller, chair of the Coalition of Labor Union Women; Claire Randall of the National Council of Churches; Jean O'Leary of the National Gay Task Force; Judith Heumann, a spokeswoman for the disabled; Carolyn Reed, head of the Household Technicians of America, and others. Several minority women who resigned later returned to the committee, deciding it was preferable to have some access to the White House rather than none at all.

The remnants of the committee continued to function under its new temporary chair, Marjorie Bell Chambers. The President later issued a new executive order, reconstituting the group as the *President's* Advisory Committee on Women, in place of the *National* Advisory Committee, thus reminding the women who was boss. Linda Johnson Robb, the late President Johnson's daughter, was named to head the committee, and its functions were severely restricted. It was even forbidden to lobby for women's programs on Capitol Hill, leaving Houston's National Plan of Action without an official advocacy presence there.

The President's circle of advisers had obviously thought that firing me would be a popular move. Instead, a Harris poll showed that the public gave Carter a 52 to 29 percent negative rating on my dismissal. After I was interviewed on the "Phil Donahue Show," I received thousands of letters of support from women all over the country. Many told of their hard lives, the kind of discrimination they faced at work and in their personal relationships, and their hopes for a better future. One woman wrote, "When President Carter fired you, he fired me."

The episode had demonstrated once again the bone-deep disdain for women held by our highest political leaders. No other constituency would have been treated the way we were. Did the President really think the committee would accept my dismissal like good little girls, without saying boo? Did he think that a national, multipartisan advisory committee composed predominantly of women leaders of prestigious national organizations would turn itself into a Carter claque and put on the back burner their responsibility to represent the interests of women who were being adversely affected by administration decisions? Did he believe we could be restricted to narrowly defined "women's issues" and not be allowed to speak out on the supreme issue of war and peace? There was, it seems, a total misreading by the President and his advisers of what the spirit of Houston was all about. Women were still being kicked around, but we would no longer cooperate servilely with those who were doing the kicking. We had our own agenda and our own organized movement.

My firing and the handcuffing of the advisory committee came at a time when Carter's popularity had already reached a low point. Although the right-wing press had congratulated him and Phyllis Schlafly sent him an ecstatic telegram, he generally took a drubbing in the newspapers for the way I had been ousted. Editorial writers cited the "double standard" of the administration, comparing the treatment given me and Midge Costanza with the "kid glove" manner in which Bert Lance and Peter Bourne had been allowed to leave the government when they were under charges of serious wrongdoing.

4

The 1980 Campaign

IN THE IMMEDIATE aftermath of my dismissal, I had avoided calling on women's rights supporters to oppose Carter's reelection. With the greater danger of Ronald Reagan looming, it was apparent that we would have a very difficult choice to make. But as Carter's domestic and foreign policies came increasingly under challenge in 1979, the political picture started to change. Massachusetts Senator Edward M. Kennedy and California Governor Edmund Brown decided to seek the Democratic nomination, John Anderson began to promote his candidacy, and the new Citizens Party, with its slate of Barry Commoner and LaDonna Harris, offered the usual third-party view that we should not have to accept the lesser of two evils in 1980.

By the end of 1979 the political split between women leaders and Carter was out in the open. On November 20 WOMEN USA — a national communications network that I had set up earlier in the year with Gloria Steinem, Brownie Ledbetter, Maggie Kuhn of the Gray Panthers, and two former Congresswomen, Patsy Mink and Yvonne Brathwaite Burke — held a press conference in Washington at which we called on women to hold off endorsing any presidential candidate until he had been tested on the issues. The candidates should have to compete with one another for the women's vote, we said. We were joined at the press conference by Iris Mitgang and other leaders of the National Women's Political Caucus.

The next move came from the National Organization for Women. At a December meeting of its executive board, the major feminist group voted to oppose Carter's reelection effort — through the November election, if necessary. NOW charged that the President's record "consisted more of illusion than reality, more of lip service than performance" and said he should be held accountable for his nonaccomplishments. "For too many years," Ellie Smeal commented, "candidates have pledged support for women's rights, but action after elections has been sadly lacking. This is a vicious circle that has to be broken."

The NOW board considered endorsing Kennedy but then decided to wait and see what happened as the campaigns progressed and the candidates responded to women's issues. It later adopted a national no-endorsement policy, although many chapters worked hard for Kennedy. After they disavowed Carter, Smeal and other NOW leaders were barred from a White House meeting of women's organizations — a meeting originally suggested by NOW — that had been called to discuss ERA strategy with the President. Instead, Smeal and other women were on the outside, picketing what they called the "showcase" meeting at the President's mansion. Press secretary Jody Powell, admitting that NOW had been disinvited, said Carter would try to survive "without the support of the ayatollah and NOW." When NOW leaders protested being linked with the man who was keeping fifty Americans hostage in Iran, Powell said they had no sense of humor.

The breaking point for NOW came after two separate ERA ratification campaigns in Florida, where there was an excellent chance of winning approval. NOW called on Carter to come to Florida to campaign in person for the amendment, but his involvement was again limited to several last-minute personal phone calls. In both campaigns ERA fell two votes short of ratification in the Florida legislature. Carter had not even been able to get a favorable vote from the legislature in his home state of Georgia when the measure came up for a second time, and in Virginia, Senate approval fell one vote short. A pro-ERA Senator there had switched to a no vote at the last minute because he said Carter's call for draft registration of women had made him change his mind. Carter was more involved in the ratification campaign in Illinois, where a state requirement for a three-fifths' majority vote impeded ratification, but he refused to enlist the federal government in the women's movement's economic boycott of the states that had not ratified the ERA. Even more to the point, he would not use the federal government's economic power to help persuade the holdout states to approve a constitutional guarantee of equality for women.

That Carter had considerable power to bring the states into line was obvious. A January 1980 NOW report compared the "ineptitude of the Carter Administration's performance in state ratification campaigns, the paralysis in exerting any power inherent in the office of the Presidency" with the lavish inducements the President had given to Florida in his intensive effort to win presidential straw votes at meetings held there in October and November 1979. To win support for himself, the report said,

> The state was drenched with $85.6 million in federal grants, a $1.1 billion loan guarantee, trips into the state by the secretaries of Labor, Defense, HUD, HEW and the heads of the Veterans Administration, the Federal Aviation Administration, the White House Domestic Council, the Vice President, the First Lady, and the President himself. In addition, 300 Floridians were invited to Washington for high-level briefings on foreign and domestic affairs that concluded with a reception in the White House, and influential Catholics were invited to the White House reception for Pope John Paul II. Others were appointed to jobs in the Administration or to federal commissions.

NOW came under attack from Sarah Weddington, who said the President would not be "goaded" into "denying federal funds based on whether a state has ratified the amendment or not." Commenting on her statement, I wrote in a December 27, 1979, letter to the *New York Times:* "But the President's executive branch and political operatives have been openly applying federal pressure on public officials in the form of grants and new programs (supported by public monies) as a quid pro quo for endorsing Mr. Carter's candidacy. One Cabinet officer was widely reported to have stated that mass transit funds would be withheld from Chicago to punish Mayor Jane Byrne for not supporting the President." I noted that this was in violation of the U.S. Code, adding, "Federal pressure to win enactment of an amendment that would benefit the female half of our population (and men too) is a totally legitimate use of executive power. But using the taxpayers' money for electoral politics is not."

The point was, if the President really wanted to get something done, he had the wherewithal to do it. Why Carter, having committed himself repeatedly to ERA, did not pursue its ratification with the same zeal he showed in campaigning for approval of the Panama Canal Treaty or his own reelection is a mystery. Perhaps, deep in his heart, he did not lust for it enough. Perhaps, too, his real feelings were revealed when he told his weekly Bible class on April 13, 1980, according to a report in the *New York Times,* that "women have gone about as far as they ought to go now."

Carter continued to create problems for himself with women's rights supporters, not only on ERA, but on continuing abortion restrictions and reductions in funding for long-standing programs affecting women, mothers, and children. Although Congress had modified some of his proposed cuts, his budget had eliminated thousands of CETA jobs even as unemployment among women was rising more sharply than among men, fourteen thousand children had been removed from Head Start because of insufficient funds, money for other women's programs was not keeping abreast of inflation, and he had backed out on his support for domestic violence and comprehensive child-care programs. His 1981 budget called for another $17 billion in domestic cuts and a 12.8 percent increase in military spending. His image as a peacemaker was being replaced by that of a hawk as he gave up on SALT II, pushed for the new MX and Cruise missiles, and made militaristic threats in the Persian Gulf area.

In what was widely interpreted as a diversionary move, stemming from his frustration over the difficulty in freeing the American hostages in Iran, Carter called for draft registration, saying that women as well as men should be included. Presidential assistant Stuart Eizenstat summoned leaders of the major women's organizations to the White House and lectured them on their responsibilities: if they were for equal rights, they were told, they had to be for draft registration of women. Once again we had to *prove* that we deserved equality. Some of the women's groups decided to remain neutral on the issue, but the NWPC, NOW, a dozen other women's organizations, and leading Congresswomen, including Patricia Schroeder of Colorado, joined me in a January 1980 WOMEN USA press conference at which we announced our opposition to drafting or registering either men or women. "When we have equality of opportunity," I added, "it will be time enough to talk about equality of sacrifice." As I indicated earlier, Carter's draft registration gimmick was a needlessly complicating factor in our effort to win ERA ratification. Our explanations that with or without the amendment the government had the power to draft women if it wanted to do so could not offset the propaganda, from Phyllis Schlafly and others, which equated ERA with dragooning women into the army.

Although I remained in close touch with some of my former advisory committee colleagues, particularly with the NOW and NWPC leadership, we could not arrive at a common strategy for ways to influence the Democratic nomination for President. (The NWPC's small Republican Women's Task Force was bracing itself for a holding action at the Republican convention.) Most politically minded women were already feeling it necessary to identify with one of the leading contenders, and because we had won our fight to require the 1980 convention to include equal numbers of male and female delegates, many women were already running — and winning election — as Carter or Kennedy delegates. Each slate had to observe the equal-division rule, and as a result there were more opportunities for women to be elected as convention delegates. Because Carter, as the incumbent President, held a natural lead, many women chose to run as his delegates, even though in a large number of instances their support for him was paper thin.

Inevitably, many feminist activists and I gravitated toward the Kennedy camp. He had achieved an excellent voting record on women's issues throughout his Senate career, and after meeting and consulting with some of us, he issued an Economic Bill of Rights for Women, which strongly supported our main concerns. By spring I had formally endorsed him, as had Gloria Steinem, Millie Jeffrey, Midge Costanza, Sissy Farenthold, and other political feminists. I followed up by campaigning hard for him across the country and was elected a Kennedy delegate. When delegate selection was completed, Carter had 980 women delegates; Kennedy, 590; there were also 59 uncommitted women delegates, and a handful of others whose views were unknown.

Meanwhile, the NWPC Republican Women's Task Force was fighting an ultra-right-wing tide that was sweeping over the party. In the absence of a firm GOP commitment to equal representation, women made up only 29 percent of the delegates to the July 1980 convention. Long before the convention opened, the task force had decided to concentrate on retaining in the 1980 platform the party's forty-year-old commitment to support of ERA. At the beginning of the year the Republican women announced the results of a questionnaire they had sent to the presidential contenders. John Anderson, Howard Baker, George Bush, and John Connally all supported the ERA and opposed a federal constitutional ban on abortions; only Anderson, however, opposed efforts by some state legislatures to rescind their previous approval of the ERA. There was a last-minute addition: Ronald Reagan, like the other candidates, had received the questionnaire months earlier, but he did not send in his reply until twenty-four hours after the task force had mailed to the media the responses of the other four men. "Reagan differs significantly from the other GOP presidential candidates on issues of concern to women," task force vice chair Pam Curtis reported. "He did not state his position on the ERA; he is the only candidate to support a federal constitutional ban on abortion; and he does not even have a position on the issues of Title 9 [the federal law banning sex discrimination in education], the drafting of women, or the federal funding of family planning programs . . . The only area in which he agrees with the other GOP candidates is that he would consider naming a woman as his running mate." (The last point was not surprising. Leaders of both parties are often willing to say they will *consider* doing something that they have no intention of doing at that time.)

But Reagan was indeed against the amendment; as he liked to put it, he was for the *E* and the *R,* but not the *A,* meaning that he was opposed to constitutional enforcement of equality for women. The Republican Party Platform Committee rejected the effort to retain unequivocal ERA support. Instead, it recognized as "legitimate" both support for and opposition to the amendment, and it also called for the appointment of federal judges who oppose abortion. On July 14, the day the convention opened, ten thousand women marched through downtown Detroit to the GOP meeting place in a demonstration of support for the ERA; leading Republican women and the nine pro-ERA Platform Committee members were visibly up front. Reagan's nomination and the adoption of his platform led to the defection of some Republican women, including Mary Crisp, the party's cochair, and a number of them later endorsed the independent candidacy of John Anderson. Other leading women Republicans stayed with the party, but they and most of the GOP Congresswomen continued to press on women's rights issues.

As TV and press coverage from Detroit broadcast the news that the Republican Party was rejecting the beliefs of some of its most prominent women, those of us working in the Democratic Party were organizing to ensure that women would be a visible and powerful force at the August convention in New York. Early in 1980 the NWPC Democratic Task Force launched a Fair Share for American Women campaign, a statement of goals that encompassed both national policy and party issues. It said candidates would be measured by their performance, not their words. "This time," a spokeswoman explained, "women want preelection promises to be the postelection policies of the country." The NWPC, NOW, and other women's organizations trained their members to run as delegates; NWPC chair Iris Mitgang claimed that some four to five hundred members were elected delegates or alternates, and NOW estimated that about two hundred of its members were delegates. But our influence at the convention spread far beyond those numbers. In this first Democratic Party convention in which equal division was the rule, women constituted 49.23 percent of the voting delegates and, regardless of whether their commitments were to Carter, Kennedy, or anyone else, they, together with large numbers of male delegates, supported overwhelmingly the program demands of the women's rights bloc.

Before the convention opened, I called a meeting in New York at which the NWPC, NOW, and other groups joined WOMEN USA in a Coalition for Women's Rights that polled the women delegates on our key issues. Their responses showed that we would be in a strong position to get our demands included in the party platform. Commitments to our main issues were scattered throughout the platform that was submitted to the convention for approval. For the first time, the platform included freedom of sexual preference among the civil rights that had to be protected legally. The proposed ERA plank not only renewed its strong support for the amendment and opposed rescission, it went beyond Carter's position by endorsing economic boycotts of the states that had not ratified and pledging that the Democratic National Committee would not meet in those states.

However, our women's coalition felt that it was important to demonstrate the party's practical commitment to ERA, and we accordingly offered additional language (Minority Report No. 10), which specified: "The Democratic Party shall withhold financial support and technical campaign assistance from candidates who do not support the ERA." We also proposed to strengthen the platform's support of abortion rights by adding a statement (Minority Report No. 11) that "the Democratic Party opposes involuntary or uninformed sterilization for women and men, and opposes restrictions on funding for health services for the poor that deny poor women especially the right to exercise a constitutionally guaranteed right to privacy." This, too, was in conflict with Carter's opposition to Medicaid funding of abortions.

The Carter campaign, which strongly opposed our two minority reports, controlled all the convention committees and had a strong whip system in place. Our women's coalition had its own floor operation, which I ran. Our caucus held daily strategy meetings and briefing sessions for women delegates, met separately with the state delegations, and maintained a highly visible presence throughout the proceedings. The first time ERA was mentioned, the delegates — women and men — erupted into cheers and waved banners and it was ERA all the way from then on. Although Carter representatives Anne Wexler and Sarah Weddington continued to pressure us to drop or modify our minority reports, we held firm. Weddington held a press conference at which she said the President could not support a platform that included our two planks and she predicted we would be defeated.

Support for our position continued to build, however, and the Kennedy campaigners, who had been neutral at first, offered to assist us on the ERA plank and released their whips to help us on the abortion rights plank if they wished. We circulated a petition for a roll-call vote, and quickly got enough signatures. After the powerful National Education Association came over to our side, the Carter campaign people finally realized that we had enough delegate support to win a roll-call vote. Tip O'Neill, who was in the chair, sent me word that our ERA plank could be passed by acclamation, and a roll call was not necessary. We had won, and the convention passed, without visible opposition, the strongest plank in support of the ERA in the party's history. In the roll-call vote on our plank supporting funding of abortions for poor women, which followed, we won by a two-to-one margin, the largest majority scored on any of the convention's roll-call votes. Freedom of choice, which had been considered too dangerously controversial to be mentioned in the 1972 platform, was now fully accepted, as it had been much earlier by a majority of Americans. In another victory the delegates amended the party charter to guarantee equal division of men and women at all future conventions and meetings, as well as on all committees, commissions, and other official bodies.

Our ten-year campaign for equal numbers of women and men had been completely won at last, and it had been won because we had succeeded in greatly increasing the number of women delegates. By winning political power within the party, women had forced the members to address our concerns. No matter where they stood on candidates, the women delegates were united on equal representation and our other issues. The increased presence of women was changing not only the face, but the structures and policies of the Democratic Party.

Evaluating the significance of what had happened at the convention in its September 1980 issue, the *National NOW Times* commented:

> At this convention the presence of women in equal numbers changed the complexion of the deliberative body, as both Carter and Kennedy whips discovered. When it came down to "bottom line" issues on which women had firm convictions — and the power to vote — the whips discovered that the issues were not tradeable and compromise was unacceptable.
>
> The difference is that no matter how strongly men think they support these so-called women's issues, the commitment is intellectual — not gut level. That's a *critical* difference.

Because women at the Republican convention had remained a minority, the NOW editorial said, "When push came to shove, they lacked the power to do anything but roll over and pretend it was acceptable." In contrast, it said, "Democratic women not only had the power of their individual votes, but they had the power also of being organized to fight for their convictions, to resist as a group the pressures to cave in, and they were invincible on women's rights issues."

It concluded that 1980 "was only a taste of things to come. With 50/50 representation at the state and national levels of the Democratic Party we will participate in 1984 very decisively, not only in the formulation of the platform, but in the nomination itself."

We were all too aware of the disparity between the party's platform and the views of its standard-bearer. Carter reiterated his opposition to the platform's revised abortion rights plank and stressed his determination to go ahead with the MX missile program, a stand that had created great controversy at the convention. Some critics said we had won a paper victory, but I felt that we had accomplished much more. Our efforts were part of a continuing democratic process in which we women were infusing our views and strength into the party's policy structures at all levels, and that process would be difficult to reverse. If women continued to work together as a political bloc, we could in time exert enormous influence on party policies and have a greater voice in selecting the kinds of men and women who would be chosen to lead the party and the nation.

Although women did not have a 1980 presidential candidate we could endorse wholeheartedly, we had laid down some of the guidelines that future candidates would have to meet if they wanted female support. The appearance of five male candidates for the Democratic presidential nomination before the July 1983 NWPC convention — and their unequivocal support for the Equal Rights Amendment and abortion rights — demonstrated that women had indeed become a national political force, a remarkable achievement that had been won in little more than a decade. Also, the policies we advocated had sharpened the distinctions between the Democratic and Republican parties, with the result that more women than men were identifying themselves with the Democrats.

Carter's renomination confronted many feminists with an immediate political dilemma. Along with other groups, the Coalition for Women's Rights had favored an open convention that would have allowed delegates to vote either for Carter or for Kennedy, regardless of their original commitment. That proposed rule was rejected on the first day of the convention, however, and although the ovation Kennedy received indicated he probably would have been a stronger candidate, we were stuck with Carter. (We don't know whether Kennedy would have defeated Reagan, but he would not have lost the Democrats control of the Senate, as Carter did. But unsatisfactory as the President and his policies had proved to be, we knew that Reagan would be a disaster for us. Political women began to move in various directions. With varying degrees of fervor, some lined up behind Carter, some supported Anderson, some endorsed the tiny Citizens Party, and others decided not to vote. Some argued that it would be better to have an outright enemy in the White House than a sometime-friend, sometime-enemy who confused and divided the women's rights camp. (In fact, NOW, the NWPC, and other women's groups reported big increases in membership and contributions after the Reagan victory.) Liberal women appointees in the Carter administration and some black women leaders led his campaign appeals to women, although the outreach and participation did not compare with that in 1976. National NOW still held off from endorsing Carter, but many of its state branches and local leaders decided to support him. In the last few weeks of the campaign, as the prospect of a Reagan victory became more evident, many women leaders were alarmed into dropping their opposition to Carter and endorsing him.

Two days before the election, an ad hoc group called WARN (*W*omen *A*gainst the *R*epublican *N*ominee) ran a full-page ad in the *New York Times.* Headlined "Reagan May Fool Some of the People Some of the Time . . . But Not Most of the Women," it was signed by seventy-six prominent women, including Republican Kathy Wilson, Millie Jeffrey, Iris Mitgang, Ellie Smeal, Gloria Steinem, Koryne Horbal, New York City Council president Carol Bellamy, author Erma Bombeck, Los Angeles political consultant Frances Lear, Myrlie Evers, Maxine Waters, former U.S. delegate to the United Nations Marietta Tree, Carolyn Reed, and me.

"There is a women's vote," the ad said. "We may not yet have a candidate we're wholeheartedly for, but we do have one we're against — because he's against everything we need for equality."

The ad outlined Reagan's anti–women's rights positions, including his statement that a wife in the work force "threatens the very structure of family life itself" and his description of the League of Women Voters as "America's New Reactionaries . . . the Rhine Maidens." It noted that Reagan had urged sending U.S. troops to ten different countries in twelve years, and said, "Women have always been more skeptical that force or militarism can really solve anything, either at home or internationally."

The ad did not directly endorse Carter; instead, it implied that women should vote for him: "Yes, we have criticisms of Jimmy Carter, and we will continue to press him. But the Democratic Platform, which opposes these Reagan positions, and the many good appointees in the Carter Administration, are the practical and preferable alternative to a real and present danger."

It concluded by urging "Americans for equality, women and men" to vote, pointing out that in 1960, 1968, and 1976, one vote per precinct could have elected a different President.

We were caught in an awkward position, yet the dilemma was not of our making. Once again, as in so many elections, we were confronted with a choice between two unsatisfactory men. We still lacked the effective power to nominate a candidate we could enthusiastically endorse. Although I was dismayed by the Reagan victory, the 1980 election results had one positive outcome: women were voting in equal percentages with men, and they were voting with more political sophistication. The electoral gender gap had opened.

5

Showdown at Gender Gap

RONALD REAGAN was declared the winner of the 1980 presidential election even before the polls had closed on the West Coast. At first glance the popular vote totals and the Electoral College tally appeared to give Reagan an overwhelming victory, the much-heralded "mandate" that he quickly claimed as his own. Yet a closer look at the voting patterns reveals a different picture. Reagan won a scant majority — 50.7 percent of the total vote — which represented only 30 percent of all Americans eligible to vote. Of those who voted for him, most gave an anti-Carter, not a pro-Reagan reason for doing so. According to the CBS/New York Times Election Day exit poll, 38 percent of those who voted for Reagan said they made their choice because "it's time for a change"; only 11 percent voted for him because "he's a real conservative." The NBC Election Day exit poll reported that fewer than half (49 percent) of those who voted for Reagan strongly supported him.

The most important story of the 1980 election results, though, was that a new and distinct political phenomenon — the gender gap — was revealed; it showed a marked difference between women and men in their candidate choice. While 54 percent of all male voters chose Reagan over Jimmy Carter, only 46 percent of women voters did so, a gender gap of 8 percent, the largest difference between women and men since the Gallup organization began compiling such data in 1952.*

On Election Day 1980, according to exit polls, nearly 46 million women went to the polls, and their votes were about evenly divided between the two major candidates: 46 percent for Reagan, 45 percent for Carter. Clearly, Reagan was not the first choice of a majority of Amercan women voters. Although 21 million voted for him, when one adds the votes for Carter and the independent, John B. Anderson, the total shows that 25 million cast their ballots for a different presidential candidate.

Reagan's professionally cultivated charm and personality were insufficient to distract women from their serious concerns. Reagan and the majority of American women disagreed sharply on two fundamental issues: attitudes toward peace and the Soviet Union, and the Equal Rights Amendment, symbolizing the whole range of women's demands for equality. The ERA battle had been publicly fought at the 1980 Republican national convention, before a national TV audience. It was clear that the 1976 platform plank supporting ERA was deleted from the 1980 version at the behest of Ronald Reagan and delegates committed to his candidacy. Reagan was consistent in his opposition to the ERA. In both his unsuccessful primary campaign in 1976 and his winning 1980 effort, he tried to position himself as an advocate of equal rights for women, at the same time contending that a constitutional amendment was neither a necessary nor desirable mechanism for achieving this goal.

Women voters weren't fooled by Reagan's lip service to

---

*In both the 1952 and 1956 presidential elections, women gave Dwight D. Eisenhower 5 to 6 percent higher majorities than men. The distinction was attributed by Gallup to women's belief in 1952 that Eisenhower would end the war in Korea, and their subsequent approval of Eisenhower's refusal to involve the United States in the Suez Canal war, an interpretation that fits in with the higher value that women traditionally place on peace. From 1960 through 1972 Gallup found only marginal differences between male and female presidential choices. A 1976 Gallup poll showed women preferring President Ford by a 6 percent gender gap; a CBS News exit poll found no sex difference in the vote.

equality: fewer than one third of the women and only four out of ten men who supported the ERA chose Reagan. Even among self-identified Republican women, defections were notable: 8 percent voted for Carter and 5 percent for Anderson.

In the televised presidential debates sponsored by the League of Women Voters, Carter had tried to spotlight Reagan's aggressive foreign policy views. The hawkish image of Reagan — which his performance in the White House has fully borne out — seemed to take, even though the Republican candidate slickly softened his militaristic views sufficiently to cost Carter some female support. Even so, according to the CBS-*New York Times* Election Day exit poll, 59 percent of the women who disagreed with the statement that we "should be more forceful with the Soviet Union even at the risk of war" voted for Carter, and another 9 percent chose Anderson, leaving Reagan with just 29 percent of their votes.

There were other issues that divided the electorate. The NBC Election Day exit poll found that 62 percent of those who felt government spending on defense and the military should be increased voted for Reagan, while 57 percent of those who favored decreasing spending or keeping it at the same level voted for Carter. (Actually, Carter also favored more military spending, but not to the same extent as Reagan.) Furthermore, 68 percent of those who believed an effective President could control inflation voted for Reagan, while 67 percent of those who felt inflation was beyond the control of any President voted for Carter. Voters most concerned about America's position in the world, cutting federal taxes, and controlling inflation gave their votes to Reagan by a two-to-one margin. Carter received the overwhelming support of voters most concerned about ensuring peace and relations with Iran and Arab countries. On economic issues the CBS/*New York Times* exit poll found that those who viewed unemployment as the most important problem preferred Carter over Reagan, 51 percent to 40 percent, while those who cited inflation as the most important chose Reagan over Carter, 60 percent to 30 percent.

Significantly, in every area of the country, in all racial, demographic, and socioeconomic categories among women of almost every type, support for Reagan was lower than men's. His highest gender gap — 17 percent, more than twice the national average — appeared among college graduates: 58 percent of the men chose Reagan, compared with only 41 percent of the women. The Reagan gender gap ran ahead of the national average in the South (11 percent), among Catholics (13 percent), professionals and union members (10 percent), the unemployed (13 percent), voters aged 18 to 21 (14 percent), and voters aged 30 to 59 (11 percent). Carter drew 84 percent of black women voters, a 7 percent margin over black men, and his biggest gender gap was the 19 percent difference in his support from Hispanic women (61 percent), compared with men (42 percent.) Only among women in the West, among high school graduates, and among those over 60 years of age did Reagan's gender gap narrow to as little as 3 or 4 percent. Reagan received a majority of the female vote — and a scant majority at that — from women who lived in the West, Protestant women, women in professional or managerial occupations, and women over 60 years of age. According to political scientists Sandra Baxter and Marjorie Lansing in *Women and Politics,* "Women who identified themselves with the 'Moral Majority' or indicated that they were very religious were much more likely to vote for Reagan than were their less religious sisters," and the religious group included large numbers of older women. (See the chart, The Gender Gap, 1980 Election.)

Carter also had a problem with women voters. In the 1976 election, he had won 48 percent of the women's vote, roughly 3 percent less than Ford. By 1980 his rate of support had dropped to 45 percent. In considering Reagan, women were trying to decide what he might do. With Carter, they were evaluating his performance and obviously found it wanting. No longer did American women believe nor could Jimmy Carter prove to their satisfaction that he understood and would act on their concerns. Only 9 percent of the women interviewed in NBC's exit poll said they could trust Carter "to do what is right just about always," while 18 percent responded "almost never."

In 1976 both President Gerald Ford and Carter, then the challenger, supported the Equal Rights Amendment. In 1980 President Carter and challenger John Anderson were both pro-

THE GENDER GAP, 1980 ELECTION

R = Reagan
C = Carter
A = Anderson

	Men			Women			Reagan Gender Gap[1]	Carter Gender Gap[2]
Percentage	R	C	A	R	C	A		
	54	37	7	46	45	7	−8	+8
Region								
East	52	39	7	43	45	10	− 9	+ 6
Midwest	55	37	7	47	45	7	− 8	+ 8
West	56	31	10	53	38	8	− 3	+ 7
South	57	39	3	46	51	3	−11	+12
Background								
White								
Black		77			84			+ 7
Hispanic		42			61			+19
Religion								
Protestant	61	33		52	41		− 9	+ 8
Catholic	56	35		43	45		−13	+10
Jewish	39	41	17	31	53	13	− 8	+12
Occupation								
Professional	61	28	9	51	39	9	−10	+11
Blue Collar	49	44	4	41	50	5	− 8	+ 6
Union Members	47	45	6	37	54	8	−10	+ 9
Unemployed	41	49	8	28	61	8	−13	+12
Age								
18–21	48	41	8	34	51	13	−14	+10
22–29	46	39	11	41	45	12	− 5	+ 6
30–44	58	32	2	47	44	6	−11	+12
45–59	59	34	5	48	44	7	−11	+10
60 plus	55	40	4	51	43	5	− 4	+ 3
Education								
H.S. Graduate	52	45	2	48	45	5	− 4	0
College Graduate	58	29	11	41	44	13	−17	+15
Affiliation								
Democrat	25	67	8	17	76	7	− 8	+ 9
Republican	91	6	3	87	8	5	− 4	+ 2
Independent	63	25	12	51	34	15	−12	+ 9

[1]Reagan gender-gap column indicates lower percentage of support from women, compared with men.
[2]Carter gender-gap column shows higher percentage of support from women.

WOMENS REGISTRATION AND VOTING RATES BY AGE AND BACKGROUND FOR 1980

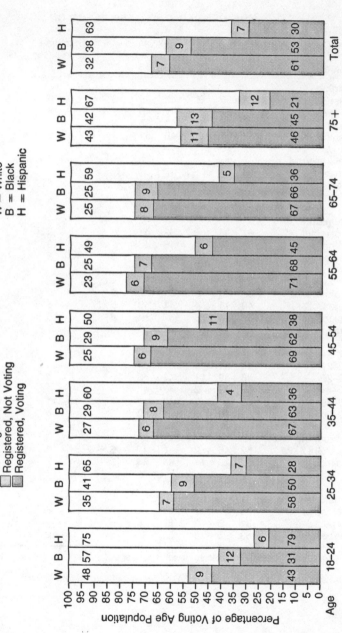

W = White
B = Black
H = Hispanic

☐ Not Registered
▨ Registered, Not Voting
▨ Registered, Voting

ERA, at least on the record, while Reagan was staunchly opposed. This gave Carter a distinct edge — 55 percent of the vote from women and 47 percent of the vote from men who favored the ERA — but what happened to the remaining votes? Eleven percent went to Anderson, four points above the 7 percent national average of the total vote that he received; the rest voted for Reagan, except for a few defectors to other third parties.

One explanation, of course, is that support for the ERA was not the "bottom line" issue in the decisions of some voters. Some of these women, fed up with Carter, believed Reagan would be a stronger President. A more significant reason, I believe, was that other women who defected from Carter were no longer content with words rather than action on this issue. Carter's waffling on abortion rights, his shift to a higher military spending policy that cut into women's programs, and his high-handed treatment of the National Advisory Committee on Women all took their toll. His economic policies were hardly more palatable to women than they were to men. Increasing unemployment threatened the slender hold low-seniority women had on their jobs, and rampant inflation caused hardships for women living on fixed incomes, those dependent on government benefits for the bulk of their income, and those living near or below the poverty line. A majority of these women are normally Democrats, and Carter retained most of their support, but at much lower levels than they had shown in 1976. On economic issues, Carter lost some support from blue-collar and union women as well. Although he won a majority of their votes, their rate of support had dropped significantly from 1976. Democrats, independents, and liberals, disaffected with Carter, gave Reagan his victory, not Republicans and conservatives.

According to the CBS/*New York Times* Election Day poll, Carter's support among Democrats dropped from 77 percent in 1976 to 66 percent in 1980, among independents from 43 percent to 30 percent, and among liberals from 70 percent to 57 percent. Reagan captured 54 percent of the independent vote, drew the support of 27 percent of liberal voters, and won 26 percent of the votes cast by Democrats.

John Anderson's independent candidacy siphoned off a

large measure of support from Jewish, independent, professional, and younger voters and from self-identified liberals — both women and men — who had voted heavily for Carter in 1976. Although Anderson won just 7 percent of the nationwide vote, 13 percent of women with college degrees, 13 percent of Jewish women, and 13 percent of women voters under 21 years of age and 12 percent of those aged 22 to 29 chose him. His 6 million votes were not enough to offset totally Reagan's 8.4 million plurality, but they more than accounted for the margin of difference between Reagan and Carter in fourteen states, thus explaining the Republican's Electoral College vote landslide.

Whether Anderson deserved the vote of women and liberals is a different question. During the campaign he did try to position himself as a "liberal" candidate on such issues as the ERA and peace, but his actual record as a Representative from Illinois was quite different. In Congress, for example, he was a conservative on economic issues; he had been a long-standing supporter of the Vietnam War, apologizing for his votes only after he got into the presidential contest; on ERA, he fell into the same "all talk and no action" category as Carter: he had never actually taken any effective steps to get it ratified in his home state, where some of the closest and most intensive vote battles had been fought in the legislature.

In 1980 the gender gap opened on presidential candidate preferences, but, happily, it closed in turnout rates. For the first time since 1944 — when 12 million American men were absent on Election Day owing to armed service duty in World War II — women voted at the same rate as men. According to the U.S. Census Bureau, 59 percent of women and men eligible to vote actually did, but the women's voting rate was higher than men's among blacks, Hispanics, and in all age categories up to 55 years old. Because women are a majority — 53 percent of the voting-age population — an equal turnout rate for both sexes means that far more women than men actually vote. In 1980, 6 million more women than men went to the polls. While the turnout rate for both sexes has been declining in all presidential elections since 1964, the percentage of women voters has been

growing over the years, and in 1980 it equaled that of men.*
This trend, coupled with the gender gap, strongly suggests that
the women's vote will play an even more significant role in
future elections, especially because there are now under way
major registration and get-out-the-vote campaigns among
women. (See chapter 11.)

1982: The Gender Gap Widens

Just before the 1982 election, *Ms.* magazine published an article
entitled "Five Reasons to Vote, Any One of Which Should Be
Enough." One reason cited was that "finally, belatedly, politicians and the media have discovered 'the women's vote.' If it
doesn't materialize in 1982, how many more years before it's
taken seriously again?" Well, it did materialize again in 1982,
much to the delight of feminists and Democrats and to the
chagrin of the White House and Republicans. In this nonpresidential election year, all 435 members of the House, one third
of the U.S. Senate, 36 governors, and many state legislators
were being voted on. For the first time since the mid-1960s,
many more women than men voted Democratic in the congressional elections. Exit polls found an overall gender gap of 6

*Reports on turnout rates vary because different standards and sources are used to
calculate the vote. Although exit polls found that nearly 46 million women voted in
1980, the U.S. Census Bureau said that 49.3 million women voted. The Census Bureau
statistics cited throughout this book are based on postelection surveys that ask respondents if they are registered to vote and whether they voted in the preceding election.
More people say they vote than actually do. However, these data provide the most
comprehensive information on a consistent and uniform basis from election year to
election year and are the most reliable source available for measuring women's political
participation against men's.

Actual registration and turnout statistics compiled by secretaries of state do not
include breakdowns by gender. Because states have different standards concerning the
kinds of data they compile and the methods they use to collect that information,
drawing an accurate national picture from state records is extremely difficult. Voter
surveys conducted by pollsters and political scientists may produce findings that differ
from those of the Census Bureau because of variations in sample size, interview techniques, and other factors. Thus, use of the Census data provides the most consistent
yardstick for measuring the voting behavior of women and men over the years. Although Asian/Pacific and Native Americans make up a significant proportion of the
electorate in several states, the nationally aggregated data for these groups are not
considered statistically reliable for analysis by sex.

percent, with women favoring Democratic candidates over Republicans 53 percent to 47 percent. For men the reverse was true: 53 percent voted Republican and 47 percent Democratic. In specific races the gender gap was even greater, and in three gubernatorial contests the women's vote provided the winning margin.

According to a study by political scientists Arthur H. Miller and Oksana Malanchuk at the University of Michigan, "In all Congressional Districts combined, women voted only 6 percent more Democratic than did men . . . But in districts without an incumbent running for reelection, the gender gap was a full 16 percentage points." Although Democratic incumbents did well with both men and women, the researchers noted that reelected Republican incumbents received less support from women than from men.

While peace and women's rights issues were seen by poll analysts as important factors in the 1980 gender gap, in the 1982 midterm elections, after two years of Reagan rule, economic issues were emerging as a key explanation of the continuing gender gap. An April 1983 Census Bureau study reported that compared with the last nonpresidential election in 1978, a sharply higher proportion of the nation's jobless had voted in 1982. Voting turnout was also up among women (many in the ranks of the unemployed), blacks, government workers, and residents of middle western and north central states, areas that had been hard hit by the depression. Ann Lewis, political director of the Democratic National Committee, asserted that she felt the markedly higher turnout among the unemployed — who generally have a low voting rate — the women, and other groups materialized because these "people had been hurt and had reason to think there was worse on the way" from White House policies.

In the gubernatorial race in my home state of New York, Democratic Lieutenant Governor Mario Cuomo defeated Republican Lew Lehrman, a millionaire businessman, by a margin of 3.2 percent, with a gender gap estimated variously by CBS, ABC, and NBC of 6.5 percent, 7 percent, and 8 percent. Clearly, Cuomo won because there are more women than men, more women voted, and they voted for him in larger percentages and numbers than men did. In this campaign, in which Cuomo had the strong backing of labor and minorities, there were sharp differences between the candidates on women's issues and social policy, and that difference showed up in the voting.

Lehrman ran an extremely expensive, highly negative, and anti–women's rights campaign, in which he used $13 million of his private fortune. His campaign literature stated that he favored the death penalty, promised to cut welfare programs, and opposed the freedom-of-choice position on abortion. In one brochure boldly headlined "A vote for Lew Lehrman is a vote for traditional family values," he attacked Cuomo for having won "the endorsement of the big-spending Liberal Party and the biggest spender of all — Bella Abzug." (As a member of Congress, I had brought $6 billion in federal funds into the state for greatly needed water resource, public transportation, and job programs.) Lehrman's tactics backfired, and with good reason. New York women knew that Cuomo shared their values and would better represent their interests as governor.

I endorsed Cuomo early in his campaign against his major opponent, Mayor Ed Koch, helped him to receive the NOW endorsement, and chaired his campaign's Women's Project, staffed by Lydia Newmann and active throughout the state. Cuomo was right on all our issues, setting forth his views and commitments in a major position paper that he presented at a public meeting with key women from throughout the state. Cuomo was as much a family man as Lehrman, but his wife was a teacher and he had a sympathetic understanding of the needs of working women. Our task was to make certain that his message got out to women and that women got out to the polls. Our Women's Project ran ads, held public meetings, distributed literature, involved a significant cross section of women in his campaign, and prepared a special mailing to prospective women voters, asking them to elect Cuomo governor and "show the independent strength of women who care about their lives, their families, their communities — and their state." Brashly — and prophetically, as it turned out — we proclaimed, "The women's vote can make the difference for Mario Cuomo." As the campaign progressed and Cuomo came under heavier attack from right-wing forces, his support from men began to erode, but support from women held firm.

Since his election, Cuomo has begun to fulfill his legislative and executive action commitments to women, and he made good on his campaign promise to appoint the first woman judge to the state court of appeals. In his first nine months in office, he appointed women to 32 percent of more than two hundred policy positions, a figure that a coalition of women's groups was seeking to increase to 50 percent.

The New York race is not an isolated example. In Michigan, Democrat James Blanchard won by a 6.8 percent margin over his Republican opponent, with a gender gap that ranged from 3 percent according to CBS, 8.5 percent according to NBC, and up to 11.5 percent according to ABC. Blanchard's campaign included appeals to women on their issues, including support for the ERA and abortion rights. His anti-ERA opponent, Richard Headlee, was labeled by *Time* magazine "an object lesson in how not to attract women voters." He had boasted during his campaign, "I have nine children [compared to Blanchard's one]. So who loves women more?" As a Michigan newspaper commented, "On that basis women should prefer to vote for Peter Rabbit." Underestimating the intelligence or belittling the concerns of women voters is not a winning campaign strategy.

Blanchard's upset victory — it was the first time in twenty years a Democrat had been elected governor of Michigan — was greatly aided by the fact that his running mate for lieutenant governor was former Congresswoman Martha Griffiths, whose deeply rooted popularity among both women and men added great strength to the ticket.

Since Blanchard was elected, women have accounted for more than 40 percent of his appointments to top positions. He counts among his cabinet-level women the heads of the departments of public health, aging services, urban and public transportation, licensing and regulation, and criminal justice. One of his appointees, Dr. Agnes Mary Mansour, a Catholic nun, gave up her vows rather than obey a church order to resign as head

of the Department of Social Services, which funds abortions for
poor women.

In Texas, incumbent Republican Governor William P. Cle-
ments lost, even though he spent $12 million on his campaign.
He, too, goofed in his perceptions of how to appeal to women
voters. When he stated that he could not find a housewife
qualified to serve on the Public Utilities Commission, his Democratic challenger, Mark White, turned that remark into a big
campaign issue and won by a margin of 7.6 percent, with a
gender gap variously estimated by the TV networks' pollsters
at between 4.5 and 8 percent. (During his first six months in
office, White appointed women to about 27 percent of top positions.) Feminist Ann Richards, who ran for Texas state trea-
surer, outpolled White by two hundred thousand votes and won
with a twenty-five-point lead over her opponent. "I stressed the
fact that I am a woman," Richards told me, "and that I would
be the first woman in fifty years to be elected statewide in Texas.
I talked openly about my involvement in the women's movement and my pride in being female." Her decision to publicize
her identification with the women's movement, rather than
soft-pedal it, clearly helped her to victory.

Male Democratic candidates running against Republican
women found that appealing to women voters on the basis of
issues offset any advantage a woman candidate might normally
have with voters of her own sex. In New Jersey, for example,
Democratic Senate candidate Frank Lautenberg drew away
women's support from Millicent Fenwick, and in Massachusetts, incumbent Democrat Barney Frank unseated incumbent
Republican Margaret Heckler in a redrawn, heavily Democratic district, running ahead of her in the women's vote. (See
chapter 9 for a detailed discussion of these campaigns.)

In the wake of the 1982 elections, some commentators
jumped to the conclusion that the gender gap represented nothing more than an automatic tendency among women voters to
support Democratic candidates. That conclusion was not borne
out by the facts. As the *Washington Post* reported in a postelection analysis, "The gender gap appears to favor candidates
perceived to be more peace-oriented and more supportive of

social programs." Those candidates were not always Democrats. In a Maine congressional race, for example, pro-choice
Republican candidate John McKernan defeated his anti-choice
Democratic opponent even though the Democratic ticket swept
most of the other races in the state. The victorious new Congressman said, "My pro-choice position was a key factor in my
election," thus dispelling the myth that a pro-choice stance is
poison at the polls.

Confirming McKernan's observation, the newspaper of the
National Abortion Rights Action League (NARAL) reported
in its December 1982 issue: "Pro-choice candidates walked
away from the 1982 elections confident that their stand on the
abortion issue was beneficial. In the U.S. Senate 69 percent of
the pro-choice candidates backed by NARAL-PAC [Political
Action Committee] won. In the House, NARAL-PAC had a 71
percent victory rate . . . Strong 1982 pro-choice returns are a
complete reversal from two years ago."

In sixty-five marginal U.S. House of Representatives races,
forty-two NARAL-backed candidates won; in thirty-nine non-
marginal House races, thirty-two candidates supported by
NARAL won, and it also claimed victory in nine of thirteen
U.S. Senate races.

NARAL estimated that election of five new pro-choice
House members, joined to the conversion of fifteen incumbents,
would provide a net gain of at least twenty pro-choice votes in
the House. It did not project any change in the voting line-up
in the Senate on abortion issues, but the widening effectiveness
of lobbying for pro-choice has succeeded in blocking approval
of an antiabortion constitutional amendment. As further indication of the reversal in the antiabortion trend among politicians, NARAL reported, "Not one U.S. Senator that 'Right-to-
Life' groups vowed to defeat after last September's abortion
vote failed to be reelected."

Pro-choice successes in 1982 state legislature races also "far
surpassed our expectations," according to NARAL-PAC coordinator Suellen Lowry. She reported that in a six-state concentration campaign, there was a 79 percent victory rate in all races
and a 72 percent victory rate in marginal contests.

A significant pro-ERA voting trend in 1982 was noted by

NOW's national newspaper, which reported dramatic gains in the state legislatures of three ERA target states — Florida, Illinois, and North Carolina — and "significant gains through the defeat of legislators who opposed the ERA and wins for both ERA supporters and pro-ERA women."

These victories came several months after the failure of the nationwide ERA ratification campaign, yet they were important auguries of success in the next campaign for ERA approval. The inability to get the three needed states to join the ratification effort touched off intensive electoral activities by women's groups in key states. In Florida, ERA had been defeated by a twenty-three to seventeen vote in the Florida Senate nine days before the June 30,1982, national deadline for ratification. Pro-ERA organizations recruited record numbers of female candidates to run in the primaries for state legislature seats. Fourteen women among twenty who ran in the Florida Senate primary survived to run in the general election in November 1982; nine won, and eight of them are committed to support ERA. The election doubled the number of women senators and the ranks of women in the Florida House increased by 50 percent. "Of the 23 senators who voted no on the ERA, 10 will not be returning," the *National NOW Times* reported. "Eight of the 10 were replaced with pro-ERA senators. A count in the Florida Senate now shows 23 pro-ERA legislators, a winning majority."

There was also a turnaround in Illinois, another crucial state in the ERA campaign. Political action by pro-ERA women's groups resulted in doubling the number of women in the Illinois Senate from four to eight members, seven of whom are pro-ERA. There are now thirty-six pro-ERA legislators in the Senate and seventy-five pro-ERA legislators in the House, enough to meet Illinois's unique requirement that a constitutional amendment must be approved by a three-fifths' majority vote. In the North Carolina legislature, twenty-six of thirty-five pro-ERA candidates backed by women's groups were elected, but no claim was made that there would be enough votes to win that state's approval of the amendment.

No gender-gap figures were available for these state legislature races, but women voters were undoubtedly the mainstays of the pro-ERA victors. There is an indisputable gender gap in the way male and female state legislators vote on ERA. A 1981 survey by the Center for the American Woman and Politics at Rutgers University showed that more than three fourths of women legislators (77 percent) favored ERA, but only 49 percent of the men did. In states that have not ratified, the disparity was even wider, with 76 percent of women legislators and only 36 percent of the men pro-ERA. However, since men compose 86.7 percent of state legislators, it is obvious that the ultimate success of the ERA depends on electing much larger numbers of women as state legislators.

Whether skeptics like it or not, the 1982 elections confirmed that the gender gap was alive and well. Some critics have cited preelection polls that predicted a higher gender gap than actually appeared on Election Day to downgrade the difference between the male and female vote, suggesting that gender-gap claims were overrated. This is an erroneous view. First, the actual gender gap of 6 percent was exactly the same as that which a Harris poll had found as early as April 1982. Second, in those states in which the gender gap did narrow, it was largely attributable to candidates who, after receiving polling data showing them in trouble with women voters, changed their campaign strategies and were able to win over the women. For example, Illinois Republican Governor James Thompson reacted to his early polls, which showed him trailing substantially with women voters, by airing television ads depicting himself as a "caring" governor and stressing such issues as education and the elderly. This strategy gave him a razor-thin victory over Democratic challenger Adlai Stevenson III in an election so close that a recount was necessary to determine the winner. Last, pollster Patrick Cadell reported his data as showing for the first time that "men converged toward women. Men have always been the lead group politically. This year showed that women can also lead."

In other words, as Election Day 1982 neared, men listened to their wives, daughters, and sisters and decided to change their votes, the reverse of what had been believed to be the traditional pattern.

6

Roots of the Gender Gap

AFTER THE 1982 election, the gender gap could no longer be readily dismissed as a temporary aberration from the "normal" way women were expected to behave politically. Finally, more than 130 years after the historic women's rights meeting in Seneca Falls, New York, and more than sixty years after women had won the vote, the kind of influence that suffragist leaders had vainly hoped women would exert over the political process had finally become apparent.

Why did it take so long to materialize? Why did the hopes of our foremothers go unfulfilled so long? Unfortunately for women, social changes that work to our benefit have a long gestation period. Our gains are won only by the expenditure of considerable amounts of our energy as we struggle to knock down the formidable barriers constantly strewn across our pathway to full equality. We have yet to achieve our goal, but we are inching toward it. Our struggle for equality, too, has to be seen in the context of larger political and social battles that engage both men and women in joint action. Full equality for women is not likely to be achieved in societies afflicted with

economic crises, mass unemployment, racism, and militariza-
tion, although these factors spur women into greater activity
and protest.

Political scientists, sociologists, and historians know that all
social and political movements undergo rather predictable
stages of development. The women's rights movement has been
no exception. Its first stage began in the nineteenth century with
the suffrage movement. If a birthdate can be assigned to such
a dynamic process as women's battle for equality, the logical
choice would be the Seneca Falls meeting in July 1848. At this
gathering — the first public meeting organized and held by
American women — Elizabeth Cady Stanton, who came into
public life through her activities in the antislavery movement,
drafted a Declaration of Sentiments that paraphrased and corrected the Declaration of Independence. She began, "All men
and women are created equal," and went on to document her
charges that "the history of mankind is a history of repeated
injuries and usurpations on the part of man toward woman,
having in direct object the establishment of absolute tyranny
over her."

Among the resolutions Stanton prepared for the meeting was
one which simply said, "Resolved, that it is the duty of women
of this country to secure to themselves their sacred right to the
elective franchise." This was considered an outrageously radical demand even by many of the women there, and by Stanton's
otherwise sympathetic husband. While resolutions calling for
equal rights and opportunities for women in the trades, professions, schools and universities, political offices, and churches all
passed unanimously, the women's vote resolution carried by
only a slender margin. Stanton and Frederick Douglass, the
noted black abolitionist leader, were its chief and most passionate advocates. Thus the struggle to enfranchise women began,
and it was to last for more than seventy years.

In the process of seeking their electoral rights, American
women learned to work together politically. They broke the
taboos against women speaking in public. They wrote and produced politically persuasive handbills, letters, speeches, articles, and books. They organized and conducted public meetings
and canvassed house to house — in the prairies, mountains, and

countryside as well as in the villages, towns, and cities. They met and held their own with public opinion makers: editors, writers, prominent citizens, heads of organizations, businesses, and unions, political party leaders, and elected officials. They raised money and gathered millions of signatures on petitions, learned to organize at the precinct level, set up card files on sympathizers and prospective voters, and helped them to register and get to the polls. They conducted lobbying and legislative-monitoring campaigns in the capitals, held mass meetings and demonstrations, and staged mammoth parades complete with auto caravans, floats, marching bands, costumes, and handmade banners.

And when that was not enough, some women summoned up their courage to picket the White House (a novel and audacious act in those days). They withstood physical attacks from irate males, and when they were arrested, they went on hunger strikes and were force-fed and brutally treated. They did all this, and more. Finally, on August 26, 1920, the suffrage amendment became part of the U.S. Constitution. I sometimes marvel at how millions of women vote without giving a thought or even silent thanks to the female sweat, tears, guts, and blood it took to win them the right to walk into a voting booth. I'm appalled that millions more sit home on Election Day, not even bothering to exercise their hard-won right to vote.

The early leaders of the suffrage movement believed that with the vote women would prove to be the cutting edge of social change. They claimed that women would have a morally uplifting, life-enhancing, and liberalizing effect on the nation. As earnestly as conservatives feared the development of an independent women's voting bloc, suffragists hoped for and counted on it. They believed, too, that women might be able to prevent future wars. And so did others. James D. Cox, the unsuccessful Democratic presidential candidate in 1920, greeted ratification of the Nineteenth Amendment with this ecstatic pronouncement: "The civilization of the world is saved. The mothers of America will stay the hand of war." But although American women tended to be more antiwar than men, even with the right to vote they lacked the political power — as we still lack it — to prevent war.

Cox's view echoed the rhetoric that suffragists had increasingly come to employ, for reasons of expediency as well as personal conviction. In the early days of the movement, Stanton and others had focused on the sexual and social liberation of the individual woman as the key to equality, and suffrage was seen as only one necessary reform in a long agenda that they hoped would revolutionize male/female relationships and society as a whole.

Although some women writers and activists continued to hold these radical beliefs, suffrage organization leaders gradually shifted to an accommodation with the prevailing view, held by women as well as men, that woman's natural role was as wife and mother in the private sphere of the home. She was the guardian of the family's spiritual values, while man's domain was the materialistic public world of commerce, work, and power. In gaining the vote, the suffragists argued, women would bring their superior home-nurtured morality into the public arena, and the social reforms they sought would protect the welfare and stability of the family. "Enlarged housekeeping" was the term temperance leader Frances Willard had used to describe politics, and the image appealed to opinion makers, who depicted women in aprons wielding brooms to clean up the nation's public messes.

The emphasis on doing good for others led to a submergence of women's personal and individual goals. Once suffrage was achieved, the vast political experience gained by women was not focused on gaining elective office or political power for their own sex or building an independent electoral base.

Women's organizations set up a Joint Congressional Committee to lobby for and monitor the progress of legislation affecting women and children, the same kind of coalition that present-day women's groups have put together in Washington. Their first victory was passage in 1921 of a controversial maternity and infancy bill that appropriated $1.25 million annually for educational instruction in the health care of mothers and babies. This was the forerunner of the present Maternal and Child Health block grant, which serves nearly 12 million low-income women and children, and the Women, Infants, and Children (WIC) program, which provides diet supplements and health care to about 2.4 million needy pregnant women, nursing mothers, and children under age five. (Quite a legacy from our activist foremothers!)

In rapid succession, under pressure from the women, Congress also passed laws protecting consumers, reforming citizenship requirements for married women, and upgrading the civil service merit system to give women an opportunity to get higher-paying jobs. Congress also approved a constitutional amendment outlawing child labor, another women's priority, but this failed in the ratification process. State legislatures, too, enacted a series of measures sought by women activists.

In the mid-1920s, however, male politicians stopped trying to win women's favor. With the passage of time, it became increasingly clear that no female voting bloc existed and that women in general voted like their husbands, if they voted at all. The problem was that although more women than men apparently continued to favor social welfare programs and peace, this difference did not show up electorally. Millions of women voted, but because it was a new and intimidating experience, they voted in far fewer numbers than men did. Only about a third of eligible women voted in the 1920 election, which came just a few months after ratification of the Nineteenth Amendment. Acquiring the habit of voting proved to be a slow process, particularly in what was still a hostile climate.

There was, too, in the suffragist community the feeling of letdown that inevitably follows an intense, all-consuming effort. Winning the right to vote was a single, dramatic issue that unified and impelled women to action. Their passionate commitment to this goal, with its promise of full citizenship and respect, sustained them through the long years of struggle. But having won the vote, women could not find any comparable simple and universal issue around which to mobilize, and disillusionment set in when they found that winning the vote had not changed their lives significantly.

In analyzing women's voting patterns in the first half of the twentieth century, political scientists Sandra Baxter and Marjorie Lansing concluded from the data that "Elizabeth Cady Stanton was right: the real obstacle to equality was not the vote but the division of lifestyles between men and women — and it was only as women became 'self-supporting equal partners with men,' as Stanton put it, that women began to exercise the hard-won right to vote in large numbers. The feminists of the early part of this century had it reversed: they believed that women playing an active role in politics would change society at its roots, but the opposite has occurred. Changes in the structure of society have brought about changes in the political role of women."

The Changing Profile of Women

Beginning in the mid-1960s, the post-suffrage women's organizations moved from their second stage of civic-minded, nonpartisan, "good government" political activity into the third stage of mass political activism. This change has had a significant impact on women's political behavior, accounting for our growing power at the polls. Political scientists have identified certain socioeconomic characteristics that serve as predictors of voter turnout for both men and women. According to the accepted model, voter turnout increases with education, employment, income, age, interest in the campaign, concern for the outcome of the election, and one's sense of political efficacy. Since the turn of the century, women's status in terms of all these measures has changed in the direction of a higher women's vote in elections.

American women, measured in median number of years of school completed, have been slightly better educated than men since 1920. In the past, women were more likely than men to graduate from high school but were less apt to have graduated from college. That particular gap has been closed. While only 18 percent of all bachelor's and first professional degrees were earned by women in 1900, nearly 50 percent of modern American women have earned their sheepskins. Women constituted 51.5 percent of all students enrolled in higher education in 1980, and today young women as a group have more formal education than their mothers.

One of the greatest changes in women's social status, with a resulting impact on political behavior, has been their entry into the labor force in large numbers. Prior to World War II, few married women were employed outside the home. While it was not unusual for single women to hold jobs, women with husbands were discouraged by social attitudes and often prohibited by company policy from working. In fact, as late as 1939, bills to prohibit married women — those whose husbands earned more than a base level of income — from working in state or local governments and in business or industry were introduced in state legislatures. More amazingly, a Gallup opinion poll at that time found that a majority of both men and women favored such legislation!

The manpower shortage during World War II brought "Rosie the Riveter" and millions of American women into the labor force — and they've stayed there ever since. In 1940, for example, just one fourth of working-age women had jobs outside the home. By 1945 that figure had jumped to 36 percent, with women holding three out of ten jobs. Today, 53 percent of all women are employed, constituting nearly half our nation's workers.

Public attitudes toward working women have also changed. In 1936 only 15 percent of the public believed that married women should have full-time jobs outside the home; by 1945 just 18 percent approved; twenty-five years later, more than half (55 percent) approved, and by 1976 the figure had risen to 68 percent. Interestingly enough, the concept of equal pay for equal work found majority support even when the public opposed married women's working. In 1945, after millions of women had worked in war production plants, a Gallup poll found 76 percent of the public in favor of equal pay, a number that had jumped to 87 percent by 1954.

But neither Gallup polls nor enactment of the Equal Pay law in 1963 affected the reality; winning a public opinion victory does not ensure economic gains, and legal guarantees of equal pay for equal work are not sufficient as long as women are segregated into jobs that are socially undervalued. Only organized activity, such as the current drive to achieve equal pay for work of comparable value, can dent the continuing economic discrimination against women.

As I noted earlier, women, compared with men, still earn only an average of fifty-nine cents on the dollar. That ratio, however, does not begin to reveal the full depth of institutional, occupational, and wage segregation of women in the work force. The U.S. Labor Department's *Dictionary of Occupational Titles* lists 427 occupations with their wage levels. In 1982 more than 80 percent of all working women were confined to a narrow range of twenty-five generally low-paying occupations: secretaries, clerks, waitresses, cleaning and household service workers, salespersons, elementary schoolteachers, librarians, and other worthy and necessary occupations that carry neither status nor adequate paychecks.

Although many women do exactly the same work as men for less pay, in most cases the practice of pay discrimination and occupational segregation begins very early. From infancy, females are socialized into different behavior patterns that influence their choice of work or career and lower their expectations. Once on the job, women often find opportunities to better themselves extremely limited. According to a U.S. Civil Rights Commission report, women at every age and educational level receive less on-the-job training than men. The supervisors who make decisions about pay and promotion are predominantly male. By one estimate, two thirds of the instances of sex wage differential in firms for equally qualified workers can be attributed to differentials in job placement.

The result is that working women earn less than men in every job category; even more flagrantly discriminatory is the fact that on average, women college graduates earn less than male high school graduates. In 1980 the median wage for all women who were permanent, full-time workers was $11,200, compared with $18,006 for men. TV commercials and newspaper and magazine articles and advertisements give the impression that glamorous superwomen dressed in elegant business suits have taken over the corporate suites, banks, and other elite professions, but, in fact, only 1 percent of American women earn more than $25,000 a year; three out of five working women earn *less* than $10,000. Minority women remain the lowest paid: despite impressive gains made by a small percentage of educated black women in the higher-salaried professions, the average wage gap for black women as a whole is 54 cents on the dollar, and for Hispanic women it is 49 cents.

Changes in the family structure have brought even more women into the work force, and they work for the same reasons that men have always worked. For most women, a job is a matter of economic survival, not of disposable income for luxuries like a second car, expensive vacations, fancy clothes, or any of the other spurious and frivolous reasons those who oppose women's economic equality would have us believe.

The concept that the typical American family consists of a working father, a full-time homemaker mother, and 2.4 children is as outdated as those old Norman Rockwell *Saturday Evening Post* covers devoted to nostalgia for a long-gone — if it ever existed — America.

Today, one out of every two married women with children under six years of age works outside the home, compared to only 19 percent who did in 1960, and nearly two thirds of women with children over six years of age hold jobs in the marketplace. More than 9.4 million American families are headed by single women. If current trends continue, by 1990 only 28 percent of American households will consist of a couple with dependent children, and another 27 percent will be composed of couples whose children have grown up and departed. Before long the 45 percent of households composed solely of adults, both young and old, will be the typical American household.

The upheaval in the life patterns of American women was depicted in human terms by sociologist Alice Rossi of the University of Massachusetts in March 1983 in a paper, "The Gender Gap in Mainstream Politics." Eighty years ago, she wrote, the average woman would "reside with her parents until her marriage in her mid-twenties, often with her mother rather than both parents since marriages were typically broken by the death of a spouse before the last child in a family married. She would have five or six pregnancies and lose two to infant mortality. She would live a hard life of domestic toil, often supporting herself and the children by taking in boarders and lodgers after the death of her husband; and she would die in her sixties. Note that her household location involved no period of solo living, since she moved from her parents' household to her husband's, then headed her own while the remaining children grew up and married, supporting herself as a widow by taking in boarders both before and after the children left home."

In contrast, today's woman "marries later and has fewer pregnancies to achieve a small family of closely spaced children. An increasing proportion experience a divorce rather than a death of a spouse, and then support their children themselves or become welfare recipients, and they live to their late seventies, having survived their husbands by five or more years . . . The effect of later marriage, high divorce rates, small families, longer lives and the gender gap in longevity have combined to produce an unprecedented phenomenon in social history: a rapid increase in solo living."

With the rising number of families maintained by single women — divorced, widowed, separated, and never-married — has come the parallel development of the widely recognized feminization of poverty. Women have become the fastest-growing poverty group in America. According to a U.S. Commission on Civil Rights report, if present trends continue, women and their children will account for almost all of the nation's poor by the year 2000.

The evidence is overwhelming: in 1983, the Women's Equity Action League (WEAL) reports, 77.7 percent of poor people were women and children, and 74 percent of the elderly poor were women. Thirty-three percent of all single-parent families maintained by women live in poverty. They represent 50 percent of the nation's 6.4 million poor families, even though they constitute only 16 percent of the total families.

In 1982 more than a third of all minority families were maintained by women, and more than half these families lived below the poverty level, despite the fact that 56 percent of minority women who headed households were in the labor force. Among poor families with children under eighteen, the poverty rate is 68 percent for blacks, 67 percent for Hispanics, and 43 percent for whites.

Taken together, these demographic changes have had a radical impact on women's role in society, how women perceive themselves, and how they seek solutions to their individual and family problems. Millions of educated, single women who live alone or in group-sharing arrangements now place higher values on personal independence, satisfying work careers, and pay and job equity, and they also expect family responsibilities to be equitably shared after marriage. In seeking greater control over their lives, they have come to rely on family planning, abortion, and child-care services, which are still grossly inadequate.

Other millions of working-class and middle-class women, as members of the two-income family pattern, have found, during economic crises, that their families are just one paycheck away from poverty. If the husband loses his job, the family has to subsist on the wife's much lower earnings, heightening her awareness of job and pay discrimination; if she loses her job, the family may also lose their home or car, or more. Unemployment insurance, welfare assistance, government job programs, low interest rates, and stability of health insurance and Social Security are all life lines for these families. Single women who head poor families, the majority of them belonging to minorities, are independent only in the sense that there is no man in the house to share their burdens or poverty; instead they have become dependent on federal assistance systems that simultaneously help them survive and lock them into hopeless lives, except for those promising, but small and threatened programs that offer job training. For millions of American women who either live in poverty or teeter on its edge, the feminization of poverty leads directly to the feminization of politics, a determination that they must have a greater say over the political, economic, and social forces that dictate the way they live. The electoral gender gap is tangible evidence of that determination.

7

The Gender-Gap Issues

THE GENDER GAP is both "something old" and "something new." In part, it represents the public expression of the values long held by women. As Maryland Congresswoman Barbara Mikulski said, "Women are recognizing that their private values are good enough to be their public values." Or, as I have often put it, "What's good for women is good for men, good for children, good for America." American female values are described by Carol Gilligan in her book *In a Different Voice* as the "ethic of care." She asserts that while men are mostly guided by a highly structured and abstract sense of equality and justice, women are more apt to be concerned with consequences, with immediate situations, and with personal relationships. "While an ethic of justice proceeds from the premise of equality — that everyone should be treated the same — an ethic of care rests on the premise of nonviolence — that no one should be hurt," she says. Congresswoman Barbara Kennelly, a Connecticut Democrat, makes the same point, remarking, "Men tend to say something is right or wrong. Women say, 'How can we help everyone?' "

It is not new for women to be more concerned than men about peace, preserving the environment, attending the needs of others, and nurturing people and the world we live in. These have long been women's socialized gender roles in the evolution of the family and society, roles that have been indispensable and at the same time sexually constricting. What is new is that the changing roles and attitudes of women have made them assert that their values should be equally shared by men, and that their ethic of care recognizes the legitimacy of women also caring about themselves as individuals. Women understand that they should operate out of self-interest (not selfishness, mind you, but enlightened self-interest), not just as protectors of others or as their sacrificial victims. Women have taken on new responsibilities — as single heads of households, as full-time workers outside the home, as coequal partners with spouses inside the home, and in joining together to seek equality and economic justice for all women.

The merging of their private values and public views has been charted in the opinion polls as well as in the voting booths, and there the gender gap assumes even larger dimensions than in the votes recorded in the 1980 and 1982 elections. The issues at the heart of the gender gap range from women's rights to their broader concerns about the economy, war and peace, the environment, and other issues related to their vision of a more rational, peaceful, and compassionate world.

As the following summary of recent polling data shows and as most analysts, including those in the White House, agree, President Ronald Reagan and the Republican Party were in deep trouble with women voters as 1984 approached. For the first time in history, there was a strong likelihood that the women's vote could and would defeat an incumbent President and oust his party from power.

Women and the Economy

Men and women express different priorities in the economic arena. Despite some improvements in the economy and a minor pickup in employment in the first half of 1983, the U.S. Labor Department reported that at the end of August 1983, the number of jobless aged sixteen and over was more than 10.6 million, compared with 6.7 million in January 1980, when Reagan took office. The overall unemployment rate for August 1983 was 9.5 percent, a shocking 20 percent for blacks, 12.9 percent for Hispanics, 23 percent for teen-agers, and 8 percent for women over age twenty; jobless rates were higher for black and Hispanic women than for whites. Although the overall unemployment rate was slightly lower for women than men, reflecting the huge layoffs in mass-production industries that traditionally employ larger numbers of men, almost twice as many females (4.2 million) as males (2.4 million) were considered labor market dropouts; women who needed jobs but could not find work had given up looking.

The social welfare program cuts that began under Carter and were continued much more deeply by Reagan as part of his plan to decimate all domestic and human services programs — the better to increase military spending — had a harsh impact on women workers, lower-middle-class women, and especially black and minority women who depended mainly on these programs not only for direct family assistance, but for job-training programs and, for upwardly mobile minority women, employment in related federal, state, local, and private-sector programs. Women's recognition of their economic vulnerability was undoubtedly an important factor in their negative views of Reaganomics.

In an interesting analysis of what he calls "the hidden agenda" of Reagan's "new class war," political scientist Steven P. Erie of the University of California at San Diego points out that in 1980 nearly one third of the nearly 38 million women in the nonagricultural labor force worked in human service jobs, compared with only 11 percent of the 47.5 million men then in the labor force.

"Social welfare employment was especially important for black women," he reported in a presentation to the annual meeting of the Women's Caucus for Political Science in September 1983. "In 1980, 39 percent of all black women were employed in the human services sector, compared with 30 percent of white women, 13 percent of black men, and 11 percent of white men. In terms of job growth between 1960 and 1980, a startling 59 percent of all new employment for black women occurred in social welfare fields, compared with 37 percent for white women, 24 percent for black men, and 22 percent for white women."

As Reagan's policies eliminated large numbers of these jobs and closed the escape hatch for women living in poverty, millions of other women — middle-class whites and minorities — were also confronted with the loss of their own jobs or unemployment among other members of their families. The result, a June 1983 CBS/*New York Times* poll showed, was widespread dissatisfaction among women with the administration's economic program and a growing gender gap. For example:

• Just 39 percent of the women, compared with 60 percent of the men, approved of Reagan's handling of the economy — a 21 percent gender gap.

• Only 21 percent of the women thought Reagan had done enough to reduce unemployment, while 34 percent of the men thought he had, a gender gap of 13 percent.

• A majority of women (54 percent), compared with 36 percent of men, thought Reagan had not done enough to bring down inflation — an 18 percent gender gap.

• Although men were equally divided on the question of whether or not the recession was over (47 percent thought it was, 48 percent did not), only 38 percent of the women believed it was over while 55 percent did not — a 9 percent gender gap.

• Only one in five women thought she had been personally helped by Reagan's economic program, while three out of ten men thought they had — a gender gap of 10 percent.

• The views of men and women on their families' financial situations were mirror images of each other: 29 percent of the men, but 22 percent of the women, thought it had improved, while 22 percent of the men and 28 percent of the women thought it was worse.

Even more pessimistic views were recorded by a July 1983 Harris survey: 61 percent of the women, compared with 53 percent of the men, thought they and their families were then worse off than they had been when Reagan took office.

An August 1983 ABC poll showed roughly similar gender gaps in the way women and men viewed the economy, and also found women more skeptical that their hard work would be rewarded. Fewer women (57 percent) than men (68 percent) agreed with the statement that if you work hard in this country you will eventually get ahead. Four out of ten women did not think that was true, while only 29 percent of men disagreed.

By September 1983, a CBS/*New York Times* survey found that only 39 percent of women, compared with 50 percent of men, approved of the way Ronald Reagan was handling the economy; 48 percent of women and 44 percent of men disapproved.

A June 1983 poll taken for the National Republican Congressional Committee by Market Opinion Research of Detroit confirmed that women consistently take a more negative view of the Reagan administration's economic performance: it found that while 62 percent of the men said the economy was better than it had been one year ago, only 47 percent of the women felt that way, a fifteen-point gender gap. There was also sharp disagreement on whether "things are going in the right direction" — 55 percent of men, compared with 39 percent of women, thought so; 51 percent of women and 36 percent of men thought the country was on the wrong track.

Women and Peace

American men and women have registered the deepest division of opinion on the issues of war and peace, with women always taking the more pacific position. Willingness to fight in wars and to commit violence has been made the ultimate social test of manhood throughout history; the role of women has been more complex. Aggressive militarism has depended on the subordination and exploitation of women, who are needed to do society's work while the men are away at war and to validate the warmakers' propaganda rationalizations that they fight to save home, family, and country. Women have been complicitors in wars and have been used in armies as workers, nurses, logistical aides, and even as soldiers, but they have not been the primary makers of war or violence. Their traditional pacifism is often seen as an expression of motherly concern for the survival of their children, just as — in times of war — their willingness to send their sons (and sometimes their daughters) off to die is praised as the highest form of patriotism. But, historically, the tendency of women has been to favor peaceful solutions and to hate war. Some female peace leaders attribute this bent to biological reasons. Dr. Helen Caldicott, a pediatrician and leader of Women's Action for Nuclear Disarmament, says, "There's nothing more powerful than the instinct a mother feels for the preservation of her children" and describes the avoidance of a nuclear catastrophe as "the ultimate parenting issue." Others say that women have been socialized into the mothering and peacemaking role and, under certain conditions, are as capable as men of being warlike and violent.

On the whole, because of their exclusion from political power, government, and military leadership, women have no vested interests in war-making policies and institutions, and feel freer to express their opposition to war and aggression.

In 1983, the great majority of American women were opposed to the continuing arms race and the prospect of a nuclear war that could destroy all human life — men, women, fathers, mothers, children. Strengthening their antiwar stance was a growing recognition that the Reagan administration was choosing guns over butter, nuclear missiles over essential domestic programs. In March 1983 an ad hoc coalition of fifty-five major national women's organizations issued a report, *Inequality of Sacrifice: The Impact of the Reagan Budget on Women,* which charged that the administration's budget cuts would have "a devastating impact on women and their families at every stage of their lives." While concentrating on domestic issues, the coalition called on Congress to "look long and hard at the President's budget and help us find an alternative which will focus on our human infrastructures rather than just defense and public works." It cited a study by Employment Research Associates of Lansing, Michigan, which found that "every time the Pentagon budget goes up $1 billion, 9500 jobs disappear for American women." The coalition statement was symptomatic of a growing recognition in the women's movement that peace is a women's issue and that its goals of equity, economic justice, and feminist values cannot be achieved in a militaristic society.

Gender-gap differences on war and peace issues showed up

long before the anti–nuclear war movement began. In an analysis of public opinion survey data from World War II to 1968, reported in Sandra Baxter and Marjorie Lansing's *The Invisible Majority,* Alfred Hero found that "females were more likely to view our entry into the two world wars and the Korean and Vietnam conflicts as a mistake than were males. Women have been more likely to support U.S. withdrawals from wars already entered into and less receptive to the idea of 'peacetime' conscription."

A 1952 University of Michigan survey reported a gender gap regarding the Korean conflict: almost half the men (48 percent), but fewer than one third of the women (32 percent), believed the United States had done "the right thing in getting into the fighting in Korea." Inversely, 45 percent of the women and 37 percent of the men believed "we should have stayed out." (The first electoral gender gap appeared in 1952, when women favored Dwight D. Eisenhower because he had pledged to end the Korean War.)

The gender gap was equally as marked in the Vietnam War period:

• In 1964 only 30 percent of the women, but 42 percent of the men surveyed felt we had done the right thing by getting involved in Vietnam; nearly twice as many men (38 percent) as women (21 percent) felt we should take a stronger stand.

• By 1969 nearly two thirds of the women (64 percent) labeled themselves doves, while fewer than half of the men (48 percent) did so.

• By 1972 Gallup found that 70 percent of the women, but only 54 percent of the men, favored troop withdrawal from Vietnam by the end of the year. (In a retrospective on the Vietnam War, a 1983 opinion poll found that only 16 percent of the men and 12 percent of the women replied that our involvement in Vietnam was "the right thing.")

Women react as strongly to threats of force and the risk of war as they do to war itself. For example, a January 1980 Gallup poll showed that only 30 percent of the women, compared with 43 percent of the men, favored using force to free the U.S. hostages in Iran.

Not only did November 1980 Election Day exit polls show a gender gap in women's perception of Reagan as a potential warmaker, but opinion polls taken during the Reagan presidency continued to show that women were more suspicious of Reagan's foreign policy, more concerned about the threat of nuclear war, and more opposed to the use of military force than men.

According to a June 1983 CBS/*New York Times* poll, only 35 percent of women, compared with 53 percent of men, approved of Reagan's handling of international issues. The same poll also found that a near majority of women (47 percent) answered yes to the question, "Regardless of your overall opinion of him, are you afraid Ronald Reagan might get us into war?" — up from 39 percent at the beginning of the year. Only 31 percent of the men held this view, for a gender gap of 16 percent. A majority of the women in this survey (56 percent) did not think Reagan had done enough to reach an agreement to reduce nuclear weapons, and only 39 percent of the women, compared with 49 percent of the men, believed Reagan "really means it" when he makes proposals for arms control.

An August 1983 ABC poll also showed women giving Reagan a higher negative rating on foreign affairs in general, on the Middle East, on the military budget, and on his nuclear weapons policy. Women were distinctly less supportive of his interventionist approach in Central America. Only 25 percent of women, compared with 39 percent of men, thought Congress should approve Reagan's request for more military/economic aid to Central America; 35 percent of women and 54 percent of men approved U.S. military exercises off the coast of Nicaragua; and only 12 percent of women and 29 percent of men approved U.S. overthrow of the Nicaraguan government.

A May 1982 CBS/*New York Times* poll found that 66 percent of women, but only 54 percent of men — a 12 percent gap — were afraid of a Vietnam-style involvement in El Salvador. In June 1983, when they were questioned again by the same polling group, only 24 percent of women, compared with 42 percent of men, favored sending combat troops to El Salvador. An August 1983 Gallup poll reported that 62 percent of the women, as against 48 percent of the men, believed we should not get involved in Central America.

A May 1982 CBS/*New York Times* poll also found that women were:

- less likely than men to think that development of the atomic bomb was a good thing (74 percent of the women and 56 percent of the men opposed its development — an 18 percent gender gap);
- more likely than men to think that the United States will get into a nuclear war; 52 percent of the women and 33 percent of the men held this view — a 19 percent gap;
- less likely than men to trust the President to make the right decisions about nuclear weapons, by 14 percent;
- less likely than men to see any justification for a U.S. nuclear first strike, by 13 percent; and
- in favor of reducing tensions with the Soviet Union, by a 9 percent margin over men.

The Harris surveys have also found meaningful gender gaps and high levels of female dissatisfaction with Reagan on military issues. Their May 1983 data show that 64 percent of women — up from 51 percent in February 1983 — worry that Reagan might get us into another war, while only 46 percent of men do, for a gender gap of 18 percent. Harris also found that men and women have different views on Reagan's big military budget. According to a June 1983 Harris survey, nearly three out of five women were opposed to building the MX missile system, and only about one in three were in favor. Men, on the other hand, were equally divided on the issue.

After the Soviet shooting down of Korean Air Lines Flight 007 in September 1983, a CBS/*New York Times* survey reported that although men and women gave equal levels of approval to Reagan's handling of the incident, women were less likely than men to say he should have taken stronger actions. Only 30 percent of women, compared with 41 percent of men, favored stronger action, and 52 percent of women against 44 percent of men agreed that "the risks of taking stronger action to punish the Russians are greater than any satisfaction it might give us." In the same poll, only 36 percent of women, compared with 46 percent of men, approved of the way Reagan was handling foreign policy; equal percentages of men and women, 40 percent, disapproved.

The day after more than two hundred U.S. marines were killed in Beirut, an October 24, 1983, ABC poll reported that 62 percent of women, compared with 34 percent of men, wanted American forces withdrawn from Lebanon.

Although President Reagan's popularity reportedly soared after the U.S. invasion of tiny Grenada, surveys disclosed continuing big differences of opinion between women and men. A November 1983 poll by the *New York Times* reported a twenty-three-percentage-point gender gap on this issue: 68 percent of men and 45 percent of women approved the invasion; 43 percent of women and 26 percent of men disapproved. On another issue, 49 percent of women feared Reagan might get the country into war, compared with 33 percent of men who felt that way, a sixteen-point gender gap.

Women and the Environment

Nuclear energy concerns women nearly as much as the threat of nuclear war. A 1979 CBS/*New York Times* poll found that 49 percent of the women, compared to 32 percent of the men, opposed building more nuclear power plants. Hard times in the economy are not enough cause for women to soften their environmental protection concerns: in a September 1981 CBS/*New York Times* poll, 48 percent of the women, compared with 41 percent of the men, favored continuing environmental improvement programs regardless of the cost. An April 1983 CBS/*New York Times* poll found that the pro-environment position had gained ground with both sexes, with 58 percent of women and men supporting environmental protection.

The National Republican Congressional Committee's June 1983 survey, however, reported that "women are extremely harsh in their assessment of air and water pollution and toxic waste." Although the NRCC did not seek to evaluate public opinion of James Watt, the bane of environmentalists who was then Department of the Interior Secretary, its poll found that a majority of the public thought the problems of acid rain, toxic waste, and water pollution had become worse in the past three years, with more women than men holding this view.

What emerges in these and other polls is a general tendency among women to take more compassionate, more nurturing, and less violent positions than men, and to question and challenge government policies. (It should be noted, however, that on many issues of war and peace, a majority of men also favor peaceful solutions, albeit by considerably lower margins than women.) Women have a broad range of social concerns, as is evident in the results of a series of 1981 ABC/*Washington Post* polls:

- 73 percent of the women surveyed, compared with 61 percent of the men, believed the government should work to substantially reduce the income gap between the rich and poor;
- 56 percent of the women, but only 43 percent of the men, favored increased spending for Social Security (not surprising, since a majority of Social Security recipients are women);
- 61 percent of the women, but just 48 percent of the men, opposed the military draft; and
- 51 percent of the women, but only 35 percent of the men, favored banning possession of handguns, except by police and other authorized persons.

Bad News for Republicans

The cumulative effect of the 1980 and 1982 elections, the public opinion polls, and its own June 1983 survey produced deep gloom in the Republican camp. The NRCC summary of the gender gap, as revealed in its own poll, reported: "Every subgroup of women is more negative towards President Reagan than their male counterparts. While the gender gap is indeed a significant problem for Reagan it is also a problem on the Congressional level. *The generic vote is more split by gender than ever . . . It is the worst it has ever been . . . and thus presents a real problem to Republican challengers and incumbents.*" (emphasis added)

The poll analysts had an explanation for the worsening gap:

"This is partially due to partisanship," they said, "as women are 8½ percent more Democratic than men as measured in this study." They also singled out certain subgroups of women who "show an exaggerated tendency to disapprove of Reagan and the Party"; namely, black women, Jewish women, Catholic women, women who have less than a high school education, women who are divorced or separated, women who earn less than $15,000 a year regardless of marital status, single women regardless of age or education, and women over fifty-five years of age. (The change in attitudes among older women reflected their lingering fears about threats to Social Security.) And as if that weren't enough, the GOP analysts complained that women college graduates are "less supportive of Reagan and the Party than they should be, given their educational attainment."

Summing up, the Republican poll gave the dimensions of women's disagreements with Reagan policies: "In addition to Reagan approval, the gender gap is most striking on women's perceptions of the direction of the country, the generic vote, the President's handling of foreign affairs, the level of defense spending, the nuclear freeze, the fairness of personal income taxes, the increase of federal spending for day care centers."

The Republicans rightly recognized that their problem extends beyond Reagan. Women have been showing an increasing tendency to identify with the Democratic Party. More than 40 percent of all women, compared with 33 percent of all men, now call themselves Democrats. Because of this gender gap, women presently are a majority constituency within the Democratic Party, accounting for 60 percent or more of the vote in the party's nominating contests.

This gender gap in party affiliation is a recent development. From 1952 through the 1970s there were no statistically significant differences between men and women in terms of party preference. Virtually identical percentages of women and men chose the Republican and Democratic parties or labeled themselves independents. More recently, however, men have shifted away from the Democratic Party, becoming increasingly independent and slightly more Republican. For women the shift has been in the other direction: a decline within the Republican ranks as more women identify with the Democratic Party.

According to political scientists, the shift can be attributed in part to generational change. Older, apolitical women in the electorate are being replaced by younger women who are more likely to be Democrats. The reverse is true for men: older, traditionally Democratic men are being supplanted by younger men who are more apt to be Republican. Thus, the largest gender gap in party preferences appears between women and men in the eighteen-to-twenty-four age group, with women 11 percent more Democratic and men 10 percent more Republican.

Women and men are also in sharp disagreement on the question of which political party is more qualified to handle the problems facing our country. In a June 1983 CBS/*New York Times* poll, more women chose the Democratic Party as better able to deal with our current and future problems generally and to control inflation in particular. Men, on the other hand, selected the Republican Party. The gender gap on these issues ranged from 7 to 12 percent. Women and men agreed that the Democrats were more likely to "keep us out of war," with women rating the Democrats 3 percent higher than men. In an earlier CBS/*New York Times* poll on the issue of unemployment — cited by both sexes as by far the most important problem facing our country today — 54 percent of the women and 50 percent of the men again chose the Democratic Party as better able to deal with the issue.

An in-house memorandum, which analyzed the ABC/*Washington Post*'s July 21–August 1983 poll and earlier surveys, concluded that not only Reagan, but also his party, was "in trouble with women as 1984 approaches." The problem was not Reagan's personality. "As many women as men like Reagan personally," the memo observed, "but fewer women like his positions and programs. The gender gap is apparently more a result of substance, not style."

Although "the traditional 'feminist' issues such as abortion and the ERA play a role in hurting the President's image," the analysis said, "they do not totally explain it." Far more important to women, it concluded, are the economy and the conduct of international affairs.

Nevertheless, there appeared to be a growing public identification of the GOP as anti-woman. Reporting on a September 1983 poll, David Garth Associates found "a tarnishing of the Republican Party's image" with regard to women's issues; 48 percent of men and women said the Democrats were better at handling these matters, while only 15 percent named the Republicans. "Whether or not President Reagan runs for reelection," the Garth analysis said, "this widespread feeling could be very damaging to Republican prospects." A third of those polled believed that Reagan's policies had hurt women. Men and women held the same views, but they differed on whether the President was personally sensitive to the problems of women: 48 percent of men thought he *was* sensitive, while 45 percent of women found him insensitive.

In still another attempt to analyze Reagan's poorer standing with women, an October 8, 1983, CBS/*New York Times* poll asked the public to explain whether there was something that bothered them as women or appealed to them as men that might not affect a member of the other sex. One fourth of all women named something about the President that bothered them as a sex. The most common answers women gave concerned Reagan's attitude toward women and feminist goals. Others cited his general style, and a smaller group mentioned concerns about war and peace.

"The President's 'women problem' extends across all demographic groups, but is particularly noticeable among well-educated, well-off women, and among black women," CBS reported. "But even among those women who approve of the way the President is handling his job, 14 percent could name something about him that bothered them as women."

In contrast, a fifth of the men interviewed found something about Reagan's style especially appealing, with better-educated and higher-income men particularly impressed by his "toughness and decisiveness" and his handling of foreign policy.

A November 1983 *New York Times* survey, taken to measure differing attitudes among women and men, found that women's perceptions of sex roles were a major element in their support of or opposition to Reagan's reelection, along with attitudes on such issues as war and peace and economic fairness.

Overall, only 38 percent of women, compared to 53 percent of men, favored Reagan's reelection, and 52 percent of women, as against 41 percent of men, thought "a new person" should be elected. Women with traditional views of male superiority — a group somewhat older and slightly less educated than other women — were much more favorable to Reagan's reelection than the majority of women, who were more critical of him. The *Times* found that 46 percent of this group, as against 33 percent of other women, said he deserved another term.

Views on sex roles were measured in part by asking whether the respondent thought men or women were more logical, more honest, or more sensitive to problems of the poor. Among women, 34 percent said they thought men were more logical, 38 percent said women were more logical, and 18 percent said there was no difference; 47 percent of men said men were more logical, 20 percent said women were, and 23 percent said there was no difference. Both sexes agreed that women were more honest (51 percent of women and 53 percent of men) and more compassionate toward the poor (69 percent of women and 64 percent of men).

Besides the fact that women who thought men more logical were more inclined to back Reagan, there were gaps among those with different views of the status of women in society. Women who felt there had been a "great deal" of progress by women into traditionally male jobs divided evenly, with 44 percent saying they favored Reagan's reelection and 45 percent opposing it. Among those who said there had not been much progress, however, 73 percent wanted a new President, and only 21 percent would stick with the incumbent.

The lowest level of support for Reagan's reelection came from unmarried, unemployed women (29 percent) and those with incomes under $10,000 (24 percent). His highest support came from women with family incomes of $40,000 or more (58 percent).

The *Times* poll also found a continuing big gap between men and women on questions relating to war and Reagan's decision to send U.S. troops to Grenada. Among men, 68 percent favored the decision and 26 percent disapproved; only 45 percent of women approved and 43 percent disapproved, a gender gap of 23 percentage points. Among women, 49 percent said they feared Reagan would get the country into a war, compared with 33 percent of men who held that view.

The poll results, the *Times* concluded (November 27, 1983), "demonstrate the persistence of a pattern that has been evident throughout the Reagan presidency. His overall popularity ratings have been more dependent on the fluctuation of his support among men than on the narrower swings in his generally lower level of support among women."

These trends may be a cause for optimism in the Democratic Party, but they should not be a source of complacency. Polls reveal only what the public thinks at the time a survey is conducted, and women's attitudes may change quickly if they come to believe that they or their concerns are being taken for granted or treated superficially by the Democratic Party or its candidates.

In 1984, from the presidential election and congressional races down to state and local contests, the gender gap will be expressed in votes — votes based on issues that have been shown to be of vital importance to a majority of American women. How women can use their power at the polls is discussed in chapter 10, but one immutable fact gives women greater power than they have ever used before: women outnumber men in the general population. If on Election Day they turn out in higher percentages than men and vote the gender-gap issues, they will defeat Reagan, Reaganomics, and Reagan Republicanism.

8

White House Cave Men/Angry Women

AFTER THE 1980 Republican Party convention abandoned its forty-year-long support for the ERA, cochair Mary Crisp of the Republican National Committee bade a tearful farewell to the delegates. Crisp, who resigned following the Ronald Reagan–backed vote, warned, "I personally believe that these actions could prevent our party from electing the next President of the United States."

Although the party looked healthy, she said, "I am afraid that we are suffering from a serious internal sickness." Reagan broke even on the women's vote in 1980, but the illness has turned out to be both chronic and increasingly dangerous to GOP electoral prospects.

One of the major gender-gap problems for the Reagan administration has been the widening disaffection among Republican women. Crisp is one of many GOP women who are at odds with Reagan Republicanism over women's rights issues, and their strong objections to White House handling of the gender gap proved to be a persistent headache for the administration.

Within days after Kathy Wilson, the Republican head of the

National Women's Political Caucus, called Reagan "a dangerous man" and said he should not seek reelection, a June 1983 CBS/*New York Times* poll was released, showing a twenty-four-point gap between Republican men and women on whether the President should try for a second term.

Aside from the astute decision of congressional Republicans to help field more women candidates, the White House reaction to the gender gap was a farcical mixture of alarm, denials,* reshuffling of female advisers, token gestures, cosmetic cover-ups, foot-in-mouth statements from Reagan, and a stonewall refusal to change any of the substantive policies and actions to which women were objecting.

The response had two aspects. One was Reagan's own obtuseness and ignorance on women's issues. (As Texas Governor Mark White joked at the 1983 National Women's Political Caucus convention, the President thinks handling the gender gap is "sitting closer to Mrs. Reagan at breakfast.") The other was that it was not just one man's personal views, but the administration's reactionary political and economic policies that were behind the treatment of women. In their scheme of things, women are expected to continue to be a source of cheap labor that can be turned off or on according to the dictates of the economy, and they are to be denied programs and opportunities that make them more independent of male authority, in the family and society as a whole.

As soon as the gender gap was identified, the White House response was to interpret it as a problem that could be managed by clever public relations gimmicks. In the post-1980 election memo that sounded the alarm, Reagan aide Ronald H. Hinckley called for "new, bold, and creative ideas" to deal with women's different perceptions of, as he put it, "what is really happening." His solution? *Communications.* He used that word eight times and "improving awareness" another three, lest anyone miss the point. New programs or changes in existing policies were scarcely mentioned. He did acknowledge that in the

---

*One White House official said it was the Democrats who had a gender-gap problem because they had less support from men than from women. This ignores the fact that women's support is more crucial because their numbers are larger; majority support by men alone cannot provide a GOP victory.

economic arena, "the President will have to improve his overall performance" and that reducing the gender gap on unemployment "required both communications and progress towards less unemployment." As for foreign policy, he noted, "How something is said is as important as what is said, particularly for the gender gap. Belligerent, bellicose, or aggressive statements will tend to increase the gap." He did not comment, however, on whether the actual pursuit of belligerent, bellicose, or aggressive foreign policies would increase the gap, or perhaps eliminate the gap by destroying us all in a nuclear war.

The Hinckley approach was also echoed by Betty Heitman, who replaced Mary Crisp as cochair of the Republican National Committee. "The reason behind the gender gap," she told a Republican women's conference, "is that this President and this administration have a terrific story to tell, but I don't think we've told it." She thought the solution was to convince women to think like men. "The majority of men in the country by far support the President, and they support him for reasons that we need to communicate to women ... The men appreciate that [Reagan] is a strong leader and understand the need for military spending."

Dee Jepsen, wife of Iowa Republican Senator Roger Jepsen and Reagan's liaison to women, dismissed the gender gap as "somewhat of a myth" and said the President had been given a "bum rap" by the media. "I think, I *know,* women are very intelligent," she said, "and if it's explained to them perhaps a little more clearly" — the reasons the President takes certain positions — "they will support him just as much as men." Like good little girls.

Jepsen was clearly out of touch with the views of a majority of American women. She is anti-ERA, opposes abortion, even when an unwanted pregnancy results from rape or incest, and believes women should be happy with the gains they've already made. Despite her role as public liaison, she refused to meet with the National Organization for Women, a group with two hundred fifty thousand members. "Appointing Dee Jepsen," a Washington feminist remarked, "was the political equivalent of giving women one of Nancy's old dresses to cheer us up."

Reagan's other adviser on women was Faith Ryan Whittlesey, his liaison to public interest groups. Like Jepsen, she had had no contact with the women's movement and made little effort to reach beyond the conservatives and Moral Majority adherents who form Reagan's base of support among women. She boasted, "I was never involved in women's issues," as if that made her the perfect choice for the job. Eventually, though, Whittlesey's nonperformance led the White House to leak word that she had been stripped of her assignment to improve Reagan's relations with women. That job was taken over by a man, Deputy Chief of Staff Michael K. Deaver, who was named to head a new unit, the Working Group on Women.

True, the President did appoint the first woman justice to the U.S. Supreme Court. (Of 121 additional judicial appointments, only ten went to women.) He did appoint two very able women, Elizabeth Dole and Margaret Heckler, to head major departments. His appointment of Jeane Kirkpatrick as ambassador to the United Nations was more controversial. She has been a strong advocate of aggressive American military policy in Central America that aims at overthrowing the Nicaraguan government and propping up El Salvador's ultra-right-wing government, a strategy opposed by a majority of American women.

Reagan apparently considers his appointments of women his best argument against the gender-gap phenomenon, and has claimed that his record on naming women to high government posts is superior to that of Jimmy Carter and any other President. Close examination of the record, however, shows that he greatly overstated the facts when he said that as of August 1983, he had appointed more than twelve hundred women to executive level positions.

According to Congresswoman Pat Schroeder, who chairs the House Civil Service subcommittee, Reagan had really appointed only eighty-eight women to executive positions. The President arrived at his own figure by including hundreds of appointments to lesser Civil Service jobs and part-time board and commission appointments. Schroeder's analysis also showed that although Reagan made 30 percent more political appointments than Carter, he named 18 percent fewer women.

One of the most acerbic comments on Reagan's appointments came from Muriel Siebert, a Republican with impeccable credentials within the business community (she was the first woman member of the New York Stock Exchange and headed the New York State Department of Banking) and within the party. "The women who represent the Republican Party at the highest levels of public life — in the Supreme Court, in the cabinet, and in Congress — have as much to do with the leadership of the party as a mannequin has to do with the management of Bloomingdale's," she charged, adding that the party was "alienating women more intentionally and effectively today than at any time since we won the right to vote."

Outlining the reasons for women's dissatisfaction within the GOP, she offered a solution: "If the party would simply reaffirm its traditional commitment to equal economic, social, and political rights for men and women; if the party would show the same kind of enthusiasm for education and nutrition that it shows for missiles and bombs; if the idea of dignity and respect for women, rather than condescension and neglect, played a more prominent part in the deliberations of the party — then I think the Republican Party in this state and throughout the nation could expect a lot more women to march in its ranks and elect its candidates than it has reason to expect today." A good solution, but there was as much chance of the Republican Party taking her advice as there was of Reagan naming me to his cabinet.

While Republican liberal women were out in the cold, traditional women and Republican women in Congress were having a hard time, too. In a brief meeting with the President in March 1983, leaders of the National Federation of Republican Women, party activists who are generally not known for rocking political boats, told Reagan that women around the country thought his "administration falls somewhere between being apathetic about women's issues to being anti-women." They handed him a written statement saying they needed help, "some tangible evidence of concern for women — the average women." They urged him to support the women's Economic

Equity Act package,* show an awareness of the working woman's needs for public/private day-care centers, and display "a sensitivity to poor women who cannot hope to educate their children without financial assistance." They also asked for concrete proof of progress on the President's so-called Fifty States Project. This was the centerpiece of what the President had offered as his alternative to the Equal Rights Amendment: a plan to identify laws in the states, as well as in the U.S. Code, that discriminate against women and to propose their piecemeal elimination. (If the same state-by-state approach had been used exclusively in the fight for suffrage, women in the solid South still might not have the right to vote. Virginia, Maryland, North Carolina, South Carolina, Georgia, Alabama, Louisiana, Mississippi, and Florida, as well as Delaware, did not ratify the Nineteenth Amendment. The southern states remain the major obstacle to ERA ratification.)

Six of the nine Republican women in the House also met with Reagan in the White House that March. They asked him not to impede adoption of the reintroduced ERA, which at that point already had 289 Representatives and fifty-six Senators as cosponsors, called for a commission to study the problem of wage discrimination against women and make recommendations, deplored the feminization of poverty, and opposed budget cuts that were having a severe impact on women and children. Congresswomen Claudine Schneider of Rhode Island, Lynn Martin of Illinois, Nancy Johnson of Connecticut, and Olympia Snowe of Maine also urged his support of the women's Economic Equity Act; the other two, Marge Roukema of New Jersey and Bobbi Fiedler of California, supported everything in the package except its proposals on insurance. White House Chief of Staff James Baker and Presidential Counselor Edwin Meese were also present at the meeting. Whittlesey, the liaison

*The women's Economic Equity Act is a five-section legislative package that would eliminate pension inequities which affect women, including divorcees and widows, and authorize IRAs for spouses; enforce collection of alimony and child support; end gender discrimination in insurance; allow tax deductions for child care and care of elderly parents and the disabled; provide child-care information and referral services; and direct all federal departments and agencies to eliminate requirements and language that are not gender-neutral.

to women's groups, did not attend and said in a July 24, 1983, interview with the *Washington Post* that she had never followed up on the meeting with the Congresswomen. "In fact," she explained, "I've been told to be very careful of that and not to initiate any contacts with members of Congress. It's inappropriate for me even to talk to them." That, she said, was the exclusive responsibility of the White House legislative affairs aide, Ken Duberstein.

As a result, four months elapsed before the Republican Congresswomen again heard from the White House. By then public opinion polls showed the gender gap worsening, Whittlesey had been relieved of her women's affairs assignment, and Deaver had set up the Working Group on Women, to which he appointed the two cabinet women, Dole and Heckler. He also invited back the six pro-ERA Congresswomen and Senator Nancy Kassebaum of Kansas. "We told him we didn't want any part of it if it was going to be window dressing. Enough is enough," said Congresswoman Schneider. "I made the point that when we're dealing with the gender-gap issue, there are two ways of looking at it — superficially through a public relations campaign or substantively through legislation. I think the White House recognizes that we've lost some time and that we female members of Congress are extremely restless." Schneider was quoted in a *Washington Post* article, whose lead paragraph said, "In the end, Ronald Reagan might not get the girl, a prospect so disturbing that his White House image makers are rewriting his script."

The remaking of Reagan's image included his appearance before a Republican women's meeting on Women's Equality Day (August 26, 1983) to proclaim his commitment to fairness and equality for American women and having his picture taken with Supreme Court Justice Sandra Day O'Connor. One Reagan effort to appease women backfired badly, leaving them angrier than ever and the President even more confused, not knowing what he had done wrong. His cave-man gaffe occurred when he appeared before twelve hundred members of the International Federation of Business and Professional Women in August to apologize for the cancellation of their scheduled White House tour. In remarks that quickly reached millions of women through television and the newspapers, Reagan said he recognized a "woman's place" and believed that "if it wasn't for women, us men would still be walking around in skin suits, carrying clubs."

A BPW spokeswoman characterized his comments as "almost unbelievable. 'Women's place' are almost code words to people who are conscious of the fact that women's place has been subordinate economically and socially for too long. We don't want to be protected, we don't want to be viewed as the civilizer, the hand that rocks the cradle, because the facts are we don't control. We are [under] the control of men in the political process and certainly economically."

National BPW president Polly Madenwald, a Republican from Oregon, called Reagan's appearance "an example of this administration's insensitivity to working women and it is an example of this administration's refusal to take us seriously." What BPW members wanted, she continued, was his support for the women's Economic Equity Act and measures to eliminate sex discrimination in insurance.

In this instance, Reagan merely added fuel to an already burning fire. Although the majority of the national BPW's one hundred fifty thousand members are Republicans, delegates to their annual convention, which had been held the previous week, voted unanimously not to support any candidate who doesn't favor the ERA, thus ruling out Reagan as their presidential choice.

At the end of September 1983, eight months after he had mentioned it in his State of the Union address to Congress and late in his third year in office, Reagan finally sent a piece of women's legislation to Capitol Hill. The proposed bill was the result of periodic meetings between the Republican Congresswomen and the Deaver group in the White House. It had been delayed, White House sources explained, until the U.S. Supreme Court issued its decision in a pension case. The ruling, which was handed down in July 1983, held that employer-sponsored retirement plans cannot under federal law provide unequal benefits to men and women. The administration bill proposed amendments to pension laws to protect survivors' (predominantly women) rights in the case of the divorce or early death of a spouse and also guaranteed that a worker who took maternity or paternity leave would not be penalized by incurring a break in service for purposes of computing pension benefits. Under the Reagan proposal, these changes, long sought by the Congresswomen's bloc and the feminist movement, would affect new workers, not people in existing plans covered by federal law.

In June 1983 the administration, without informing the GOP women, had also sent a child-support enforcement proposal to Congress, and it languished without support because women members were already backing stronger bills that had been introduced by Congresswoman Roukema and others. The issue was of great importance to women because, as NOW President Judy Goldsmith pointed out, "After divorce, men's income goes up 42 percent and women's goes down 73 percent. One of the major reasons is that most men do not make child-support payments." (In 1981 less than half the women who were awarded child support by a court received the full amount, and more than a million others received nothing. In 1982 only 15 percent of divorced or separated women had alimony agreements, and three of ten of them never received any payments.) Roukema had been urging administration support for her bill. The legislation finally sent to Capitol Hill by the White House was not as effective as Roukema's bill or other child-support measures, nor was its pension-reform proposal as comprehensive as the pension section in the women's Economic Equity Act.

At this writing, the Republican Congresswomen were still negotiating with the White House on legislation to provide tax deductions for child and dependent care and for spousal IRAs, and there was no chance the administration would agree to the women's movement's demand for an end to gender discrimination in insurance policies. Reagan was at one with the giant insurance industry in opposing such legislation. Thus, it was evident that after three years of lip service to women, Ronald Reagan was not even willing to support the modest women's Economic Equity Act package, despite its endorsement by such groups as the National Federation of Republican Women. If he had to choose between ignoring women in his own party or offending his big-business backers, he knew where his allegiance lay.

The only proposal left in Reagan's bag of goodies for women was his highly touted project to eliminate sex discrimination from the laws of the federal government and the fifty states, but in late August this became the focus of national ridicule and name-calling after the defection of a Justice Department woman employee, who denounced the project as a sham.

The charge came from Barbara Honegger, who had worked in Reagan's 1980 campaign, then was appointed to a post in the White House Office of Policy Development, where she and another aide first proposed the Fifty States Project, and finally moved to the Justice Department's Civil Rights Division. For eighteen months — until her resignation — she had been project director of the Attorney General's Gender Discrimination Agency Review. Honegger told her story in a lengthy article in the *Washington Post* and resigned after it was published, saying of the President's commitment to equity for women, "Frankly, my dear, I don't think he gives a damn."

Honegger said she had supervised an immense computer-assisted search to identify any sexually discriminatory practices or language in the U.S. Code, the Code of Federal Regulations, and in any policy, practice, or program of any federal department or agency. The presidential executive order under which she was working called for changing the problem laws and regulations and implementing these changes in the departments and agencies after the identification process was completed.

Beginning in June 1982, Honegger said, three reports, including a complete listing of all sex discriminatory federal laws and practices, were sent to the White House, "but not a single law has been changed." Her project was barred from proposing solutions to the problem laws, she said, and a working group directed by a presidential assistant, which had been assigned to propose corrections, was disbanded by the White House after its first round of recommendations. Moreover, the Task Force on Legal Equity for Women, which was supposed to supervise the third stage of implementing changes, was left leaderless when its chair resigned and was not replaced. It had no funds, no staff, and no office.

The administration hit back by trying to depict Honegger as a kook. Justice Department spokesman Tom DeCair called her a "low-level munchkin" and "disgruntled job seeker," and the chief White House spokesman, Larry Speakes, ridiculed her by saying that the only important role she had played was in dressing up as an Easter bunny for the White House egg-roll event.

At a press conference, where she was flanked by feminist leaders, Honegger said it was the wife of Edwin Meese III, the President's counselor, who had worn the bunny costume. She herself had attended the party "in street clothing of an appropriate nature," she said. "They're trying to discredit the source. They know they can't discredit the content because I've fully documented everything I said."

As for the Fifty States Project, which Honegger said she had thought up at the Republican 1980 nominating convention, all that had resulted was a booklet listing what the fifty states had already done on their own to identify discriminatory laws, without any assistance from the federal government. While still on the job, Honegger had called the White House to propose that she help the states conduct an exhaustive computer search of their legal codes for sexist laws and practices. She said she was thanked but told that it was "not something that the White House wants to expend any financial or political capital on."

Two weeks after Honegger denounced the program, the Justice Department obtained Reagan's approval of most of its recommendations to eliminate sexually discriminatory language from about a hundred laws. Of these, fifty-one would be corrected by a bill introduced by Senator Bob Dole, Kansas Republican, and the President also favored changes in forty-seven other laws. These involved language updates, such as references to widows but not widowers, and to "able-bodied men." When a *New York Times* reporter asked if the proposed changes were merely cosmetic, William Bradford Reynolds, assistant attorney general for civil rights, replied, "That's right." So much for Ronald Reagan's proposed alternative to the Equal Rights Amendment.

As every move the administration made to improve the President's image with women turned sour, Reagan tried still an-

other gimmick: he had the Republican National Committee
hire his daughter Maureen as its consultant on women's issues.
She accompanied him at his Women's Equality Day appearance in California, during which he accused feminists of being
hypocritical for not supporting Republican women candidates.
Wrong again! When his daughter ran in the California Republican primary for the U.S. Senate, she was endorsed by state
feminist organizations, but her father failed to support her
because she favored abortion rights and the ERA. She lost the
primary. Incidentally, the Women's Campaign Fund supported
thirty Republican and sixty Democratic women in the 1982
campaign; all met its requirement that they be pro-ERA and
pro–freedom of choice, the criteria that made them unaccept-
able to the President. Other feminist political organizations,
such as the National Women's Political Caucus, have also supported Republican women candidates.

The Reagan Record: Unfair to Women and Children

If what Ronald Reagan pretended to do *for* women was a sham,
what he did *against* women and children was only too real and
hurtful. It was nothing less than a massive, across-the-board
attack on every government program affecting women and children that had been laboriously won over a period of decades.
For years Reagan had earned an easy living as a General Elec-
tric spokesman, peddling his "free enterprise" ideology on the
banquet circuit and telling his favorite "welfare cheat" horror
stories, which usually featured a mythical woman who drove in
her limousine to pick up a welfare check. His audience of
expense-account, tax-finagling businessmen with their three-
martini luncheons loved that story. Inside Reagan's packaged
"nice guy" exterior was a tough reactionary who, unlike
Scrooge, was not a candidate for repentance. Instead, once in
the White House, Reagan set about trying to enact the entire
right-wing agenda, regardless of the human suffering it would
and did bring.

In his August 26, 1983, Women's Equality Day speech, Reagan claimed that the best thing he could do for women was to
improve the economy and reduce inflation. As the polls

showed, a majority of women did not think he had done so, as far as the effects on their personal lives were concerned. Reagan's anti-inflation program was based on an induced depression and mass layoffs. His unprecedented increase in military spending was accompanied by a staggering federal budget deficit of more than $200 billion and high interest rates that threatened to bring an international economic collapse.

Millions of women and male members of their families lost their jobs, and even after economic recovery had been proclaimed, more than 10 million Americans were officially unemployed. More than $300 billion in national income was lost as a result of the deepest depression the economy had suffered since the 1930s. Reduced inflation did not bring down prices, but simply slowed the rate at which they rose. The costs of food, clothing, and shelter — major components of middle-class and poor-family budgets — were still too high for millions of Americans; many lost their homes through mortgage foreclosures, and small-business failures were widespread. For working women, Reagan's statement in his 1983 State of the Union address that he would "not tolerate wage discrimination based on sex" had a hypocritical ring because his administration was busily removing government protections that offered women and minorities their only hope of a fair break in the job market.

After Reagan took office, two and a half million more women sank into poverty, and the national poverty rate increased to 15 percent, the highest level in seventeen years, with the traditional have-nots — women and minorities — the prime victims. Hunger, soup kitchens, and breadlines again became part of the American scene, and doctors reported the reappearance of malnutrition and other hunger-induced illnesses in children. Reagan professed to be "perplexed" at reports of mass hunger and ordered a study of the problem which his own policies had brought about.

In response to Reagan's call for a study group, Geraldine Harvey, executive director of Newark Emergency Services for Families in New Jersey, said, "More and more people are both hungry and homeless. We have a national epidemic and that's still an understatement." Her remarks appeared in a *New York Times* article on August 4, 1983, which also quoted Martha

Ballou, director of Minnesota Governor Rudy Perpich's Task Force on Emergency Food and Shelter: "I don't know why the Reagan Administration is so perplexed about the extent of hunger when they've created most of it themselves with the cutbacks in the food stamp program and the virtual demolition of the commodities distribution program."

Federal funds for food assistance were among the major targets of Reagan's initial budget cuts. Child-nutrition programs were cut by $1.46 billion. Of the 26 million children who were getting free or subsidized school lunches before Reagan took office, 3.2 million were dropped from the program because of the changes he effected. In 1982 an estimated twenty-seven hundred schools stopped participating in the lunch program because the new Reagan rules made it impracticable for them to continue.

A dramatic increase in the number of children living in poverty or close to it was reported in April 1983 by Alice Rivlin, then director of the Congressional Budget Office. Over the 1960s, she told a House committee hearing, poverty rates for children fell from almost 27 percent to 14 percent. However, she said, "The proportion of children who were poor rose slightly over the 1970s, and in the last three years it has risen dramatically, from 16 percent to almost 20 percent. More than one fourth of all children now live in households with incomes below 125 percent of the poverty level — an income equivalent to about $9000 for a family of three." Many of these children live in single-parent households, Rivlin said, pointing out that in the last three years federal welfare benefits to these households had declined significantly. "The number of children living in poverty," she said, "will probably remain high in the near future and may continue to increase."

In March 1983 the Coalition on Women and the Budget issued a report titled "Inequality of Sacrifice: The Impact of the Reagan Budget on Women." The coalition of fifty-five national organizations, with millions of members, ranged from feminist groups such as NOW, the NWPC, and WOMEN USA to the YWCA, Girls Clubs of America, League of Women Voters, American Association of University Women, and American Nurses' Association. They declared:

The fiscal year 1984 budget presented by the Reagan Administration to Congress calls for inequality of sacrifice by the women of America. If enacted, the budget cuts proposed by the President will have a devastating impact on women and their families at every stage of their lives. The reason for the "gender gap" — differences in voting patterns of women and men — should no longer be a mystery to the Administration or to anyone else. Women understand that the cumulative effect of the budget cuts on women — women in families, girls and young women, women in the work force, and older women — are unfair and place an unconscionable burden on them.

The coalition had also found a discriminatory pattern in the proposed 1983 fiscal budget cuts. "Congress turned back some of the most egregious cuts," it said, "and [we] hoped that the Administration had learned from the experience. Apparently, it had not."

Among the Reagan actions cited by the report:

• At a time of unemployment and family stress, there is no relief for some mothers who are trying to make ends meet. There are cuts in programs for the education of their children, in programs providing medical care, in nutrition, family planning, and employment training programs.

• Large cuts in educational programs that benefit girls and women are also slated. The Women's Educational Equity Act, Title 4 of the Civil Rights Act of 1964, and Title 4 of the Indian Education Act of 1972 are all marked for extinction. The Vocational Education Act and the Adult Education Act would be folded into a block grant, with a cut in appropriations of nearly two-thirds. And further cuts are proposed in student financial assistance.

• Elimination of the Work Incentive Program, which was designed to offer job counseling, training, placement, and support services for recipients of Aid to Families with Dependent Children. At a time of high unemployment, the low-skilled, low-wage worker — usually a woman — needs assistance in finding employment. Yet WIN is targeted for zero funding.

The coalition also noted that older women were faced with higher Medicare costs and that the postponement of a cost-of-living adjustment left them with fixed incomes for another six months, while their bills for food, rent, utilities, and medical care were rising.

In analyzing the Reagan budget allocation, the coalition said that "in matters the Congress and President can control directly, i.e., appropriated dollars, the percentage spent on direct benefits to individuals is reduced by over 50 percent. The defense expenditures increase from 29 percent to 40 percent when viewed this way. The cuts have brought . . . dramatic shifts in growth to military spending, paralleled by cuts in human services."

What we seek, the coalition said, "is an alternative to the 'supply side' model of economic recovery which increases the defense budget at the expense of women and families. We ask for a 'nurture side' solution, which nourishes all Americans as it decreases the deficit. We ask for an economic program which focuses resources on building the nation's entire infrastructure — not just its buildings, highways, and pipelines. We believe that the human infrastructure — the lives of our people and their families — must be our first priority."

But Reagan wasn't listening, and his government not only pursued its attack on human services but also cut away at affirmative action and other programs designed to give women better work opportunities.

Although women account for approximately 33 percent of the federal work force, in 1981, after Reagan ordered mass firings of government employees, women constituted 45 percent of those who lost their jobs. According to a congressional study of federal agencies, minority personnel were dismissed at a rate 50 percent greater than whites in 1981. In 1982, in proportion to their percentages in the federal work force, two minority workers were laid off for every white worker.

Reagan's Justice Department virtually abandoned the affirmative action policies of the past twenty years, stating that it would no longer advocate hiring goals and timetables even in cases in which courts had identified blatant discrimination. The scope and effectiveness of the Office of Federal Contract Compliance was drastically limited by a new policy that exempted about 76 percent of all companies doing business with the government from having to file affirmative action plans, and by reducing back-pay awards to victims of discrimination.

The Equal Employment Opportunity Commission, which had worked effectively under Eleanor Holmes Norton in the Carter administration, became significantly less active after Reagan's election. In the first three quarters of 1982, only seventy-two equal employment opportunity lawsuits were filed — 73.9 percent fewer than in 1981. In fiscal 1982, only 761 back-pay awards were made, compared to 4336 in Carter's 1980 fiscal year.

The administration's attitude toward affirmative action was exemplified by James Watt's snide remark in September 1983 that an advisory panel he had set up was ideally balanced because it included "a black, a woman, two Jews, and a cripple." Watt's remark, which got a response of laughing approval from his Chamber of Commerce audience, created an uproar in Congress and the media. Republicans joined in demands for his resignation, but while Reagan refused to fire him, the pressure finally led to his stepping down. Reagan did, however, fire a majority of the presumably independent U.S. Civil Rights Commission. It had been critical of moves by the departments of Education and Justice to limit enforcement of Title 9 of the Education Amendments of 1972, which barred schools that received federal funds from discriminating on the basis of sex or race. The commission included two Republican women, Jill Ruckelshaus and Mary Louise Smith, a former chair of the Republican National Committee. Ruckelshaus, whom Reagan later dismissed from the commission along with Smith, charged that the President's Justice Department "has moved consistently toward a narrowing of federal civil rights enforcement policies in education," without any legal justification for doing so. Smith cited Reagan's granting of tax exemptions to two southern private colleges that practiced racial discrimination (a move later ruled unconstitutional by the U.S. Supreme Court) and charged that the administration's policies "jeopardize not only equal education protections for women, but also fundamental civil rights guarantees against discrimination based on race, color, national origin, age, and handicap in all federally assisted programs." (Subsequently, Reagan agreed to a compromise with Congress on the make-up of the Civil Rights Commission, but reneged on an understanding that Ruckelshaus and Smith would be reappointed.)

Further evidence of the administration's hostility to civil rights protection came when the Justice Department took the unusual step of filing a brief on behalf of Grove City College in Pennsylvania, which contended that it did not have to comply with Title 9 because it did not receive direct funding from the federal government, although many of its students were receiving federal loans and grants. In a reversal of ten years of government policy, the Justice Department argued that Title 9's ban on sex discrimination applied only to specific federally funded educational programs (in this case, the student loan office) but not to other programs at the same school. In backing the college's appeal to the U.S. Supreme Court, the government brief made the narrowest interpretation of Title 9, one that would exclude from antidiscriminatory protection such major aspects of school life as athletics, vocational guidance and counseling, and health services. Students denied jobs given to males only or women athletes denied access to gym facilities would have no legal recourse.

Congresswoman Claudine Schneider led congressional opposition to the Reagan move. She, with 220 cosponsors, introduced a bill declaring that Title 9 should apply broadly to any institution that receives federal assistance and filed an amicus curiae brief, which was signed by a bipartisan group of fifty members of the House and Senate. It passed.

Meanwhile, the administration continued to demonstrate its intention to scuttle programs that assisted women and minorities. All five women engaged in the women's Educational Equity Act program were fired or reassigned, while the five male employees were retained. The program, which among other assignments finances training programs for women who wish to enter nontraditional careers, had already been marked for zero funding in the 1984 Reagan budget.

Reagan's opposition to the ERA and abortion rights came as

no surprise; he encouraged the Republican opposition to the reintroduced ERA, which was defeated in the House, and used his office to encourage attempts to win congressional approval of a constitutional amendment restricting or outlawing women's access to safe, legal abortions. He also sought regulations making it more difficult for young women to obtain contraceptives and family planning services. His 1982 budget had slashed by more than 25 percent funding for federal family planning services.

With the President's approval, the Department of Health and Human Services announced a "squeal rule" regulation, requiring federally funded family planning clinics to notify parents when teen-agers received prescriptions for contraceptives. This rule applied only to female teen-agers because male contraceptive devices are over-the-counter, nonprescription items.

According to independent studies, the parental notification regulation would result each year in about thirty-three thousand additional unwanted teen-age pregnancies (already a major national problem), with young women foregoing the use of family planning services for fear of parental reprisals or opposition. Although federal courts struck down the regulation as an unwarranted interference with the right to privacy, Reagan remained determined to implement it and supported an expedited appeal of the court decisions.

In June 1983, when the U.S. Supreme Court, in a six-to-three decision, reaffirmed the constitutional right to reproductive freedom, the President expressed his "profound disappointment" and called on Congress to "make its voice heard" and pass legislation to overrule the high court. He praised his appointee, Associate Justice Sandra Day O'Connor, for her dissenting decision, in which she contended that the Congress was the appropriate forum for regulation of abortion.

All Reagan's blundering attempts to overcome the gender gap foundered on the solid rock of his anti-woman actions as President. On every national issue on which a majority of American women had expressed their opinions — whether they touched on women's rights or domestic or foreign policy — Reagan took a contrary view, which he backed up with the full might of his governmental power. He succeeded in further angering the nation's large feminist constituency and alienated women from every social, economic, racial, and age group, including large numbers of women in his own party.

In 1984 the cave men were still in control of the government, but millions of angry women were waiting to go to the polls to vote them out of power.

9

Ms. Supercandidate

ONE WOMAN'S DREAM of more females holding political power is another man's nightmare. How else to explain Senate Majority Leader Howard Baker's reaction when he arrived in the chamber one morning in August 1983 to find Senator Nancy Kassebaum presiding and the only other woman Senator, Paula Hawkins, speaking at the microphone, while various female pages and secretaries were also plainly visible? It was all too much for Baker, whose own daughter, Cynthia, had shaken him up in 1982 by running for Congress without asking his permission.

"Frankly," Baker told the *New York Times*, "I do not know if I am more proud or more frightened by a total takeover by the female population here in the Capitol. It is obvious that we mere mortal men are not required anymore, and I just want to plead with my biological counterparts not to forget about us guys out here.

"I also hope," he said, "that the press will not dwell on the reports that the Senate was a fixture of decisiveness and harmony, in an unprecedented fashion, during this time, which will no doubt come to be known as 'The Women's Hour.' "

But is it the women's hour? Is the presence of two women in what was once the most exclusive men's club in the nation enough to make the ninety-eight men tremble about a female takeover?

Unfortunately, the worries of male politicians are premature. The electoral gender gap has not yet been translated into the practice of women voting for women by significant margins.

History, custom, overt discrimination, and popular prejudice have all played roles in the dearth of women in elective and appointive office. Political scientists and candidates themselves have found that much more demanding criteria are applied to women than to men in politics. Female politicians are usually expected to be superwomen in their abilities, backgrounds, and performances; laxer standards are applied to male politicians, who are endowed with authority and respect simply by virtue of being male.

The National Women's Political Caucus has undertaken an in-depth study of the relationship between the women's vote and the successes and failures of women politicians. A nationwide survey by the Gallup organization, conducted for *Redbook* magazine in November 1979, found that although 65 percent of women and 58 percent of men said they were concerned about the small number of women in Congress, there was a lingering bias against female candidates among both men and older women; women aged eighteen to thirty-five and women college graduates were more favorable to female candidacies.

More recent polls show increasing public acceptance of the changing political role of women; 80 percent say they would support the election of women to Congress and the presidency. A September 1983 nationwide survey by David Garth Associates found that 83 percent of the respondents said that a party's nomination of a woman for Vice President would have no effect on their vote. Eight percent said it would make them more likely to vote for the ticket, balanced by 7 percent who said they would be less likely. Women and men responded almost identically to the question.

When asked a more general question, 18 percent said they

would be more likely to vote for a woman candidate for public office, 10 percent said they would be less likely, and 68 percent said it would make no difference. The response also revealed a gender gap: 24 percent of women said they would be more apt to vote for a woman, as opposed to just 13 percent of the men.

In response to another question, 59 percent of men and women said there were too few women elected officials, and only 3 percent said there were too many. The greatest support for women candidates came from blacks (80 percent), part of a pattern in the survey that found blacks supporting feminist positions in higher numbers than any other group, even self-described liberals. As members of a group made sensitive to discrimination through personal experience, blacks were more ready than other groups to identify discrimination as a barrier to women in politics, according to the survey analysis.

In the November 1983 *New York Times* poll cited earlier, 51 percent of women and 45 percent of men said they believed Congress would do a better job if more women were elected. The response among women was also linked to their support for Reagan's reelection. Among women who thought Congress needed more women members, only 33 percent favored Reagan's reelection; among women who thought the presence of women would make no difference in Congress, 50 percent supported the President's reelection.

Encouraging as these responses are, judging from electoral results there still appears to be a real conflict between conscious acceptance of a political role for women and the apparently unconscious resistance to women in high political office. The gender gap reflects changing attitudes, but it will take quite a while for voting behavior to overcome the present reality and past practices of overwhelming discrimination against women in government. Consider the numbers: since the founding of our constitutional government in 1789, there have been 10,957 members of Congress. Only 116 have been women. The first Congresswoman was Jeannette Rankin. A Republican and a pacifist, she was elected to the House, in 1916, from Montana, one of the western states that had already enfranchised women. Rankin got to Washington in time to lead the House floor debate on the suffrage amendment and help get it passed, but she is best known for the vote she cast against American entry into World War I.

The first woman to serve in the Senate — Rebecca Felton, an eighty-seven-year-old suffragist — sat there in 1922 for only one hour. There had been a special election in Georgia, in which Walter George was picked to replace a Senator who had died. The governor, formerly an opponent of suffrage, decided to court the votes of the newly enfranchised women of Georgia by honoring the venerable women's rights leader. His token act was to appoint Felton to serve as Senator until George was sworn in. The Senate, agreeing to a temporary suspension of the rules, allowed Felton to take the oath of office and hold court on the Senate floor. After an hour of this shadow play, she was escorted out, the *real* Senator from Georgia was sworn in, and the men got back to business. Felton certainly knew she was being used, but she believed that even symbolic acts have their value, and she wanted American women to know that there could and should be women in the Senate.

Women were members of the House and Senate in the years that followed, but many got there as a result of what came to be known as the "widow's game." Of the 101 women who have served in the House, thirty-seven were selected to fill vacancies caused by death or resignation. In most instances, they were the widows of deceased legislators and were appointed or elected because it was taken for granted that they would vote exactly as their husbands would have. All but two of the fifteen women who have served in the Senate were initially appointed or chosen in special elections to replace their husbands. The exceptions are the two present women Senators, Nancy Kassebaum and Paula Hawkins, both Republicans but holding different views. Kassebaum is generally sympathetic to women's rights and ERA, and Hawkins takes an extreme right-wing approach.

Among the women Senators, only two served more than one term. Hattie Caraway, a Democrat from Arkansas who was elected to fill her husband's seat in 1931, was the first woman to get into the Senate after Felton's token appearance nine years earlier. (A traditionalist, she remarked after the suffrage amendment was ratified, "I'll just add voting to cooking and sewing.") A protégée of the late Huey Long of Louisiana, she ran on her own when her interim term ended and was reelected twice. She was also the first woman to chair a committee, the first to conduct Senate hearings, and the first to preside over the Senate.

Margaret Chase Smith, a Maine Republican, came into the House in 1940 as a replacement for her dead husband, served there for almost nine years, and then was an outstanding Senator for twenty-four years. In 1972 she was unexpectedly defeated by a Democrat, who had campaigned hard while she adhered to her honorable but impractical custom of not campaigning in her home state while the Senate was in session. An independent Republican, Smith had her most shining moment in 1950 when she took the Senate floor to attack her Republican colleague, Joseph McCarthy. "I do not want to see the party ride to political victory," she said, "on the Four Horsemen of Calumny — fear, ignorance, bigotry, and smear." She was the first Republican to speak out against McCarthyism.

Over the years, Democratic women have outnumbered Republican women in Congress almost two to one. Some remarkable women of both parties appeared from time to time, but until recently they had no specifically female base of support and their abilities were consistently ignored by the congressional leaders. Only seven women ever got an opportunity to chair committees, but four headed minor committees. Congresswoman Martha Griffiths of Michigan, one of the ablest women (or men) ever to serve in the House, was made chair of the Select Committee on the House Beauty Shop! Just three women chaired full legislative committees: Leonor Sullivan, a Missouri Democrat, who headed the House Merchant Marine and Fisheries Committee; Mary Norton, a New Jersey Democrat, chair of the Labor Committee and the District of Columbia Committee; and Edith Nourse Rogers, a Massachusetts Republican, who chaired the Veterans' Affairs Committee.

Looking back over the experiences of women in Congress from 1917 to 1976, an official government history, *Women in Congress*, notes:

There is almost a bittersweet quality to many of their careers: one has a sense that too many talented women missed the chance to prove themselves. Several women of promise were prevented from seeking reelection for financial reasons: they could not raise the money for an election campaign. Others entered Congress too late in their lives to build the kind of power necessary to have any impact on public policy.

Many women stood out for their strong identification with humanist issues: peace, child care, health and welfare, and other social issues. And regardless of their party or political ideology, the vast majority supported some form of women's rights. Women as different as Katherine St. George [a Republican] and Martha Griffiths [a Democrat] both worked hard on the Equal Rights Amendment. Many women introduced bills and pressured for the passage of many different versions of what became the Equal Pay Act. Still others joined to support the inclusion of domestic workers in minimum wage coverage.

A Woman's Place Is Everywhere

In 1970, although I had never before run for public office, I became a candidate for Congress from Manhattan's Nineteenth District, and won after an upset primary victory in which I defeated a seven-term Democratic machine male politician. Reflecting the new perspectives of the women's movement, my campaign theme was "This Woman's Place Is in the House — the House of Representatives." It was a catchy slogan and became one of the most popular mottos in other women's campaigns. It was soon expanded to "A Woman's Place Is in the House and Senate," and its latest version is "A Woman's Place Is Everywhere." (After I won, my older daughter, Eve, said, "Thank God, we're getting her out of our house and into *their* House.")

We were still in the early days of the feminist revival, and a woman running for major elective office was sufficiently novel to attract a lot of press attention and volunteers. My campaign workers came mostly from the ranks of the new women activists and men involved in the feminist and antiwar movements as well as from the many community organizations working on neighborhood and city problems. On August 27, women in major cities throughout the nation held meetings and parades to celebrate the fiftieth anniversary of the suffrage amendment's ratification, and in New York more than ten thousand of us surged down Fifth Avenue in a spirited demonstration that we called Strike for Women's Equality. As we marched, we felt the power of togetherness and our own potential strength. I had just turned fifty, too, and was thrilled by the new independence and assertiveness of women, qualities that had always marked my own life.

Discrimination wasn't anything new to me (every woman runs into it, whether she admits it or not), but neither my temperament nor intellect had ever allowed me to accept the notion that I belonged to an inferior sex. Raised as an Orthodox Jew, I love the strong sense of justice and compassion that is the core of our religious code of behavior. But it was hard for me to accept the segregation of the sexes in our synagogue, where women had to sit in the balcony, unseen and unheard. My father died suddenly when I was thirteen, and I broke tradition by reciting the Kaddish for him, a ritual that in the custom of those days was reserved for his male relatives. Every morning for the following year I went to the synagogue on my way to school to recite the holy prayer for the dead. No one tried to stop me, and as I stood in a corner reciting my mourner's prayers, I came to understand that one way to change outmoded traditions was to challenge them.

When I was young, it wasn't that easy to challenge the traditions of Harvard Law School. When I was ten, I had decided that I wanted to be a lawyer, and at the all-women Walton High School and at Hunter College I had been elected student body president, good training for the law. Everyone told me that if I wanted to be accepted as a lawyer, I should go to the best law school, but when I applied to Harvard, I received a letter stating that it did not admit women. In 1942 only 3 percent of the nation's lawyers were women. I was outraged (I've always had a decent sense of outrage), so I turned to my mother. In those days there was no women's movement, so you turned to your mother for help. "Why do you want to go to Harvard, anyway?" she asked. "It's far away and you can't afford the carfare. Go to Columbia University. They'll probably give you a scholarship, and it's only five cents to get there on the subway." Columbia did give me a scholarship, the subway did cost only five cents in those days, and that's how I became an advocate of low-cost public transportation.

(Harvard finally agreed to admit women to its law school ten years later. Former Congresswoman Elizabeth Holtzman recalls that when she was a student there, from 1962 to 1965, the faculty included a professor who didn't believe that women should be called on as part of the regular Socratic method of classroom interrogation. Instead, he established a "ladies' day" and once a week all the women students were questioned in front of the entire class.)

While I was at Columbia, my future husband, Martin Abzug, courted me in an unconventional manner. He typed my term papers while I studied in the library, and before we married we had long discussions about who would do what. It was agreed that I would work at my legal career even after we had children, and we raised our two daughters together. It was not the kind of formal prenuptial contract some couples now enter into, but our informal understanding of respect for each other's work has endured throughout our marriage, which is still going strong after thirty-nine years.

I worked as a civil rights and labor lawyer and conducted a general practice as well. I handled divorce cases in which my clients were all too often women who had been trained only for marriage and home and suddenly found themselves facing poverty when their husbands left them. I practiced law full time from the day I got out of law school until I ran for Congress, and was always active in politics and liberal causes.

For ten years I was also political action director for Women Strike for Peace, a network that thousands of us women had formed spontaneously in 1961 to protest the resumption of nuclear testing by the Soviet Union and the United States. In large and small delegations, we made frequent visits to the New York and Washington offices of our legislators, presenting them with statements, petitions, and arguments in favor of a treaty outlawing nuclear testing. Our big picket lines outside the White House impelled President John F. Kennedy to comment, "I understand what they were attempting to say . . . their message was received." When the partial test-ban treaty was approved in 1963, many commentators attributed its passage to fear of the "mothers' vote." We, too, believed the signing of the treaty was in large part a result of our campaign, but it was only a small victory. Although the treaty sent testing underground, ending the atmospheric fallout of radioactive strontium 90 and other cancer-causing elements, the arms race escalated.

Our peace work flowed naturally into the campaign to get U.S. troops out of Vietnam. I organized a Seventeenth Congressional District Peace Action Committee in the "silk stocking" district of Manhattan's East Side. We formed open caucuses to pressure for approval of anti–Vietnam War resolutions in each of the local Democratic Party clubs, which until then had been supporting President Lyndon B. Johnson's Vietnam policy. Our committee had a thousand or so members — students, teachers, working women, housewives, business people, professionals, scientists, artists, writers, and so on. Ultimately, no political meeting or election in the district took place without our involvement, and no candidate for any level of political office ran without seeking our endorsement, which was always contingent on the candidate's support for withdrawal of our troops from Indochina.

I also worked in coalition with the late Allard Lowenstein to help organize the national "dump Johnson" movement in 1968, after Johnson, contrary to his election pledge, escalated the war in Vietnam. My role was to encourage independents and anti-Vietnam peace activists to enroll in the Democratic Party. Many of these activists were disillusioned with the party and its prowar policies and had despaired of being able to effect change through the political process and by their votes. But they responded to our campaign, and we registered thousands of women and men in the Democratic Party all over the country. They became involved in the party reform movement and the Eugene McCarthy and Robert F. Kennedy campaigns, hoping to create policies that would bring peace and take us out of the war in Vietnam.

I had been working all along to elect a variety of male politicians who I believed would support or, better yet, fight for the programs I cared about most. In 1969 I poured all my energies into a campaign to reelect New York Mayor John V. Lindsay, who was in a tough three-way race. I organized a Taxpayers

Campaign for Urban Priorities, which brought together 160 community groups in an activist coalition in support of Lindsay. "New York Spends More on War than on New York" was the headline of one of our ads, which spelled out in shocking detail how more of our tax money was being used to kill people in Vietnam and build unneeded nuclear missiles than to help people in our city, which was beginning to fall apart at the seams.

After Lindsay's victory, some colleagues and I met with the mayor at City Hall. I urged him to continue the community coalition, issue-oriented approach we had used for his reelection and to develop and lead a national campaign to change our nation's lopsided war priorities. He couldn't see it. My activist, organizing brand of politics was not his style.

"Don't you want to be a judge or the head of the housing department or something?" he asked me, assuming I wanted a personal reward for helping to reelect him.

"No," I said. All I was interested in was changing the direction of government policy.

"You're always so critical of politicians and government," he said. "Why don't you try it yourself, and you'll find out how hard it is."

"You're right," I said. "I think I will." Then and there, I decided to run for Congress. It was like a light switch being turned on in my brain, that "click" which my friends at *Ms.* magazine call the moment of recognition of a feminist truth. I had been working hard all those years to elect men who weren't any more qualified or able than I, and in some cases they were less so. I realized that if I had strong beliefs and ideals about how our country should be run, I could best work for them right up front, out in the open, in my own way. The gender gap in political office was too wide and deep to be left unchallenged.

In talking to other women who have gone into politics, I found that many experienced similar clicks. A woman would be lobbying an elected official, briefing him on an important national or community issue, and suddenly she'd realize that she knew more about the matter under discussion than the man she was trying to convince. "What's so special about this guy?" she'd ask herself. "I could do just as well, and probably better."

All it required was a closing of the perception gap, with the woman focusing on herself as a legislator and leader, not as the usual behind-the-scenes worker and supplicant. In the 1970s those individual clicks were becoming a chorus — a small one, but with the promise of more to come.

I stressed three major themes in my campaign — peace and Vietnam, a reordering of our spending priorities, and, as my slogan indicated, women's rights. As far as I can tell, I was, with the possible exception of Jeannette Rankin, the first female candidate to win election to Congress in a campaign that stressed women's equality issues.

When I ran in 1970, there were only nine women among the 435 members of the House, and Margaret Chase Smith was holding the fort alone in the Senate. Among the outstanding Congresswomen were Martha Griffiths; Edith Green, an Oregon Democrat who chaired a subcommittee that held pioneer hearings to document discrimination against women in education; Shirley Chisholm; and Patsy Mink, the first and only Asian-American woman ever elected to Congress. Mink played a major role in the fight for Title 9 of the Education Amendments Act, which bars sexist discrimination in educational institutions, and the Women's Educational Equity Act. She became a special friend of mine. Although they had not campaigned as feminists, all four were strongly for women's rights.

In an interview published in the *Wall Street Journal* on October 8, 1979, Griffiths spoke for many of us: "If we could get issues women understand and get women voting for or against candidates on the basis of them, we could rapidly change the face of America." Green said the mere presence of women on congressional committees could make a difference. "Women have their antennae up for subtle bias in legislation that might slip by men," she said. (My antennae were always at full alert when, as a member of the Public Works Committee, I attached and got passed a nondiscrimination requirement in every bill we voted on.) Chisholm, in her usual spunky style, stressed that it was not enough for women just to get into Congress. The way they got there was equally important.

"There's a difference," she said, "between a woman fighting

every obstacle in her way to show she has the skills, talent, and intelligence for the job and the woman who's 'behaved herself beautifully' so many years that the 'gentlemen' feel it's time to give her a chance. We don't want women coming to Congress who are going to 'behave,' because they won't help us." And she gave me a boost: "Bella is going to be like me. She'll rock the boat."

Chisholm and I had known each other since 1968, when I led a Women Strike for Peace delegation to her office to urge her to include a call for U.S. withdrawal from Vietnam in her maiden speech. She did so, in stirring language.

The 1970 elections raised to twelve the number of women in the House. The newcomers were Ella Grasso of Connecticut, Louise Day Hicks, a Bostonian elected on a single-issue anti-busing program, and me. Grasso stayed for two terms, then was elected governor of Connecticut, the first woman to serve as head of a state in her own right, without having succeeded her husband. Hicks left after one term to run unsuccessfully for mayor of Boston. We were an unlikely, but perhaps symbolic trio: I, the liberal activist; Grasso, the conventional politician who had risen through the Democratic Party ranks; and Hicks, a conservative. I was polite to Hicks but became close friends with Grasso, an honest, straight-talking woman full of political savvy and humor. We were about the same age and each of us had two children and a supportive husband. A devout Catholic, she opposed abortion rights, but supported the women's movement on its other issues and worked with Chisholm, Mink, and me in opposition to the Vietnam War. Her premature death deprived us of a highly effective and appealing national political leader, and I lost a dear personal friend.

Among the losers in the 1970 elections were two women of polar extremes: Myrlie Evers, widow of the murdered civil rights leader Medgar Evers, and Phyllis Schlafly, who was not yet notorious as a right-wing apostle, though she was practicing. Evers, who ran as a peace candidate in California, had been picked by local Democratic leaders to be a sacrificial token in a heavily Republican district. That was typical of the kind of political opportunity offered to women in both parties. Schlafly, a Republican, ran in a strongly Democratic district in southern

Illinois. She was quoted in the press as saying, "I don't believe in women's rights, I believe in chivalry." Apparently there weren't enough knights in shining armor around to elect her.

In 1968 Shirley Chisholm had the distinction of being the first black woman elected to Congress. Since then there have been only four others — Yvonne Brathwaite Burke, California Democrat, and Barbara Jordan, Texas Democrat, both elected in 1972, and the current Congresswomen, Cardiss Collins, an Illinois Democrat who for a time headed the Congressional Black Caucus, and Katie Hall, an Indiana Democrat. Chisholm and Jordan retired, and Burke left to run unsuccessfully for statewide office in California.

On her arrival in Congress, Chisholm had put up a fight when she was assigned to the House Agriculture Committee, saying, "There are no farms in Brooklyn." She won reassignment to the Education and Labor Committee. I tried hard to get on the Armed Services Committee, an occult male domain that functioned as a blank-check committee for the Pentagon. I felt it was important to get to the source of the military overspending that was depriving us of funds for our real needs, and also to demonstrate that as a woman and peace activist I could bring to the committee a different concept of what was required to assure our national security. I was turned down and, in compensation, got two other choice committee assignments, Public Works and Government Operation. My challenge helped put two male liberals — Ron Dellums, a black Democrat from California, and Les Aspin, a Wisconsin Democrat who is more an arms "control" than a disarmament advocate — on the committee, and two years later newcomer Patricia Schroeder, a Colorado Democrat and feminist, was appointed. She has become an expert on military systems and a continuing annoyance to the Pentagon.

Women Make a Difference

Just as women in the postsuffrage era were believed to vote in the same way as their husbands or fathers, women in Congress until recent times were expected to vote as the husbands they replaced would have voted or in accord with the dictates of their party leaders in the House. A distinctive change occurred with the renascence of the women's movement and the election to Congress of women such as Mink, Chisholm, myself, and others. The new women coming into the House were more activist, more visible, and certainly more independent than some of our female predecessors, and this was true of women in both parties. We were seen as more liberal, and we were often joined in our votes by the more senior women members of Congress, who were reacting to our presence, the changes among women, and the demands of organized feminism.

During my six years in Congress (from 1971 to 1977), a majority of the women, except for a few die-hard conservatives, voted together in favor of the gender-gap issues, supporting measures for women's equality, peace, economic justice, and a safe environment. From that time to the present, Congress-women from both parties have often been found on the same side of an issue.*

When I entered Congress, all but one of the women members were fighting for approval of the ERA. Increasingly, we came together informally to discuss and coalesce around other women's rights legislation — Title 9, the Women's Equity Act, equal credit legislation, child care, Social Security coverage in their own names for homemakers, and flextime — and against efforts to weaken federal regulations that enforce social welfare programs. Some of the Congresswomen who joined us in the next few years — Burke, Barbara Mikulski of Maryland, Schroeder, Helen Meyner of New Jersey, and Elizabeth Holtz-man of New York — came with strong commitments to women's issues, and others became converts to feminism. I was the first to introduce a Social Security for homemakers bill, and Burke and I collaborated on the flextime legislation.

Representative Lindy Boggs, a Louisiana Democrat who was first elected to replace her husband, the late Hale Boggs, was initially quite conservative and still votes against abortion rights, but now she says, "The more you sit here, the more aware of the inequities you become." Republican Congress-

---

*For a detailed analysis of Congresswomen's voting patterns, see Kathleen A. Fran-kovic, *Sex and Voting in the U.S. House of Representatives, 1961–1975. American Politics Quarterly* 5 (July 1977): 315–30.

woman Olympia Snowe of Maine, who frequently votes against her party's positions, believes it is the responsibility of women in Congress to ensure equity for women. "If we don't, who will?" she asks.

Schroeder and Snowe cochair the Congressional Caucus on Women's Issues, which was formally organized in 1977. It recently decided to include men, recognizing the dependable bloc of Congressmen who can be counted on to vote with the women members on their issues. The caucus's 125 members include twelve Democratic and two Republican Congresswomen and Senator Kassebaum. Each female member contributes $1500 to the caucus operations, while the male members pay $600, a reverse kind of economic discrimination. The caucus limits its executive committee to women members.

Under the Reagan administration, the caucus, through its educational arm, the Women's Research and Education Institute, issued a report showing the adverse effects on women of the proposed domestic budget cuts. The caucus members also persuaded the House leadership to include job-creating provisions for women in two jobs bills that were considered and voted on by the Ninety-seventh and Ninety-eighth Congresses. The bills had concentrated only on construction and mass-transit programs, areas in which few women are employed. The caucus is also the prime mover behind the women's Economic Equity Act package.

Most important is the cooperation of the women's caucus with the congressional black and Hispanic caucuses. Just as the joint efforts of women and minority voters can prove to be enormously significant as a progressive force for change, the close cooperation of these three caucuses in Congress can certainly help move our legislators to take more advanced positions. The three caucuses testified jointly on affirmative action regulations after President Reagan, deriding affirmative action as a "racial spoils system," sought to weaken them. They also initiated a letter, which was signed by two hundred members of Congress, opposing Reagan's firing of three members of the U.S. Civil Rights Commission. They have worked to prevent women business owners from being pitted against black and minority business owners on the issue of "set aside" funds for small-business owners. Both groups need separate set-asides, they have insisted.

In answer to the question, Will electing more women to Congress change anything? I think the evidence adds up to a strong yes. Flora Crater, editor of *The Woman Activist* newsletter, analyzed the voting records of members of Congress for the years 1974 and 1975 and found that eleven of the fourteen Democratic and four of the five Republican women members had voting records that were more liberal than those of their party leaders. Both Democratic and Republican women opposed increases in military spending more frequently than did their male colleagues. All nineteen women members voted against providing aid to U.S.-backed rebel military forces in Angola, a vote in which five Republican Congresswomen opposed the wishes of their leaders. A substantial majority of the nineteen women voted, in opposition to the leadership of both parties, against financing the new B-1 bomber, against providing military aid to the Chilean dictatorship, and in favor of banning the use of government funds to plan assassinations or influence foreign elections. All but two of the nineteen voted to override President Gerald Ford's veto of a bill to control strip mining and another to create a public works jobs program.

In the current Ninety-eighth Congress, liberal voting patterns predominate among the twenty-two women in the House (fourteen Democrats and eight Republicans); in the Senate, Republicans Kassebaum and Hawkins are usually divided on women's rights and peace issues, with Kassebaum taking a more liberal stance. She joined eighteen Congresswomen in cosponsoring the reintroduced Equal Rights Amendment, which was again submitted to Congress immediately after its June 1982 deadline for ratification had elapsed. A majority of the women House members support abortion rights and the nuclear freeze and oppose the MX missile, the neutron bomb, nerve gas, and covert U.S. military aid to opponents of the Nicaraguan government, positions that Kassebaum has also taken on some votes.

These recent votes reflect a continuation of the independent voting stance of the women members, and some Republican members — Olympia Snowe, Claudine Schneider, and Marge

Roukema, as well as Nancy Kassebaum — often challenge their party's positions.

The Double Standard

The women with whom I worked in Congress and the present members are, on the whole, exceptionally able, dedicated, and selfless legislators. Call them superwomen or survivors — either way, to get to Washington they had to overcome obstacles that would have discouraged many of their male colleagues. Women usually start without formal party support or encouragement, without wealthy financial backers, and without media support, and most have to run against incumbents, which stacks the odds against them. Although more women have been running for office in recent years and doing fairly well in state and local contests, the numbers are still against them. Even though there are twice as many women in Congress today as when I arrived there in 1971, they still constitute only 5 percent of the House, 2 percent of the Senate, and only 13 percent of the state legislatures. At this writing, there was one woman governor, four lieutenant governors, and only thirty-four women serving in statewide offices. Despite the more enlightened climate, many Americans still have difficulty accepting "A Woman's Place Is in the House . . . and in the Senate." As Ruth Mandel wrote in her book, *In the Running: The New Woman Candidate,* "Centuries of history and custom have taught that women belong in the private sphere. Rather than seeking elective office, a single woman is still thought to be better off seeking a good husband; instead of serving in office, a married woman is expected to be serving her husband's and children's needs first."

Mothers of young children are particular targets, whether they aim for the Congress or lower office. When Pat Schroeder was elected to Congress, she moved to Washington with her two young children and lawyer husband, who had agreed to change jobs so they could be together. When voters asked her how she could be a mother and a Congresswoman at the same time, Schroeder would say, "Because I have a uterus and a brain, and I intend to use them both."

Cynthia Kukor ran against an incumbent city alderman in Milwaukee several years ago. A divorced mother with three young children, she was not only grilled about her status, but her opponent's supporters organized a group called the Concerned Mothers for the Kukor Children. Kukor decided to make no apologies for wanting to be a public official. When asked what kind of a mother she could be if she were elected, she replied, "I'd be just as good a mother as the incumbent is a father to his children." A sign of the changing times: she won almost three to one in her blue-collar neighborhood.

Male opponents find it expedient to make constant references to their female challengers' physical appearance or gender, and the press often uses society-page-style prose in reporting on campaigns involving women. Roxanne Conlin, who ran unsuccessfully for governor of Iowa in 1982, is a bright and effective prosecutor who has never lost a jury trial. Covering her campaign, the *Des Moines Register* published six photos showing the different hairstyles she had worn in the last eleven years, indicating that they were more concerned with her hairdo than with the serious issues she was raising. Barbara Mikulski, elected to the House in 1976, says her physical appearance is always cited in the Baltimore press. For example, a typical story says, "Barbara Mikulski, who is short and rotund, in her uphill fight against the political machine, said today, 'No more expressway in southeast Baltimore.' " But, she points out, the press never describes her male opponents as "middle-aged, potbellied incumbents who are facing a downhill race against Barbara Mikulski." Kathy Whitmire, Houston's first woman mayor, had an opponent who always referred to her as "the little lady" and kept saying, "You need a big man for mayor." When he refused to debate her in a run-off contest, Whitmire ran a full-page ad, which read, "Jack Hurd, come out and fight like a man." She won.

Sometimes, though, sexist sniping at women candidates can be hurtful, as Martha Keys, a Kansas Democrat elected to Congress in 1974, discovered. Between her second term and her campaign for a third, she had been divorced and married a colleague, Congressman Andy Jacobs of Indiana. Her male opponent campaigned against her with the slogan, "Martha doesn't shop here anymore." There were two insinuations in this attack: her loyalties had shifted from her home state of Kansas to her husband's state, and she was neglecting the traditional housewifely role as the family shopper. No criticism was directed against her husband for marrying a legislator from another state. She lost; he was reelected.

Congresswomen and female candidates are held to higher moral and ethical standards than men are. The public is generally cynical about the male-run political machinery, all too ready to believe reports of widespread corruption, bribery, and even criminal acts by elected officials. Women are usually looked on as being more honest, reliable, and independent, and, therefore, less subject to being influenced by special interests. When Mary Anne Krupsak was running for lieutenant governor of New York in 1975, her slogan was, "She's not one of the boys." She understood the public's interest in political independence, and it helped her win.

Because women must toe a higher line, when they appear to transgress they are punished more severely.

An unfounded charge of financial impropriety was believed to be a major factor in the defeat of Roxanne Conlin. During the campaign, it was revealed that she and her husband had availed themselves of legal tax shelters, with the result that they had paid no income tax. The charge dogged her to the bitter end, dominated the headlines day after day, and may have turned her winning campaign into a losing one. Conlin's husband was in the real estate business, where tax shelters are an accepted practice; ironically, one of Conlin's major campaign proposals called for tax reform, which would have eliminated her husband's tax-shelter advantage.

Nancy Kassebaum, however, escaped unscathed from a campaign charge that she had failed to disclose her family's finances or explain inconsistencies in her income tax payments. In contrast to the way many women candidates are treated, Kassebaum received kid-glove handling from the press in Kansas, where she benefited from the prestige of being the daughter of the venerable and highly respected Alfred Landon, Franklin D. Roosevelt's Republican opponent in 1936. Kassebaum, too, is bothered by the way women politicians are described in the media. She said, "Someday I am going to hit someone over the head for calling me diminutive and soft-spoken. But," she added quickly, "I am."

Madeleine Kunin, who was an outstanding lieutenant governor of Vermont, was defeated when she ran for governor in 1982, and she believes a major reason is that it is "much more difficult for a woman to get elected to an office which few women have ever held, simply because of the lack of precedent, both for the candidate and for the voters. The higher you go, the harder it gets. I faced little bias in my race for lieutenant governor, partly because the office does not have an enormous amount of real power (although it has symbolic power) and because it is both legislative and executive.

"However, our associations with the position of chief executive are so predominantly male historically that it takes a giant step to envision a woman in that role. It can be done, but it means facing a bigger hurdle.

"It's also more difficult for a woman at that stage to develop a comfortable style of political leadership that is both female and 'tough' in the traditional masculine sense. A woman has to prove her adherence to a traditionally male-defined leadership system. That sometimes sets up difficult contradictions within herself — because if she is too feminine, she is not tough enough, and if she is too tough, she has abandoned her femininity. The alternative is to develop a female political voice which redefines our view of leadership and allows it to be more flexible and accommodating to the values of our time, and the values of both sexes."

Kunin's comments are right on target with my experiences in my political career, during which I have been and still am often described as "aggressive," "abrasive," and "strident." Friends and coworkers have observed, and I concur, that had I been a male politician with my record of accomplishment in Congress and the movements for social change, the adjectives would have been transformed into "strong," "courageous," and "dynamic."

Why Women Lose

Political women call it Catch-22. It works like this: women candidates lose because they don't have enough support; they don't have enough support because they don't have enough money to conduct effective campaigns; they have trouble raising money because people think they're losers; and round and round it goes. It doesn't always work that way, but there's no doubt that the money problem is one of the major obstacles to women's winning elections. In testimony before a House Task Force on Elections, on June 23, 1983, a representative of the Women's Campaign Fund said: "In 1982, two women ran for governor and lost; three women ran for the U.S. Senate and lost; fifty-five women ran for Congress; thirty-four lost. Overall, fewer women than men run and more women lose. Women lose in primaries; women lose to incumbents; women lose because they are consistently outspent by male opponents.*

In 1980 women challengers were outspent nearly two to one, and in 1982 the odds became more than two to one. According to the WCF, in an average House race in 1982 a woman challenger raised $133,000, compared with $170,000 raised by male challengers and $285,000 raised by male incumbents. There were exceptions, of course. Katie Hall, running from a predominantly black district in Indiana, won election to a vacated congressional seat although she spent virtually nothing. In Tennessee, Cynthia Baker spent about $1.25 million — considerably more than her opponent — on her try for Congress, but won only 34 percent of the vote. Her youth and inexperi-

---

*Although there is an upward trend in the number of women running for Congress, the total numbers of candidates and victors remains extremely small: In 1970 13 of the 25 women who ran for the House were elected. In 1972, 16 of the 32 women who ran for the House were elected. In 1974, 19 of 44 women candidates were elected to the House. In 1976, 52 women ran, and 18 were elected to the House. Patsy Mink, Gloria Schaffer — Connecticut's Secretary of State — and I were all defeated in our Senate races. In 1978, 16 of 45 women who ran for the House won. Two women ran for the Senate and Nancy Landon Kassebaum was elected. In 1980, an all-time high of 57 women ran for the House and 22 were elected. Paula Hawkins, Florida Republican, won a Senate seat. In 1982, 22 of 55 women candidates won House seats. In Senate contests, Millicent Fenwick, Harriett Woods, and Florence Sullivan, a Republican-Conservative, were all defeated. In the same time span, the number of female state legislators almost tripled, rising from 362 in 1973 to 992 in 1983.

ence were probably the crucial factors in her defeat. The only successful woman challenger of a Republican male opponent was Marcy Kaptur of Ohio, who was outspent two to one but achieved victory nonetheless.

As mostly outsiders, women face the tough problem of running against incumbents, who have high reelection rates. (In 1978, for example, 94 percent of House incumbents and 60 percent of Senate incumbents were reelected.) Women also lack access to anything comparable to the old-boy networks, through which the establishment perpetuates itself and raises funds for its favorite legislators. Campaign spending is running wild, but not in the direction of women. In 1982 election spending totaled $343 million, a 44 percent increase over 1980. That money came primarily from the political parties, special interest Political Action Committees (PACS), and individual and family sources. In what has become scandalous proportions, the big campaign money comes from the major PACs, and although there are PACs that raise money for women, minorities, and liberals, they do not match the resources of the conservative and right-wing PACs dominated by big-business men. Of the $35 million in PAC contributions that went into congressional elections in 1982, only $4 million went to challengers, and women candidates received just 7 percent of these funds, reflecting both their paucity of numbers and lack of financial support.

All nine incumbent Democratic Congresswomen were reelected in 1982; they were more successful than women challengers in raising money. Pat Schroeder was the only one who was outspent by her opponent (he received considerable assistance from the Republican Party), but she won. Only two of these Democratic incumbents received financial help from their party, and that was minimal. All but one of the Republican women incumbents were also reelected. The exception was Margaret Heckler, who spent $966,621 on her campaign, compared with the $1.5 million spent by her successful Democratic opponent, Barney Frank, also an incumbent. Heckler, however, received more than $63,000 from her party, compared with the $9600 that Frank received from the Democrats.

Reflecting its base of support, the Republican Party traditionally outspends the Democratic Party, sometimes by staggering proportions. The October 16, 1983, *Washington Post* reported that Republicans spent $214.9 million in the 1981–1982 election campaign, compared with the Democrats' $39 million. The Republican Senatorial Campaign Committee alone outspent its Democratic counterpart by nearly nine to one, distributing $48.9 million, as against the Democrats' $5.6 million.

Nancy Sinnott, executive director of the Republican Congressional Campaign Committee during the 1982 campaign, estimated that her party's huge financial advantage "might have kept the GOP's twenty-six-seat loss in the House from becoming forty-five seats." Apparently the Republicans also spent their money more wisely than the Democrats. According to *Washington Post* columnist David Broder, in 1982 "the GOP targeted about $2.5 million of late contributions to embattled incumbents; the Democrats squandered more than $6.3 million in unspent contributions to 32 incumbents who ended their campaigns with more than $100,000 each in the bank." That unspent money could have helped women challengers win.

The high cost of election campaigns is perhaps the single most important factor in discouraging women from running for office, and the only way to overcome that is to reform campaign finance laws. I believe women should work for laws that would provide public financing of U.S. House campaigns, with an overall limit of $180,000 per campaign, including matching funds from voluntary tax contributions. A lid, scaled to the population of the state, should also be placed on expenditures for Senate seats.

No campaign should be allowed to receive more than a total of $50,000 from all PAC sources. To encourage individuals to contribute more to candidates, they should be allowed a 100 percent tax credit, instead of being allowed to take only a 50 percent credit on up to a $100 contribution, as now provided.

One of the biggest loopholes favoring millionaire candidates is that they can spend any amount of their own money; they should be prohibited from spending more than $20,000 of their personal and family funds. The U.S. Supreme Court sanctioned unlimited personal spending on the grounds that it was an exercise of free speech, the same criterion it applied in sanctioning unlimited campaign spending by independent committees, another practice that favors the rich and right-wingers. I concur with law professor Archibald Cox that the Supreme Court should review its decisions in the Buckley and Schmidt cases, which approved these spending loopholes.

Free broadcast and TV time and newspaper advertising space should also be made available to candidates, with public subsidies if necessary. Most Western democracies ban paid political advertising on TV and radio. These campaign reforms would go a long way toward curbing the excessive influence of big PAC expenditures, a problem well documented by Washington writer Elizabeth Drew in her book, *Politics and Money.*

Party Attitudes Toward Political Women

Despite, or perhaps because of, its opposition to women's rights goals, the Republican Party has been more politically astute and responsive than the Democrats on the issue of supporting women candidates. First in reaction to the Watergate scandal and more recently in response to the gender gap, the Republican National Committee and its affiliated campaign committees have found it politically advantageous to back women candidates who run against Democratic incumbents and for open seats. They have actively recruited, trained, and financially supported women candidates with notable success. They are reaping the benefits of picking up seats in Congress and the state legislatures and scoring a public relations victory of sorts. By pointing to Republican women officeholders and their support of their candidacies, the Republicans can deflect in part the criticism that the party is oblivious to women's goals and aspirations. In the process, they are taking their best shot at winning a larger share of the women's vote, hoping perhaps that a woman candidate will draw strength for the entire ticket. Republican policies appear to be a bit more palatable to the public when they are presented by a woman candidate, according to Senator Richard Lugar of Indiana, who chairs the National Republican Senatorial Committee.

In an August 21, 1983, article in the *Washington Post,* Lugar outlined what he called a frankly politically motivated plan to elect more GOP women. He proposed a concerted drive by the Republican Party "to stamp itself as the party of the woman elected official," and said he was ready to make the following pledges: "I am prepared to commit the NRSC to the maximum legal funding and support for any Republican woman who is nominated next year, regardless how Democratic the state or apparently formidable the Democratic candidate. I am prepared to consider direct assistance to women candidates even prior to their nomination, a sharp departure from our usual policy."

Furthermore, he said, "The party should commit itself formally, in its platform and perhaps its rules, to the goal of nominating women for at least half of all significant offices between now and our 1988 National Convention. One step toward that end might be to award bonus delegates to the 1988 convention to states meeting or approaching that goal."

Lugar made clear that the party was interested in promoting women who would oppose what he called "a small subset of women whose agenda . . . has less to do with uplifting all women than with resuscitating moribund liberalism." And just in case anyone missed the point, he said, with hope, "Elect enough Nancy Kassebaums and Paula Hawkins and people will stop paying attention to Jane [Fonda] and Bella." Lugar's statement, of course, blurred over the distinction between such fairly liberal Republican women as Kassebaum, Schneider, Snowe, and Nancy Johnson of Connecticut, who are often at odds with Republican policy, and Hawkins, who has consistently voted against women's interests.

The Democratic Party's track record on women candidates is not as good as the Republicans. Women's demands for support of their candidacies have usually been met with two shopworn excuses: "We don't have any money" and "We can't get involved in primaries." I have long believed that the Democratic National Committee and its party apparatus must take a much more affirmative and activist position to ensure that more women are elected to public office. On this issue the Republican Party is outsmarting the Democrats.

My view is that the Democratic Party should publicly support viable women candidates in races targeted by a coalition of women's groups before the primaries are held. Preprimary support is essential if significantly greater numbers of women candidates are to win general elections.

Second, the party should aggressively seek out and obtain financial and other forms of support for women candidates from party leaders, affiliated party organizations, and interest groups prior to the primary and for the duration of the campaign.

Third, the party should establish and adhere to a standard that a meaningful proportion of all the skills, resources, and financial and other forms of assistance usually provided to Democratic candidates should be directed to women candidates who are identified with the goals of a majority of women voters.

Finally, the party should adopt a national action plan to publicize its commitment to support women candidates in races targeted by the women's coalition, encouraging the cooperation of state parties and developing a training/outreach/publicity program that seeks to increase dramatically the number of women holding office at every level.

As a matter of fact, I think it would be a good idea to have a constitutional amendment requiring fifty-fifty division in the U.S. Senate, with each state electing one male and one female senator.

To date, many requests have been made of the Democratic Party, through the national committee and its chairman, asking support for women candidates and allocation of funds to maximize the gender gap by supporting mass registration drives among women voters. Not a great deal had happened, at this writing. At a July 1983 Democratic National Committee (DNC) meeting, which I attended as a newly elected member, the Women's Caucus passed a resolution that incorporated some of the proposals I made above. It specifically asked the Democratic Party, at its national and state levels, to "target for support women candidates for open seats and against vulnerable Republicans, with the goal of electing two Democratic women to the U.S. Senate in 1984, with a comparable gain in the U.S. House of Representatives." It asked for funds to support women's registration drives, and also called the attention of Democratic candidates on the congressional and state levels to the issues raised in the letter of the Women's Presidential Project, which was signed by more than two hundred Democratic women. The letter asked the Democratic candidates for President to state in detail their positions on a broad range of public policy questions.

As I indicated earlier, the DNC, the Democratic Senatorial Campaign Committee (DSCC), and the Democratic Congressional Campaign Committee (DCCC) operate on shoestring budgets, often in the red. But crying poverty will not serve to get the party leadership off the hook where women candidates are concerned. Changing old practices that, wittingly or not, blatantly favor men politicians would be more convincing proof that the party is dedicated to equality.

The DSCC and the DCCC, for example, are notorious for distributing funds to incumbents first and challengers later. This policy is foolish and damaging. Simply by virtue of holding office and having financed previous campaigns, incumbents begin with an enormous advantage over challengers in fundraising abilities, name recognition, and political organization. They need help the least, but receive the most. Since so few Democratic women serve in Congress, this incumbent preference policy does little for our cause. It diverts resources away from those trying to unseat Republican incumbents and puts an additional barrier in the path of women running for open seats, since they have to wait until after the primary for party help, while their Republican opponents are likely to have been fully funded from the start. Women who challenge incumbent Democrats in primaries are completely frozen out by the party committees, despite their professed policy of primary neutrality.

In 1982 the DNC did set up the Eleanor Roosevelt Fund to raise and distribute contributions to women candidates. It's a nice gesture, but they seem to have missed the point. What we need is not just our own little fund — and you can believe that it will be *little* — but equal access for women candidates to the party's total financial resources. That's a commitment we've yet to win. The DSCC and the DCCC, which have more money than the DNC, should set up special units to seek out and encourage women to run for office, then use their considerable resources to help elect them.

Here's another low-cost suggestion, which could easily be implemented, to assist women candidates substantially if the party were truly interested in doing so: the party could, if it would, provide such valuable in-kind services to women office seekers as opposition research, computerized targeting, polling data, and pooled consulting advice.

The we-don't-get-involved-in-primaries excuse doesn't hold up, either. It's a known fact that Democrats as well as Republicans target seats to be vacated by incumbents or those held by persons they perceive to be vulnerable. The parties then go out to persuade, cajole, and encourage candidates to run in these races. Who does the recruiting? White men. Whom do they recruit as candidates? White men. How do they entice these white men to run? By offering financial support and campaign services. They actively discourage any challengers, except the anointed one, from running, turning down requests for help with the pious demurral, "We don't get involved in primaries."

Recruitment tactics could be used for the benefit of women candidates rather than against them, but the old-boy networks flourish among Democrats as well as Republicans. They're just not very eager to have us join their club in the Senate or House.

You would think the Democratic Party would be embarrassed by the fact that the party which purports to be a strong advocate of civil and equal rights has no female or black Senators and only one governor. You would think the leadership of a party dependent on women and minority voters for nearly two thirds of the support it receives in elections would be more responsive to these constituencies. You would think the Democratic leadership would draw the same conclusions from gender-gap surveys as the Republicans and recognize that backing women candidates would make excellent political sense. You might think so, but you would be wrong.

For the 1984 Senate races, the Democratic Party early on got its white-male candidates rather neatly lined up in front-row position, ignoring and often actually excluding potential women candidates. In New Hampshire, for instance, Republican incumbent Gordon Humphrey was targeted for defeat.

To whom did the Democrats turn? To Congressman Norman D'Amours, a reluctant candidate whom they persuaded to run even though Dudley Dudley, who, as a representative on the Governor's Council, is the highest-ranking Democratic woman elected official in the state, had been seriously exploring a senatorial bid. D'Amours would be the stronger candidate, they alleged, despite the fact that the district Dudley represents on the council is larger than D'Amours's congressional district. Without any encouragement from top Democrats, Dudley then decided to try for a House seat. If the Democratic brass were really serious about electing women to the U.S. Senate, they would have used the same forces to line up the Senate nomination for Dudley rather than for D'Amours.

In the Senate contest in Minnesota, Democratic Secretary of State Joanne Growe, one of the party's highest vote getters, faces primary opposition from Congressman James Oberstar. Although Growe has been elected to statewide office, while Oberstar represents the rather remote northeast corner of the state, the party made no effort to discourage his candidacy, thus denying Growe the kind of help that had been given D'Amours in fending off potential primary opponents.

In Colorado, Democratic Lieutenant Governor Nancy Dick, a strong women's rights and peace advocate, decided to run against the incumbent Republican Senator, William Armstrong. Rather than jump in firmly behind Dick's candidacy, the Democratic leadership kept trying to figure out ways to persuade Democratic Governor Dick Lamm to run for the Senate seat, despite his repeated disavowals of interest in the contest. Had he changed his mind, Nancy Dick presumably would have been expected to bow out gracefully in deference to the male candidate.

The Senate Obstacle Course

The U.S. Senate is considered the breeding ground of future Presidents, and many Senators start their national careers by serving first in the House of Representatives. That's the process for men, but the rules change when women are involved. Only one woman Representative, Margaret Chase Smith, made the transition to the Senate. Other female House members have hoped to move up to the Senate and some of us have actually tried, without the success that would have come more easily if we had been men. Martha Griffiths and Edith Green both worked in the House for twenty years, without ever getting the party recognition or support they deserved for winning higher office. (Griffiths now presides over the Michigan Senate as a grand dame of politics, brandishing her famous finger to admonish legislators, whose parents are her contemporaries, to behave. She is, no doubt, performing admirably, but what a loss to our nation that she could never bring her formidable abilities to the Senate.)

Although Barbara Jordan retired after three terms in the House, reportedly because of ill health, there were rumors that she had been politically disappointed. She had wanted to be Attorney General in the Carter administration, it was said, but the President appointed instead the infinitely forgettable Griffin Bell, a Georgia crony. The Texas Democratic Party also reportedly coldshouldered Jordan's hopes that it would back her for a Senate nomination. The party was perfectly prepared to use her at national conventions as a token image of its democratic spirit, but not to give her the political opportunities it afforded to men with far inferior talents. The irony was that Jordan had been a loyal Texas party machine adherent throughout her early career.

Ironic, too, is the circumstance that neither of the two present women Senators had served in the House or had much state political experience, whereas Griffiths, Green, Jordan, Mink, Holtzman, Fenwick, and I would have been, I say without any fake modesty, extremely knowledgeable and notable additions to the Senate.

Although the political realities differ in every contest, there were some similarities in the experiences Mink, Holtzman, and I had when we tried for the Senate.

Patsy had served in the House for twelve years when she decided to seek the Democratic nomination for Senator in 1976. She was an outstanding legislator, an advocate of women's rights and civil rights, and author of the women's Educational Equity Act. No one fought harder for the interests of her state than she did. Many were the times I would seek a vote from her on an issue of urban transportation or economic development that my committee was interested in, issues she would normally support, but if they conflicted in any way with the needs of her state, she would say no. Yet when she relinquished her House seat to try a run for the Senate, the Democratic Party and the influential labor and money groups in Hawaii supported a male politician, Congressman Sparky Matsunaga, against her. He spent twice as much as she did, and defeated her. Patsy later became president of the Americans for Democratic Action and in 1982 won a seat on the Honolulu City Council, which she now serves as president. I am certain she is doing a fine job there, but that does not justify her absence from the national political scene. She is a woman well qualified to be Secretary of State or to serve in another cabinet post.

In my own case, after serving three terms in the House, I felt it was a worthwhile risk to run for the Senate in 1976. With the defeat of Margaret Chase Smith, there would be no women in the upper house, and no woman had ever been on a major party ticket as a candidate for the Senate from New York, an anomaly in view of the state's large and active population of feminists and its key historic role in the suffrage movement and other liberal crusades. As Chisholm had predicted, I had rocked the boat in my six years in the House and become one of the leaders of the progressive bloc of white and black legislators, a creative advocate of women's rights legislation, author of a provision that allowed transfer of interstate highway funds to public mass transportation, and a coauthor of the amended Freedom of Information Act and the Privacy and Sunshine laws. I had also been up front in the campaigns to cut off congressional funds for the war in Indochina and to impeach Nixon and Agnew. I had brought $6 billion into New York State for programs of transportation, public works, economic development, and water and sewage programs. In my district I conferred with community people almost every weekend, and my office staff ran a highly organized constituency service program. Contrary to the claims that my oft-cited "abrasive" personality would alienate my colleagues, I had been voted by them the third most influential member of the House in a *U.S. News & World Report* survey. House Speaker Tip O'Neill had even decided to campaign for me, an unusual intervention by a congressional leader in a Democratic primary.

But in spite of my record and the disgraceful absence of women from the Senate, the chair of the New York State Democratic Party, Joe Crangle, sought a male candidate to oppose me for the Democratic nomination. He succeeded in recruiting Daniel Patrick Moynihan, who had served in the Nixon and Kennedy administrations and held many neoconservative views that did not reflect the prevailing Democratic temper at that time. The male incumbent the Democratic nominee would oppose in the general election was James Buckley — younger brother of William Buckley Jr. — an ultraconservative who had squeezed into office in 1970 because two liberal men had opposed each other in a three-way contest. Senator Buckley had an almost zero record on issues of concern to New Yorkers. I had been tracking his performance closely while we were both in Congress and knew he would be easy to beat.

Not only did Moynihan run against me, but two well-known liberals, Ramsey Clark and Paul O'Dwyer, also entered the primary after I had announced my candidacy. My fourth opponent was a millionaire builder, Abe Hirschfield, who provided the comic relief. Trying to outdo my feminist credentials, he insisted in one debate that he believed in women's rights, too. "In my household," he said, "I am the head and my wife is the neck, and the neck twists the head." (Some said she hadn't twisted far enough.)

I lost the primary by less than 1 percent of the vote, and Moynihan went on to win the general election. I drew more votes than Moynihan in all the rural counties and upstate cities and in two out of the three major New York City suburbs. My liberal vote, however, was split in the city by Clark and O'Dwyer, who had been lagging far behind Moynihan and me throughout the campaign; they refused to withdraw in my favor even though they were requested to do so by many who considered them spoilers. Another blow came from Arthur Ochs Sulzberger, the publisher of the *New York Times*, who, unknown to the public, set aside an eight-to-two vote by the newspaper's editorial board to endorse me and instead wrote an influential editorial supporting Moynihan. My campaign could not afford Election Day polls, but the press reported that I had received a higher percentage of women's votes than men's; however, the margin was not quite large enough to overcome the division in liberal ranks.

The primary campaign was illuminating in showing that even the most liberal men did not regard the absence of women from the Senate as a grievous wrong that should be remedied. During one debate Clark claimed that it was inherently sexist for me to conduct a campaign that included the women's representation issue and lectured me on what a "truly liberated" woman should do: namely, ignore the fact that she is a woman or that a special effort was needed to break down the barriers against women in the nation's foremost legislative body. When I reminded Clark that he had fought to open up the system to blacks and Hispanics, he said that was different. (It's standard practice for men who talk about blacks not to mention that more than half of them are women and to forget Shirley Chisholm's celebrated remark that she had encountered more discrimination as a woman than as a black.)

O'Dwyer, my other liberal opponent, admitted that if a black candidate had been seeking the Democratic nomination, he would have thought twice about running, but his doubts did not extend to preventing me from winning the nomination. After the primary he called me to express his regrets, but during the campaign itself both he and Clark, whose overall political views were similar to mine, concentrated on attacking me for criticizing Moynihan.

Other women candidates and I have learned the hard way that although a liberal male politician may take the correct stand on women's issues, he cannot be counted on to advance the democratic principle of women's representation if he himself feels threatened by competition.

Former liberals are even more hostile to potential women opponents. A case in point: Mayor Ed Koch of New York City, with whom Mario Cuomo and I, as well as others, competed in a 1977 mayoralty primary, persistently attacks me and sets me up as a target whose name he thinks he has merely to drag into a discussion of an issue to show how unpalatable it is. In a March 1982 interview in *Playboy* magazine — in which his sneers at rural folk later lost him the Democratic gubernatorial nomination to Cuomo — Koch called me, among other things, "bigmouth," "very pushy," and "aggressive." On the other hand, he refers to himself fondly as "Mayor Mouth."

If I were the only woman political leader Koch attacked it could be put down as a simple case of mutual dislike (there's certainly plenty of that, on both sides), but he has also made a point of stomping on other progressive women political leaders. In the summer of 1983 he went on a national campaign, attacking the Democratic Party for being too liberal and accusing it of pandering to women on the ERA issue. He called Carol Bellamy, president of the New York City Council, a "horror show" and a "pain in the ass" when she took a more liberal position than he on some municipal matters. As council head, she is next in line for the mayoralty. She was elected at the same time that Koch became mayor, winning three hundred thousand more votes than he received, and that did her in with him.

Koch has also singled out for harsh attacks the two most progressive women in the City Council and went out of his way to undermine Congresswoman Elizabeth Holtzman's 1978 race for the Senate, although he purportedly supported her after she won the Democratic nomination. Holtzman, who had served three terms in the House and was a smart and energetic legislator, was engaged in a three-way contest. Her opponents were the Republican-Conservative Alphonse D'Amato and the incumbent Senator, Jacob Javits, who had lost the Republican primary but remained in the race on the Liberal Party line, creating a split in the liberal vote. Javits, who was old and seriously ill, was importuned to withdraw by those who feared a victory by D'Amato, a man considerably less qualified than Holtzman or Javits; he was an adamant opponent of abortion rights and ultra right wing in his views. Javits held on to his failing candidacy, however, with the result that Holtzman lost by a narrow margin. Koch did his bit by providing photo opportunities at City Hall, where he posed in friendly fashion with D'Amato, and kept referring to Javits as the finest member of the U.S. Senate, which may have been his belief but was hardly helpful to Holtzman. She also encountered the traditional problems of women candidates in raising money. The Democratic Senate Campaign Committee gave her $49,000, compared with the $700,000 D'Amato received from the Republican committee. The Democratic establishment was generally slow to offer her campaign assistance or help from crowd-drawing speakers. Most of the elected officials who campaigned with her were women.

When Holtzman later ran for district attorney in Brooklyn, Koch endorsed her male opponent, who saturated the airwaves with a commercial that featured a female voice saying, "Liz Holtzman is a wonderful woman. I would love her for my daughter but not for my district attorney." This time Holtzman won; her opponent was a weak candidate and the crudely sexist commercial backfired.

Then there's Harriett Woods, who, in 1982, ran for the U.S. Senate seat from Missouri against incumbent Republican John Danforth and came close to victory, winning 49 percent of the vote. Although she had twenty years of public service to her credit, including eight years in her city council, a stint as highway commissioner, and was in her sixth year as a member of the Missouri Senate, state Democratic leaders rejected her candidacy because, as she put it, they thought she was "too liberal, too urban, and even worse, a woman." The party's male establishment contended that Missouri was too conservative a state to accept as a candidate a woman who was pro-choice and pro-ERA.

According to press reports, the state's other U.S. Senator, Democrat Thomas Eagleton (who is anti–abortion rights), asked Woods to get out of the race because Burleigh Arnold, a veteran Democratic fund raiser and banker, wanted to run. This was a man who had never held or sought public office before. Woods, strongly backed by women's organizations and the constituency she had acquired during her long public career, refused to bow out and won the Democratic primary two to one against a field of ten male candidates. She was the party's official nominee, but the token support she got from the Democratic establishment did not compare with the help the GOP lavished on the incumbent Danforth. When polls showed

Woods closing in on Danforth, she recalls, "The Republicans really came in. They took over and threw all their resources into it, brought in all sorts of people. As for the Democratic Party, it was just 'Good luck.' " A particularly bitter point with Woods is that the day before the election, Senate Majority Leader Howard Baker arrived to campaign for Danforth and claimed that Woods would close down McDonnell-Douglas, a major aerospace firm, which is the biggest employer in Missouri. "That was balderdash, of course," Woods says, "but I had no one to counter with. I didn't have any of those troops. I didn't have any Senators to speak for me."

Danforth achieved his narrow victory by spending about twice as much money as Woods. She did succeed in raising $1,250,000, but the last quarter of a million came into the campaign only in its last five days, too late to be used effectively, even though the polls showed her running neck and neck with her opponent. Money and political support are necessary early in a campaign; the Democratic Party has not been forthcoming with either for women candidates when they most need help.

At present, public opinion surveys show Woods to be one of the most popular politicians in Missouri. She is running for lieutenant governor and will undoubtedly look to the Senate again. She put together an impressive support coalition of farmers, workers, women, senior citizens, students, and small-business men. They won't go away. Will the party please step in?

Some political analysts wonder why women candidates have not had a bigger, more decisive gender-gap vote in their favor, although they usually get more votes from women than from men. Until recently, many women candidates made a point of insisting that they were not running because they were women, that voters should not vote for them because they were women and should support them only because they were better qualified than their male opponents. This might be the correct policy in a unisex world, but when last I looked we were still living in a society that blatantly discriminates against women and shortchanges their particular needs. Pretending that being a woman will not affect your interests or performance in Congress is an approach that will neither mobilize a large women's vote nor convince women that they will be electing a representative more attuned to their needs and goals than the average male politician. If a woman candidate says, "Judge me as you would a man," it encourages voters to regard political office as the natural habitat of men, who provide the role models that a woman must emulate to succeed. This is a mistake. Women candidates have special strengths and should not try to conceal them.

Even women's rights advocates sometimes tend to downplay their special credentials and views, I have discovered in talks with women candidates and leaders of women's organizations. In several cases, women candidates who were members of the NWPC or were known as feminists or as advocates of the ERA, abortion rights, and economic equity for women told me they felt it was unnecessary to refer to their activities in behalf of women during their campaigns because "everyone knows of my association with women's causes" or "everyone knows of my identity as a feminist." Many women who used this approach lost their races. In other instances, leaders of women's organizations have admitted to me that they sometimes advised feminists to move more assertively on other issues and concerns because their identification with women's demands was evident and did not have to be stressed.

A contrary view is held by Claudine Schneider. When she first ran for office she did not campaign as a woman or on women's issues, but her experiences in the House changed her mind. "I never considered myself a feminist before I got this job," she says. "But then I started looking at the laws and I recognized that many of them were written with a slant against women. We Congresswomen not only represent the men and women in our district, but since women are such a minority in this body we feel the responsibility and weight of representing all American women." When she was reelected in 1982, the polls showed that she won 58 to 42 percent among male voters, but 62 to 38 percent among women.

In Harriett Woods's campaign, a TV commercial stressing her strong support for abortion rights was yanked at the last minute, on the advice of her male media consultants. In retrospect, she and others believe that may have been a mistake, depriving her of a winning margin. She lost by only 26,000 votes out of 1,543,000. Woods believes that her pro-choice position on abortion was instrumental in her near win and says experienced politicians now agree that "abortion is no longer a dangerous campaign issue." Just a slightly larger turnout of women voters aroused by a more forceful stand on their issues could have elected her to the Senate.

Frances Lear, a Los Angeles political consultant and generous and helpful supporter of women candidates, argues that it is essential to develop a larger corps of female media and campaign consultants to bring their own special insights and values into campaigns to elect women. I agree.

The failed campaign of Millicent Fenwick, the New Jersey Republican who tried to move up from the House to the Senate in 1982, presented a difficult problem for feminists, who wound up on both sides of the question of whether they should support her. As more women enter politics, this will become an increasing dilemma for the gender-gap bloc of voters: How should we balance a woman's positive record on legislation specifically relating to women and children against a partially or totally negative record on broad social policy questions affecting the economy and foreign affairs? And even trickier: Should a woman with a good record be supported if her election would give control of the Senate to an administration and party that is generally opposed to our goals? (As it happened, even with Fenwick's defeat the Democrats were not able to win back control of the Senate in 1982.)

The NWPC endorsed Fenwick and the New Jersey NOW decided to endorse her Democratic opponent, Frank Lautenberg, a strongly anti-Reagan, liberal millionaire businessman. Fenwick and I had hit it off as soon as she arrived in Congress in 1975. She is a woman of enormous grace, style, wit, and the independence that always attracts me. We became good friends, and she had the kindness to say, after I left Congress, that she felt she was "losing her right arm." During her Senate primary contest, conservative candidate Jeffrey Bell quoted this remark to illustrate her closeness to "the liberal Democrats." We often joked that she should have said she was losing her *left* arm.

During her years in the New Jersey legislature and in Congress, Fenwick was a strong partisan of the ERA, abortion rights, and women's legislation and voted to cut off funds for the Vietnam War. One of her best stories was about the time a male colleague in the state legislature rose to speak against passage of a state ERA. "I don't think women should have equality," he told her. "I think women should be kissable, cuddly, and smell good." Whereupon Fenwick replied, "That's funny, because that's how I've always felt men should be." And, she added, "I hope for your sake you haven't been disappointed as often as I've been."

I did not follow Fenwick's record closely after 1976, but I understand that on several votes she favored President Reagan's economic proposals and budget cuts even though they adversely affected important women's programs that she had previously supported. She continued to be an advocate of the ERA, reproductive freedom, family planning, and consumer protection and stood firm against right-wing demands for school prayer, tuition tax credits, and other proposals. Knowing her as well as I do, I find it hard to characterize Millicent Fenwick as a Reagan Republican.

In explaining the decision of the New Jersey NOW to oppose Fenwick and endorse Lautenberg, Ann Baker of NOW set forth the cause for its action in a letter to the *Washington Post* on September 2, 1983, responding to a charge by Senator Richard Lugar that feminists were guilty of hypocrisy in "the betrayal of Millicent Fenwick." In her primary campaign against the conservative Jeff Bell, Baker said, Fenwick "discouraged the endorsement of organizations identified with advocacy of women's issues, or of women candidates." Not only did she have a higher record of support for Reagan legislation than other moderate Republicans, but she had the President come to New Jersey to campaign for her, Baker noted.

In contrast, Lautenberg actively pursued NOW's endorsement and agreed to make women's rights one of the central issues in his campaign. His presence in the Senate could be a factor in the Democrats' possibility of rewinning control of the upper body in 1984; yet, I have strong objections to the widening phenomenon of millionaires using their fortunes to get into the Senate. Lautenberg spent almost $4 million of his own money in a campaign in which he outspent Fenwick by $5.3 million to $3 million. A relative unknown with no previous electoral political experience, Lautenberg had the money for round-the-clock saturation TV and radio commercials that made him a household name overnight. Fenwick, who objected on principle to spending personal money, had to put $876,717 of her own money into the campaign. (Few women in politics have private fortunes they can dip into for their public careers.) She received very little money from PACs — $14,499 as against the $142,077 that Lautenberg received; she opposed PAC contributions, again on principle. On the other hand, she received $428,696 from the Republican Party, while her opponent got only $74,500 from the Democrats; clearly, he didn't need the party's help that much.

Granted that Fenwick chose the path of expediency in emphasizing her agreements with the Reagan administration rather than her deep differences on women's rights and other issues, I believe there should be some recognition by women's groups of the positive role an unusual woman like Millicent Fenwick had played in Congress and the New Jersey legislature in the past; neutrality by NOW would perhaps have been a signal that a 100 percent voting record is not the only measure of a candidate, and that once in the Senate, Fenwick might have regained some of her independent spirit and value as a champion of women's rights. It is impossible to determine whether the NOW endorsement provided Lautenberg with his narrow winning margin or whether it may have produced a larger percentage of women's votes than he might have received anyway. The probability is that for the voters of New Jersey, a state hard hit by Reaganomics and unemployment, it was the Reagan endorsement, not the NOW rejection, that sank Fenwick.

In another 1982 contest, women's rights groups were united in opposing the reelection of Margaret Heckler, veteran Republican Representative from Massachusetts, because of her antiabortion stand and her vote for Reagan's budget. She was handily defeated by a proven Democratic liberal, Barney Frank. I had also been very friendly with Peggy Heckler in Congress and found her to be, with the exception of her antiabortion position, a strong advocate of ERA and women's and other social programs. When as a young lawyer in 1966 she started her political career, she had wanted to run as a Democrat, but received no encouragement. Instead she ran in the Republican primary against Joe Martin, former Speaker of the House and then its minority leader, and to everyone's surprise, including her own, she won. Her loyalty to the Reagan administration, however, proved too much for previously admiring voters. After she was defeated, Reagan was quoted as saying, "Gee, I'm sorry Heckler lost. She was a good little girl."

Reagan later appointed Fenwick to a diplomatic post in Italy and named Heckler to his cabinet as secretary of the Department of Health and Human Services, where she has committed herself to his antiabortion policies. If Reagan is using Heckler in an attempt to cover up his gender gap, she probably thinks that she can mitigate the harshness of his social welfare program cuts by working on the inside of the administration. That is the choice Heckler made, but it is not the kind of patchwork choice women voters have to make. They are powerful enough to elect an administration that will strengthen the health services and other programs needed by women and their families without settling for the present Reagan tactic of using women officials as cosmetic cover-ups for bad policies.

A Woman President?

Why not? Isn't it time? Hasn't a Gallup poll shown that 80 percent of the American public say they would vote for a woman candidate nominated for the presidency by her party?

Actually, there are several good reasons why a woman might run for President. The first, of course, is to win the nomination, win the general election, and become the chief executive of our nation. The second is to raise important issues and come to her party's nominating convention with enough delegate support to influence its choice of a nominee, to shape the substantive policy issues of the general election campaign, and to bargain for future concessions. A third reason is to make a symbolic but necessary point — that the presidency should not be considered a white-male preserve and that a woman, white or black, or a black man has the right to run and be considered on her or his merits.

Unfortunately, even with all the momentum of the gender gap that should have pushed the women's movement into daring action, we seem to have missed the boat on running a woman for President in 1984. I argued strongly in feminist meetings for that tactic, but it foundered on the questions of "Who?" and "How?" and the continuing self-doubts that afflict even the strongest women leaders when they're up against the male-dominated political system. They also tend to feel that they have to wait for that moment when the male power structure decrees that our time has come. That will indeed be a long wait.

Although some women have just gone ahead and sought the nomination — as Shirley Chisholm boldly did in 1972 — others hesitate to take the plunge without guarantees that they will have the complete unified support of the women's and allied movements. Men who want to run for office discuss it with their peers, but they don't ask for permission. They do it.

A case in point is the self-propelled move of Jesse Jackson. Spurred by his desire to see greater representation of blacks in government and greater response to the economic and other needs of the black community, Jackson first undertook a major registration campaign and then used that campaign to test the waters for his presidential candidacy. By running for President, Jackson, together with other black leaders, could develop a bloc of delegate votes that would give them considerable negotiating clout at the 1984 Democratic convention.

Unfortunately, the situation is different for women. We have created the gender gap by our votes, but we still suffer from a credibility gap. We have yet to prove to the doubting Thomases and Thomasinas of the world that a majority of women voters would unite behind a woman's presidential candidacy. The solidarity of black voters — especially since the election of Mayor Harold Washington in Chicago and Mayor Wilson Goode in Philadelphia — and the overwhelming response of blacks to mass registration drives have given credibility to the view of black men and women as a united, anti-Republican voting bloc. That women could achieve the same unanimity is greeted skeptically, an attitude that has some basis in that the gender gap has not yet emerged as a big enough factor even in the election of women to lesser offices.

The media, that "great mentioner" in which candidacies are usually launched, still have trouble taking the idea of a woman President seriously, although they're becoming more accustomed to and enlightened about the notion. Women are not found in the places that are the traditional steppingstones to the highest office in the land — the U.S. Senate, the ranks of governors, or former Vice Presidents who assume the role of heir apparent. That is perceived as an insuperable obstacle, but I don't agree that it should be.

Another barrier to a woman's presidential candidacy is the same old problem of money, or the lack of it. Without a nationally recognized name and carrying the label of underdog at best, a woman candidate would face enormous difficulty in bankrolling a campaign. Not enough male "fat cats" would invest in a woman's candidacy, and too few women have developed the habit of giving large sums of money to their sisters who seek political office.

Aside from the superhigh standards set by women political leaders, the major and most deeply felt reason for the Democrats' reluctance to promote a woman candidate was their fear that the stakes were too high. Getting rid of Ronald Reagan and ousting the Republicans from control of the White House was too important a goal to risk dividing the Democratic Party over the question of a woman's presidential candidacy. Now was not the time. I certainly share the determination that there be a massive repudiation of Reaganism at the polls; yet the feeling lingers that we missed an opportunity in not projecting a woman candidate around whom we could focus our demands, organize broad support among women, and demonstrate our strength at the convention.

As I write this, a movement is shaping up to demand inclusion of a woman vice presidential nominee on the Democratic

1984 ticket, and the Democratic male candidates have already
agreed to give serious consideration to the idea. Considering
and actually selecting a woman running mate are two different
matters, but for the first time in American history there is real
interest in the proposal in the Democratic Party, as well as
apparent public support.

The idea first came up at the initial New York meetings of
women leaders, which led to the formation of our Women's
Presidential Project in the fall of 1982. (See chapter 11.) After
we failed to reach a consensus on the tactic of running a woman
for the presidency, I suggested that we promote a woman for
the vice presidency. That was regarded as a more achievable
goal, and I was asked to prospect the field for possible candidates. I called several Congresswomen and other prominent
women to inquire whether any would be prepared to wage an
active campaign for the nomination, around which women
could rally delegate support. All were interested in having their
names mentioned, but, perhaps understandably, they were un-
willing to wage active campaigns at that time, in the absence of
what then appeared to be a lack of public interest.

The situation changed, however, as continuing reports about
the gender gap and the potential power of the women's vote
showed that we were in a strong bargaining position. The Democratic male presidential candidates had all responded with
utmost respect and solicitousness to the detailed questionnaires
our Women's Presidential Project had sent them, and, in appearances before the NWPC convention and the subsequent
NOW convention in Washington, almost all agreed to consider
naming a woman running mate. The idea spilled over to the
Republican Party; there was speculation about whom the
Republicans might choose, and *New York Times* writer Tom
Wicker suggested in a September 12, 1983 column that Reagan
would be well advised to replace George Bush with a woman
nominee if he wanted to win reelection in 1984.

As opinion polls showed strong public support for the idea,
the media began spotlighting potential women candidates, and
the thought of a woman Vice President no longer seemed
strange. Whether or not a woman does appear on the 1984

ticket of either or both parties, we have succeeded in projecting into the national debate the theme that women have a right to share in the highest political leadership of our country and, even more important, that our people want the values and guidance of women. In proposing a woman for the vice presidency we have also provided an effective vehicle through which women can express their frustration at having had so little direct representation in the higher councils of government decision making.

One way women can use this vehicle is through the process of delegate selection for the nominating conventions. In February 1984, the states start selecting convention delegates pledged to a particular presidential candidate. Might it not be a good idea at the same time for aspiring candidates to pledge support for a woman vice presidential candidate? Although the states do not provide for selecting such a candidate in the way a presidential nominee is selected or supported, campaigns at the grassroots level as well as nationally could produce sufficient delegate pressure at the Democratic convention to convince the presidential nominee that it would be good politics to choose a woman as his running mate.

Congresswomen, former Congresswomen, mayors, appointed officeholders, and others are being mentioned as possible nominees, and more candidates will probably emerge. Some women's organizations may get behind a particular woman candidate; others may prefer to ask delegates as they pledge themselves to a presidential candidate to pledge their support for a woman Vice President, with the name to be filled in at the convention — provided, of course, that the woman selected has a proven record of commitment to women's rights and the other gender-gap issues.

In this way, an idea whose time has come may actually give Americans their first opportunity to vote for a woman on a major national party ticket.

Even if a woman is not nominated for Vice President in 1984, the debate on this issue has had the effect of increasing public consciousness of the need to support women for all high political offices, for President, Vice President, governor, Senator, House member, mayor, and state elective office.

As the gender gap persists, women public officials and candidates will be more likely to identify themselves as feminists and to support the gender-gap issues, and with good reason, for they will benefit from the gender-gap vote that favors the election of more women.

Run, women, run. This is the time to step out front and center. As many more women run, many more will win.

10

Power at the Polls

NINETEEN EIGHTY-FOUR could be a watershed year in American political history. It marks the first time that women, through their voting power, their numbers, and their organized strength, could decide who will be the next President of the United States, which party will control the Congress, who will reside in the governors' mansions across the nation, who will serve in our state legislatures, and who will fill thousands of elective posts at the town, city, county, and state levels.

The gender gap has been established as a political fact of life. It is endlessly being measured, dissected, probed, analyzed, and debated by pollsters, academics, sociologists, politicians, the media, and by women themselves. Most agree that it is not a flash in the pan, a sometime thing. It will remain. Like the highs and lows on a seismic chart, the gender gap reflects the rumblings of powerful subterranean social forces that are now surfacing and changing the political attitudes and behavior of American women. It is a product of the conditions under which American women live, work, think, and feel, and it has been greatly influenced and shaped by the women's movement in its ongoing struggle for the ERA, reproductive freedom, economic justice, peace, and the other social improvement issues with which so many American women have come to identify themselves.

The gender gap is not a cause in itself. It simply measures differences in opinions and voting patterns of men and women, and it will narrow or vanish only when millions more men adopt the attitudes and beliefs already held by a majority of women and large numbers of men — or when government policies change. It will *not* vanish if Ronald Reagan and his successors think that all they have to do is to sweet-talk women into imitating his male supporters, accepting the macho views of the war hawks or settling for smaller paychecks and dead-end jobs.

Although polls show that men and women favor women's equity goals in almost equal percentages, the intensity of male support does not measure up to that of women, nor is it as decisive in how they vote. What may be only token, fashionable approval on the part of men is strong, overriding conviction on the part of those women who represent the active feminist constituency. Using various in-depth studies as a basis, I estimate their electoral strength at about 10 million, but allied with them are many more women who are linked, with varying degrees of commitment, to the gender-gap issues.

Some political scientists have identified the 1980 electoral gender gap as a pro-ERA, pro-peace vote, and the one in 1982 as primarily an expression of economic dissatisfaction. Others pinpoint the latter as a vote by professional working women, mostly over age thirty; a vote by single, divorced, poor, and minority women, a majority of whom are Democrats; an economic self-interest vote; and a "vulnerability" vote by women who perceive themselves as a disadvantaged or vulnerable minority dependent on the good will of the male power structure.

But no one theory can explain the gender-gap phenomenon. American women are a very diverse group, and certain factors may have more influence than others on how women decide to vote. Compassion, a yearning for peace, concern about the environment, the desire for economic security, and equality are shared by most women, but the degree to which a particular factor motivates a particular woman or group of women may vary. For example, working women, lower-middle-class women, welfare recipients, and the unemployed may be pulled by their economic self-interest more strongly than higher-income professional women or homemakers whose concern is less about economics and more about the issues of peace, environmental protection, and equality, for their children as well as for themselves. But the important message of the gender gap is that women do join together across *all* racial, social, and regional lines in stark opposition to President Reagan and his policies.

I believe that in 1984, women will defeat President Reagan or any stand-in for the policies he represents. Millions of men and women will vote against the President, but it is women's votes that will provide the margin of difference between victory and defeat.

Women, too, will be voting in coalition with other powerful anti-Reagan forces — environmentalists, blacks, Hispanics, and other minorities, union members and working people, the poor and unemployed, gays, and Jews — who can be expected to give a majority of their votes to the Democratic presidential candidate. Many of these constituencies overlap and women appear in all of them. Strengthening their voting numbers will be millions of Democrats who defected to vote for Reagan in 1980 and have been thoroughly disillusioned with his policies. Large numbers of Republican women will also defect, either to vote for the Democratic candidate or to oppose Reagan by remaining neutral or voting for a third-party candidate.

The key to a victory for women in 1984 can be summed up in two words. *Register. Vote.*

We cannot take for granted, however, that women will automatically go to the polls, even if they are dissatisfied with Reagan Republicanism. Here are some hard facts on the past and potential strength of women in the electoral power struggle:

- One out of three eligible women did not bother to register in 1980; that adds up to 27.3 million women who threw away a

once-in-four-year opportunity to have a voice in running this country.
* Some 55.7 million women did register, but 6.4 million of them
did not follow up by actually voting.
* According to the Census Bureau, 49.3 million women voted,
but 33.7 million did not.
* In 1980, 9 million more women than men were eligible to vote,
but on Election Day women voters outnumbered men by only 6
million.

Because of population growth, even more women are eligible
to vote in 1984. They will again outnumber men at the voting
booths. The bigger the female turnout, the better the prospects
that the gender-gap issues will prevail and that we can have a
new team in the White House. The most important point to be
made about participating in an election is that every single voter
should think of herself as providing the one vote that can make
a difference. Reagan's victory in 1980, all the "landslide" non-
sense aside, rested on some hairline margins. For example:
Reagan would not have been elected if one out of every
twenty people who voted for him had stayed home. He would
have lost if just 881,743 voters in sixteen states had decided to
cast their ballots for Carter instead. That is just *1 percent* of all
those who voted nationally, requiring a switch of only 4666
votes in each of the congressional districts in those states.
The Democrats would have won if more women, blacks, and
Hispanics had voted in key states. Reagan's plurality in the ten
largest states was less than the number of all nonvoting white
women in each of those states; less than the number of nonvoting black men and women in Michigan, New York, and California; less than the number of nonvoting Hispanic women and
men in California, New York, and Texas.*
In 1980 Carter carried six states (Georgia, Hawaii, Maryland, Minnesota, Rhode Island, West Virginia) and the District
of Columbia, winning only forty-nine Electoral College votes of
the 270 necessary to elect a President. He could have carried

*The U.S. Census Bureau provides voter turnout data for white, black, and Hispanic
women and men by race and sex only on a national basis. State data used here for these
subgroups are based on information from the Joint Center for Political Studies and the
Southwest Voter Registration Project, which provide data for race only, as well as on
Census Bureau reports.

New York if just seven out of one hundred nonvoting white women or one of every six nonvoting black women and men had gone to the polls and voted Democratic. Or Illinois, if one of every three nonvoting women had voted Democratic. In Pennsylvania, one of every six nonvoting white women, and in Michigan, one of every four nonvoting white women could have provided the swing votes. In North Carolina, just six of every hundred nonvoting white women or seventy-five of every thousand nonvoting black women and men could have made the difference. Overall, slight increases in voting turnout by women and minorities in sixteen states, ranging from 1915 more voters in Massachusetts to 199,597 in New Jersey, could have brought Carter the Electoral College votes he needed.* It could be said, and I would agree, that Carter's record as President was just not good enough to inspire women or minorities to flock to the polls, but many excellent candidates have also been sunk because of voter apathy, indifference, or legal obstacles that prevented people from voting.

In 1984, however, after four years of Reagan rule, women's organizations, blacks, and the Democratic Party will be mounting major registration drives (see chapter 11) in the correct belief that the more people who vote, the stronger the chances of sending Reagan back to his ranch for a permanent vacation. You can be certain that the Republicans will also run intensive registration and get-out-the-vote drives among their solid constituencies, and since the GOP can easily outspend everyone else, women will have to use all their political and community organizing skills and creativity to enlarge and get out the women's vote.

To increase women's registration 3 percent above the 1980 level, we must register 1,757,000 more women. We would then have a formidable force of more than 60 million women registered to vote in 1984 — 4.6 million more women than were

---

*Alabama, 9 electoral votes; Arkansas, 6; Delaware, 3; Illinois, 26; Kentucky, 9; Maine, 4; Massachusetts, 14; Michigan, 21; Mississippi, 7; New Jersey, 17; New York, 41; North Carolina, 13; Pennsylvania, 27; Tennessee, 10; Vermont, 3; and Wisconsin, 11. These 221 votes, added to Carter's 49 Electoral College votes, would have made the required 270 votes.

registered four years ago. *This is a practical and achievable goal* — and women have never had a stronger incentive than they have now to reach that goal.

How Reagan Can Be Defeated

Predicting the outcome of presidential elections is risky business, yet it's one of America's favorite political games. So, if you like numbers, let's play. Otherwise, move directly to chapter 11, which tells women about the work we must do to defeat Reagan — hard, serious work, though if we can get a little fun out of it along the way, all the better.

Carol Casey, a political scientist, has constructed three electoral models of what *could* happen on Tuesday, November 6, 1984, all based on an overall 3.2 percent increase in voter turnout as compared with 1980. In these models, women's registration would increase by a conservative 2.5 percent (compared with our 3 percent goal) and their turnout rate on Election Day would be up by 4.1 percent, to 63.5 percent. Male registration would increase by 2.3 percent and voting turnout would increase by 2.3 percent, up to 61.4 percent.

Model 1 projects the Democratic presidential candidate defeating Ronald Reagan by 5.8 points, with a gender gap of 10.7 percent. It assumes that there will be a strong pro-women's rights Democratic candidate who will generate enough interest to boost registration and turnout by women and minorities, and also pull a solid vote from white male Democrats. (These models do not take into account votes for minor party presidential nominees, which would probably not change the relative percentages of votes cast for the major party nominees.)

Model 2 projects the Democratic presidential candidate defeating a Republican candidate other than Reagan by a narrower margin of 2.2 points, with a gender gap of 7.4 percent.

Model 3 projects a real squeaker, with a Republican (other than Reagan) running with a woman vice presidential candidate and winning by a mere 1.4 percent, with a gender gap of

4.1 percent. But if Reagan should run and replace George Bush with a woman vice presidential candidate, that gesture in itself would not be enough to compensate for his antiwoman record, and he would probably lose anyway. Any Republican advantage to adding a woman to the ticket would be canceled out if the Democrats did the same. Democratic women would then have no reason to switch to the GOP and there would be no special appeal to cause independent women to vote more heavily Republican.

In all these scenarios, Ronald Reagan is out, one way or another, and the gender gap is decisive in two of the three models. The projections take into account Reagan's solid base of support among white, college-educated men, including young men, in the GOP and independent categories. They are likely to register and turn out in large numbers for Reagan. He also had (as of August 1983) the support of 40 percent of all blue-collar workers, which cuts into the white Democratic male vote the most. That figure, however, is subject to change, depending on economic and employment factors as well as the effectiveness of the AFL-CIO campaign for Democratic candidate Walter Mondale.

Who are the constituencies among the electorate that will probably vote against Reagan and for the Democratic nominee? They include the gender-gap women, traditional loyal Democrats, and, with some overlap, the following groups:

• College-educated women. These tip the balance to the Democratic candidate, particularly among the independents, who register and vote at high rates.

• The poor. They represent 15 percent of the national voting-age population: 12 percent among whites, 35.6 percent among blacks, and 29.9 percent among Hispanics. The unemployed (more than 9 percent nationally) are also prospective Democratic voters, but will probably not vote in large numbers. Only 34.1 percent of the jobless voted in 1982.

• Single heads of households. Although data are not available to allocate them across party lines, it can be expected (based on their responses in public opinion polls) that 58 percent of white female single heads of households will vote Democratic.

• Lower-middle-class and union-member households. In households where annual income is under $20,000 or union members are present, Reagan has registered about 40 percent approval, with women showing less support than men. Union homes gave a 20 percent edge to Democratic candidates in 1982.

• Blacks. The models project a record number of about 10 million black women and men voting, and their votes will be overwhelmingly Democratic. An August 1983 *Newsweek* poll reported that 76 percent of blacks disapprove of Reagan's performance as President, 56 percent think the situation of blacks has deteriorated under his presidency, and only 20 percent — the lowest percentage since the question was first asked in 1969 — think blacks are doing better today than they were five years ago. Reaganomics has given blacks good reason to turn out at the polls in record numbers. According to the Census Bureau (August 1983), the black unemployment rate was double that for whites, black median family income was just 56 percent that of whites'; more than a third of blacks lived below the poverty line, nearly three times the rate for whites; 70 percent of poor black families were headed by women, and 41 percent of all black families were headed by women with no husbands present. Louis Harris has predicted that the black vote will go more than 90 percent against the Republicans. "In 1984," he said, "it is entirely conceivable that the black turnout [rate] will equal that of whites. If it does, it means that Ronald Reagan is going to have to win the non-black vote by ten points or better."

• Hispanics. In 1980 Reagan won the support of about 36 percent of all Spanish-speaking voters, a larger share than a Republican candidate normally receives. His support from Hispanic women was considerably less. In 1984 he may have greater difficulty within the Hispanic community; only Cuban-Americans in Florida — about six percent of the national Hispanic voting-age population — can be reliably counted in the Reagan column. The much larger Hispanic voting bloc — Puerto Ricans and Mexican-Americans, located in the pivotal states of California, Illinois, New Jersey, New York, Texas, and throughout the Southwest — tend to cast 80 percent or more of their votes for Democrats. Public opinion polls show that these Hispanic voters share women's displeasure with Reagan and have also been adversely affected by his policies. A June 1983 CBS/*New York Times* poll found that 35 percent of all Hispanics approve of Reagan, and 75 percent consider their family finances to be worse than or the same as they were a year ago. The poverty rate for Hispanics is 30 percent overall, and 55 percent for families headed by Hispanic women. Republican political operatives admit they need 35 percent of the Hispanic vote to offset their expected losses among black voters.

Past election results and current public opinion polls suggest that other key voting groups would join in the gender-gap coalition to defeat Reagan. Among them are:

• Environmentalists, who oppose the Reagan administration's policies that favor private industry's interests over conservation and the health and safety of the public. According to a Louis Harris survey, 12 percent of all voters are members of environmental organizations, and another 14 percent have contributed to such groups. These voters cut across all political, demographic, and ideological lines, giving the Democratic candidate an edge with women and men who would not otherwise fall into the category of prospective Democratic voters.

• Jews, who account for about 4 to 5 percent of the total vote in a presidential election, are expected to favor the Democratic presidential nominee over Reagan. They represent a key voting bloc (about two-thirds Democratic) in California, Illinois, New Jersey, and New York. About 90 percent register and vote.

• Gays, about 10 percent of the population, are expected to cast two thirds of their votes for the Democratic candidate. A highly organized and motivated constituency, they make up a particularly important voting group in California, New York, and Texas. Not only did the 1980 Democratic Party platform accept sexual preference as a civil right that should be protected legally, but lesbians, many of them single heads of households, professionals, and working women, regard Reagan as especially antagonistic to their lifestyle as well as their economic and social requirements.

• Peace and nuclear freeze activists, who number in the millions, strongly oppose Reagan's military posture in Central America, his huge military build-up, and his cold war rhetoric and policies in arms limitation negotiations with the Soviet Union.

• Independent and liberal voters, who care about many of the above issues, are also expected to vote for Reagan in lower percentages in 1984 than they did in 1980.

All these groups are overlapping rather than discrete entities. All include women. Each varies in registration and turnout rates. But, together, they compose the solid core of the progressive coalition that can defeat Reagan and elect a Democratic President in 1984.

MODEL 1

(Reagan Is Defeated)

	Democratic Vote (in thousands)		Reagan Vote (in thousands)		Total (in thousands)	
Men	22,896	47.1%	25,674	52.9%	48,570	45.8%
Women	33,371	57.8%	24,367	42.2%	57,738	54.2%
	56,267	52.9%	50,041	47.1%	106,308	100.0%

In this projection the gender gap in both the Democratic and Reagan votes is 10.7 percent, and women vote three to two in favor of the Democratic candidate. In the voting-age population of 170 million, 62.4 percent, an increase of 3.2 percent over 1980, cast ballots; 63.5 percent of women vote, a 4.1 percent increase over 1980, and 61.4 percent of men vote, a 2.3 percent rise. (See chart p. 94)

Black women: registration increases by 5 percent, turnout by 7 percent, and they vote 90 percent Democratic.

Black men: registration and turnout both increase by 5 percent, and they also vote 90 percent Democratic.

Hispanic women: registration increases by 3 percent and turnout by 5 percent; they vote 76 percent Democratic.

Hispanic men: registration increases by 3 percent and turnout by 4 percent; they vote 70 percent Democratic.

White Democratic women: registration increases by 3.3 percent and turnout by 4.8 percent; they vote 80 percent Democratic.

White Democratic men: registration increases by 2.7 percent and turnout by 3.2 percent; they vote 74 percent Democratic.

White Republican men: register at the rate of 75 percent with 71.9 percent turnout; they vote 90 percent Republican. (Republicans, owing to their high socioeconomic status, register and vote at high rates.)

White Republican women: 75 percent register and 70.9 percent turnout; they vote 85 percent Republican. (Turnout for Republican women is lower because of their lack of enthusiasm for Reagan and unwillingness to vote for another candidate.)

White independent women: a 3.3 percent increase in registration and a 4.8 percent increase in turnout; they vote 51 percent Republican.

White independent men: a 2.7 percent increase in registration and a 3.2 percent increase in turnout; they vote 55 percent Republican.

This model is based on a narrower gender gap within groups than current public opinion polls show, but on a large national gap because of the higher percentages of women voting. The Democratic winner's plurality is 6,226,000 votes, about 14,313 votes per congressional district, and Reagan loses by 5.8 percent.

To overcome the Democratic candidate's advantage with women, Reagan would need 59.3 percent of the male vote to win. Since minority men are likely to vote according to the model, he would need 65 percent of the white-male vote for reelection.

MODEL 2

(A Republican Other Than Reagan Loses by a Narrower Margin)

	Democratic Vote (in thousands)		Republican Vote (in thousands)		Total (in thousands)	
Men	22,896	47.1%	25,674	52.9%	48,570	45.8%
Women	31,444	54.5%	26,294	45.5%	57,738	54.2%
	54,340	51.1%	51,968	48.9%	106,308	100.0%

In this projection the gender gap in both the Democratic and Republican columns is 7.4 percent. Registration and turnout figures remain the same as in model 1, as does the male vote. The women's vote changes, with the Republicans picking up 3 percent more of white Democratic women's votes, 5 percent more of Republican women's votes, and 4 percent more of Independent women's votes. The Democratic winner's plurality is 2,372,000 votes, just about 5,447 votes per Congressional District, and the Republican loses by 2.2 percent.

MODEL 3

(A Republican Other Than Reagan Runs with Woman
Vice Presidential Candidate and Wins)

	Democratic Vote (in thousands)		Republican Vote (in thousands)		Total (in thousands)	
Men	22,896	47.1%	25,674	52.9%	48,570	45.8%
Women	29,565	51.2%	28,173	48.8%	57,738	54.2%
	52,461	49.3%	53,847	50.7%	106,308	100.0%

In this projection the gender gap is only 4.1 percent, not enough to prevent a Democratic defeat by 1.4 percent. Registration and turnout figures remain the same as in Model 1, as does the male vote. The women's vote changes, with the Republicans picking up 2 percent more votes from blacks, 2 percent more from Hispanics, 6 percent more from white Democrats, 10 percent more from white Republicans, and 7 percent more from white independents.

The winner's plurality is 1,386,000 votes, just 3,186 votes per Congressional District.

The Winning Plan

Life, with all its surprises, often confounds prophecy — the 1984 election outcome can be affected by accidents or illness, international crises, unexpected changes in the economy, fatal campaign errors by either nominee, the Democrats' failure to appeal sufficiently to women voters, or the failure of women themselves to vote in the predicted numbers — but the models and projections given above are carefully calculated, realistic indicators of the decisive power women can demonstrate in the coming elections. The players and scenarios may change, but women as a cohesive, organized political force are here to stay. Now the task is to see that our *potential* power is translated into *actual* power. Election Day 1984, and everything we do until then, will be the test of our strength.

Earlier, I projected the need to register 1,757,000 more women to vote in 1984. This amounts to about 4000 *additional* women in every congressional district of the nation. Individuals in every C.D. and state who are interested in strengthening the electoral clout of women should work in their communities, organizations, and political coalitions to reach or surpass that target goal of newly registered women. Each state will probably have a number of organizations working together to maximize the anti-Reagan vote, and their resources and lists can be used to help pinpoint the potential gender-gap women.

The ten states with the highest number of Electoral College votes are likely to be selected by the presidential campaigns as their prime targets in 1984. Women, too, should concentrate their strongest efforts in these Big Ten states: California (47 Electoral College votes), Florida (21), Illinois (24), Michigan (20), New Jersey (16), New York (36), North Carolina (13), Ohio (23), Pennsylvania (25), Texas (29).

California and Texas are considered to be states that are leaning toward the Republican candidate. New York, Illinois, Pennsylvania, Michigan, New Jersey, Ohio, and Florida are considered toss-ups, states that could go either way. North Carolina is considered leaning toward the Democrats.

Together, these ten states command 254 Electoral College votes, just sixteen votes short of the 270 votes needed to elect a President. If they conduct an effective campaign, the Democrats are believed to be fairly certain of winning Georgia (12), Hawaii (4), Maryland (10), Massachusetts (13), Minnesota (10), Rhode Island (4), West Virginia (6), and the District of Columbia (3), a total of 62 electoral votes. Eight other states considered to be leaning toward the Democrats could provide another 71 electoral votes: Alabama (9), Arkansas (6), Kentucky (9), Louisiana (10), Mississippi (7), South Carolina (8), Tennessee (11), and Wisconsin (11). Realistically, the Republican candidate is expected to carry at least 16 states with 83 electoral votes.

Various winning combinations of state electoral votes can be put together from these figures. Even if the Democratic candidate gets the combined 146 Electoral College votes from the "fairly certain" states and the marginally Democratic states, he will still be 124 Electoral College votes short of victory. This deficit can be made up by carrying at least 4 of the 10 largest states (California, New York, Illinois, and Pennsylvania, for example), for 132 votes. But should California go Republican, the Democrats would need victories in Ohio, Michigan, and New Jersey to offset that one loss.

The women's vote can make the key difference in these states. If we apply our 1.7 million goal to the Big Ten, our task will be to register an additional 7,265 women in each of their congressional districts, ranging from about 95,000 in North Carolina to 327,000 in California.

This is an achievable goal.

Concentration of registration efforts by women in particular states should also be keyed to such factors as the strength of women's organizations and other groups working together there in coalition for the same goal, the existence of interesting state and local political contests that will help pull out a big vote, and other conditions favorable to promoting mass registration campaigns and a large turnout at the polls.

Projecting specific numerical registration targets can facilitate enlistment of new voters and get-out-the-vote efforts. If women's groups in a particular state set a goal of registering 40,000 additional women voters, for example, that number can be allocated among the various congressional districts, and within each C.D., specific goals can be assigned to the smaller election districts. Registering several hundred women on familiar neighborhood turf is a task that is achievable and seems less intimidating than meeting big-number targets. Interest among women can be promoted by having election districts and congressional districts compete with each other to see who can register the highest number of women, with special awards, prizes, or other recognition going to the individual or area that scores the highest.

Not only the presidency and the vice-presidency are at stake. Republicans now control the U.S. Senate by a five-seat margin. Democratic victories in Colorado, Minnesota, and Oregon, where women candidates are likely to be running, coupled with wins in Iowa, New Hampshire, North Carolina, Tennessee, and Texas — races expected to be close — could return the Senate to Democratic control.

How this winning plan can be made to work on the national, state, and local level, assisted by the efforts of individual women, is described in the next chapter.

11

Mobilizing the Majority

THROUGHOUT THIS BOOK, I've presented the evidence to show that women can — and probably will — play a deciding role in the next election. When the women's vote is acknowledged as the crucial factor in determining who wins and who loses elections, women will finally achieve public recognition for their political influence. With it will come an increased opportunity for women to participate as equal partners with men in shaping public policy decisions. That is our ultimate goal, but our success depends on millions of women throughout the country realizing that we, as women, share common interests and attitudes toward issues, that our views *can* become public policy, and that our path to political power begins with the basic steps of assuring that more women register to vote and that they use their votes on Election Day to forward women's interests. Our impact and influence will be more strongly felt if we actively encourage more women — especially those who traditionally do not register and do not vote — to join with us in casting their ballots in 1984 to elect our friends and defeat our foes at every level of government.

According to an August 1983 ABC poll, many unregistered and nonvoting Americans find it inconvenient or difficult to get to registration sites and polling places, don't think there are real differences between the candidates on the issues, and don't believe that their vote will make a difference in an election or in determining what the government will do. We can overcome these logistical and informational problems, expand the women's electorate, and fulfill the potential promise of women's political power if we make women's voter-registration, issue-education, and get-out-the-vote activities a priority for 1984. First, we can make it easy for women to register to vote by signing them up where they work, at their homes, at meetings and events they normally attend, on college campuses, at social service agencies — wherever they congregate. Second, we can educate them about the issues in campaigns, the candidates' positions and voting records, and the importance of their vote, for every vote *does* count and candidates *do* differ in their attitudes toward women's issues. Third, we can help make voting convenient by offering rides to the polls, providing day-care services, and explaining how voting machines work. Each excuse for not voting can be met with an explanation, and every obstacle can be removed from the path to the polling place if we are willing to make a commitment of our time and energy for this purpose.

Getting people to the polls is not a new strategy or a recently discovered, innovative method for winning elections. Political machines before the turn of the century were created specifically for this function, and the reputations of political bosses rose or fell with their ability to deliver votes on Election Day. The women's movement can learn a lot from their techniques. The process is easy to explain — identify your supporters, make sure they are registered, and get them to the polls on Election Day — but more difficult to implement on a precinct-by-precinct, election-district-by-election-district basis throughout the country. What I'm calling for is a "back to basics" approach to achieve women's political power. We are the ones who can organize and mobilize our own constituency most effectively, and this is the best way to do it. Politicians respect political power above all. Once we prove that the women's vote can be decisive as to who will win or lose elections on a regular basis, we will win recognition for our views.

The WOMEN USA Model for Mobilizing the Majority

Soon after the 1980 election, I organized a meeting in Washington of heads of major women's organizations, Congresswomen, and others who had worked to increase women's political participation. I knew that Reagan's ascension to the presidency was a major setback for the women's movement and that American women were destined to become the primary victims if his administration implemented the policies he had advocated. My purpose was to alert women about our danger by publicizing Reagan's intentions and to begin immediately to organize effective opposition to his proposals.

This meeting was also the catalyst for organizing the February 4, 1981, national women's lobby day, organized by WOMEN USA with help from NOW. Thousands of women who belong to all the major organizations representing women, civil rights, labor, peace, and other constituencies convened in Washington, D.C., to voice their reasons for opposing Reagan's budget proposals directly to their senators and representatives. This action led to the formation in 1982 of the Coalition on Women and the Budget, which provided the first detailed analysis of the impact of the President's proposed budget on American women.*

These were important, highly visible, national demonstrations of women's growing political interest, sophistication, and influence, but I still felt that something more was needed to create a closer connection in the minds of women between their votes and their power to influence public policy.

Since the founding of the National Women's Political Caucus, a variety of organizations had come into existence to advance the women's agenda by pursuing all avenues of political activity. We rallied, we lobbied, we trained women candidates

---

*The coalition has continued to provide this vital information on an annual basis, most recently in the form of its eighty-two-page report titled "Inequality of Sacrifice: The Impact of the Reagan Budget on Women," published in March 1983 with the endorsement of fifty-five organizations concerned about women's equity issues.

and raised money for their campaigns. We tracked the voting records of incumbents and assessed the performance on our issues of each administration. We drafted legislation and pushed for its enactment. We fought for the ERA and against those who blocked its ratification. We worked within the political parties and changed their rules to accommodate us and our concerns. We provided information about women's status in society, their changing roles, and current needs. We brought our message to women throughout the country through the news media and to the attention of our elected officials by our personal presence in the White House, in the halls of Congress, and in the state legislatures. All this and more we had done, yet it had not been enough to bring us victory. I believed then, as I do now, that another component was vitally necessary — to build at the grassroots level a self-sustaining voting bloc of women united by our common interests as women with the shared goal of using our votes, not just in a specific campaign, but from election to election. As we had progressed on so many fronts in our battle for women's rights, we had taken a more piecemeal approach, organizing women in particular areas for certain candidates or referenda in selected elections. We had usually worked with registered women who habitually voted. Rarely had we included voter-registration and get-out-the-vote drives as the focus of our efforts. With the limited time and resources at our disposal, we had not concentrated enough on building our political clout by expanding our active electorate. The lessons of the 1980 election were clear. The time was ripe for launching such a project, and WOMEN USA took the initiative.

On September 19 and 20, 1981, I, as president of Women USA, convened a special meeting of key women political leaders and heads of the major women's organizations to explain what our analysis of the women's vote in 1980 had revealed and how our organization was prepared to act on these findings to mobilize women voters.

Well before women's voting patterns had captured public attention or press interest, my colleague Mim Kelber had closely examined for WOMEN USA the election data from the 1980 election to probe the components of the gender-gap phenomenon. She shared her findings at this meeting, pointing out that the gender gap, while it included women who held strong opinions on the ERA, abortion, and other feminist issues, extended well beyond this base to include women from very diverse backgrounds. In our view, the gender gap that had emerged in 1980 was indicative of a long-range trend toward the development of a distinctive, issue-oriented women's voting bloc. We believed this trend could be accelerated and the voting bloc extended if these unifying issues formed the basis for women's voter-registration and get-out-the-vote efforts. Carol Casey presented a report outlining the political situation in each state and suggesting specific target areas and techniques for developing a women's voter program that would produce a similar gender gap in the 1982 elections. Thus, armed with the knowledge provided in the Kelber and Casey reports, the cooperation of other women's organizations, and the indispensable assistance of Frances Lear, WOMEN USA Fund, Inc., under its president, Brownie Ledbetter, began a pilot project in six states with the expressed goals of:

• initiating at the grassroots level new coalitions of women united by common interests, issue concerns, occupation, or neighborhood to conduct women's voter-registration, issue-education, and get-out-the-vote drives;
• enhancing the organizational and leadership skills of these women as individuals and as groups to develop a publicly recognizable women's voting bloc on women's issues;
• bringing more women — especially those in groups with low rates of registration and turnout, such as minorities, single heads of households, and the young — into active electoral participation;
• heightening public awareness of the issue concerns, potential political power, and policy objectives of women.

We targeted California, Iowa, Missouri, Ohio, Oregon, and Texas to ensure a geographical, social, demographic, and economic mix for testing mobilizing strategies with diverse groups of women, and hired indigenous organizers.

Under the guidance of a national field director and after a briefing and training session, the organizers tailored their own programs to the women in their communities. In every instance, we worked on a nonpartisan basis, neither endorsing nor opposing any particular candidate or party. Rather, we sought to inform women about the impact of government decisions, pending legislation, and national issues whose bearing on their daily lives had not yet been articulated. We encouraged them to measure all candidates against their own yardsticks of priorities and to vote according to their conscience — and political consciousness — on Election Day. We stressed the importance of their using their votes as a means to effectively express their policy preferences by choosing to support candidates whose public positions reflected their own personal views. We asked them to join with us in getting more women to register and to vote on Election Day, drawing them into our project as a way of developing their political skills while building up their self-confidence and sense of belonging to a significant cooperative effort for advancing women's goals through political participation.

The experiences of our organizers illustrate the kinds of techniques and innovative ideas that can be used by women's groups to conduct successful registration, issue-education, and get-out-the-vote campaigns, regardless of the community. Each model can be adapted to suit local circumstances and for outreach to diverse types of women.

In four areas in two of our targeted states — Toledo and Columbus, Ohio, and Alameda and Sacramento counties in California — we conducted a preelection survey of potential voters to ascertain women's opinions on a number of current issues. The survey was used as an organizing vehicle to achieve several purposes simultaneously. First, our organizer could begin building a women's vote coalition at the local level by asking women's organizations, issue groups, and professional associations for their input on the questions to be asked and for volunteers to complete the survey. The idea of polling women in the community was very appealing to these groups and they participated willingly because they could appreciate the value to be gained from the results. Second, the actual process of conducting the survey stimulated women's interest in the issues they were questioned about and made them more apt to be attentive to candidates' positions during the campaign. Third, publicizing the results of the survey focused press and public attention on women's issues and the women's vote in the campaigns. In both states, we found that women in communities as diverse as Toledo and Sacramento, Columbus and Berkeley, held similar views on important issues, confirming locally what national opinion polls had already shown and what was to be affirmed in the 1982 election results. The women we interviewed were overwhelmingly in favor of the ERA, the pro-choice position on reproductive rights, a bilateral nuclear freeze, cutbacks in military spending, handgun control, and government funding of jobs, housing, Social Security, and other domestic programs. The California women cited equal pay for work of comparable value as their priority issue.

After the surveys were completed, press conferences to announce the results were held in each community in late October. In each case we received extensive publicity — newspaper, radio, and local television coverage — which underscored our message that women were thinking about the issues and were prepared to vote their convictions at the polls. Candidates in these areas recognized the significance of the surveys and began to take more forceful public positions on the issues we had identified as being most important to the women in their communities.

In their voter-registration drives, all of our organizers used the general themes "A Woman's Vote Counts" and "A Voting Woman Can Make a Difference," keying into specific issues in their areas. In California, for example, economic concerns were highlighted in messages describing the feminization of poverty in America and citing the impact of the Reagan administration's budget cuts on different groups of women to link working women, senior citizens, homemakers, students, and the poor. In Iowa, our organizer found that women's concerns about nuclear war united low-income women, students, and women on Indian reservations, and films like *The Last Epidemic,* about nuclear war, and *Whose Budget Is It Anyway?* were shown to dramatize the importance of using women's votes to express their opinions on these issues.

In Kansas City, Missouri, our organizer developed "A Woman's Agenda for Kansas City," which included the issues of peace, the need for funding shelters for victims of domestic violence, and providing adequate day-care facilities, to link students, working women, and black women in the northeast neighborhoods. In Oregon, the theme "A Woman's Vote Counts" was particularly appropriate, given the fact that a recent state representative candidate won the nomination, after a recount, by just two votes. In Texas, local economic concerns, such as jobs, pay equity, and day care, provided the focus for organizing Hispanic women.

In each state, WOMEN USA's organizers initiated contact with local groups to explain that the project had the time-limited objective of registering more women to vote, organizing them around the basis of their issue concerns, and getting them to the polls on Election Day. Once it was clear that WOMEN USA would provide the expertise and direction necessary for a successful drive, these groups (varying in size from fifteen to forty-five in different areas) participated willingly, contributing volunteers and other resources. The coalitions that WOMEN USA forged at the local level linked groups with diverse memberships and agendas who had not worked together in the past, uniting them around the specific objective of mobilizing the women's vote in 1982 and helping them build a continuing relationship based on trust and shared experiences.

Once the voter-registration drives were completed, the issue-education component of the project intensified. Get-out-the-vote activities began the last weekend in October and continued through Election Day. In California, WOMEN USA spokespersons appeared on radio and television talk shows to discuss the gender-gap issues and stress the importance of a high women's turnout in the election. Public service announcements urging women to vote, created by Frances Lear and recorded by Lena Horne, Loretta Swit, Rita Moreno, Bonnie Franklin, and Jean Stapleton, were aired on local radio stations in all the targeted states. In Texas, our organizer prepared get-out-the-vote materials in Spanish and English, and took the initiative to write, produce, and air a public service ad, asking women to vote, which appeared on local television stations.

Traditional techniques, like mailings and phone calls to newly registered women voters and women contacted through our issue-education activities, were used to stimulate turnout. Our volunteers passed out leaflets and registered women at public transportation sites, on college campuses, outside office buildings, at factory gates, in targeted neighborhoods, at day-care facilities, at cheese lines and social service centers, and at shopping malls, reminding women to vote on the basis of their issues and self-interests. We proved that "A Woman's Vote Counts." In one state legislative district in Iowa, for example, a woman candidate, running against an incumbent representative who opposed the ERA, won by just fifty-two votes after WOMEN USA had registered more than one hundred women in her district alone.

Blacks in Kansas City, Missouri, Hispanics in El Paso, Texas, Native Americans and rural women in Iowa and Oregon, and women of all races and backgrounds in California and Ohio were receptive to our message. A postelection survey commissioned by WOMEN USA Fund and designed, structured, and analyzed by Dr. Barbara Farah of the Russell Sage Foundation and the University of Michigan and Dr. Ethel Klein of Harvard University showed that the women contacted by our pilot project, like women interviewed in 1982 national Election Day exit polls, shared a common policy agenda on gender-gap issues, regardless of their race, geographic background, or socioeconomic status. According to the Farah-Klein report, "In five states, an overwhelming majority of the respondents, ranging between 71 percent and 94 percent, felt that the President's economic policy was hurting most Americans. A similarly high agreement was reached in these same states where women felt any budget adjustments should favor increasing social programs at the expense of lowering military expenditures. More than four out of five of all women surveyed supported a nuclear freeze and approved of the ERA. This pattern held true for women of all races, educational levels, and employment categories."

In an open-ended question that asked respondents to identify the "one issue that was the most important in the election," economic concerns were most often cited, with women listing specific issues like unemployment, taxes, and Social Security, rather than the economy generally. According to Farah and

Klein, these women "were most concerned about getting jobs and keeping them; they were more concerned with the specifics of economic survival than the more broadly defined aspects of economic health that included inflation and interest rates. This emphasis on labor force issues was true for homemakers and working women, women with a college education, and those less educated women in the electorate. Party divisions did not change this overall emphasis on unemployment and jobs."

The women interviewed were also asked to identify "the most important problem facing women today." The survey results showed that women's equality issues were most often cited, while unemployment and jobs ran a consistent second. The basic response pattern held true across state lines and among women of different educational levels, employment status, and party affiliation, with only slight differences among black, Hispanic, and white women. Farah and Klein concluded that these data "suggest that a mobilizing effort organized around the issues of jobs and women's equality would find a receptive and responsive audience among all types of American women."

The survey went on to probe whether women associated specific candidates with issues. Most of the women identified Democratic candidates as being "better able" to deal with the issues women cited as most important to them. Many of those surveyed were Democrats, but independents made similar judgments, and 41 percent of the Republican women in Ohio chose the Democratic gubernatorial candidate as better able to handle problems important to women. In their analysis, Farah and Klein state, "These data suggest that both Democratic and Republican women will ignore their party affiliation and vote for a candidate of another party if they perceive that candidate to be better able to deal with their issues. Thus, mobilizing women to vote on the basis of their issue concerns has as strong, if not stronger, impact as party attachment."

Finally, the survey found that "women's voting decisions in 13 out of 19 electoral contests — from congressional to gubernatorial to other state level contests — were based on women's choice of the candidates who were best able to solve the problems that were most important to women. Party identification for most of the women surveyed was only of secondary impor-

tance in their voter choice." Furthermore, the women interviewed in our survey held positions on each of these issues. The
low percentages of "no opinion" and "don't know" responses
suggested to the analysts that WOMEN USA Fund's organizers "succeeded in getting women to learn and take positions on
women's issues."

The experience of WOMEN USA in our pilot project and the
survey results give guidance — and hope — to women who
want to increase women's registration and turnout as a means
of demonstrating women's political power. The postelection
survey provided independent data to substantiate what our
organizers had reported and the originators of this project believed would be the case. Building on the knowledge gained in
the 1982 pilot project, WOMEN USA Fund has expanded its
efforts for 1984, targeting many more areas and reaching out
to thousands of women who can, by their votes, join in forming
a politically powerful gender-gap coalition.

Coalitions and Collective Efforts

In the summer of 1982 a small group of leaders in the women's
rights movement, academics who have studied the role of
women in politics, and women who now hold or have held
elective office and prominent positions in government, spent a
weekend at Frances Lear's Vermont home, discussing our next
steps for advancing women's role in the political process.

Our original purpose was to discuss the formation of a national women's "think tank" and center at which women writers, philosophers, political pragmatists, and policy experts
could congregate to reflect on and exchange ideas that would
facilitate women's political action. The need still exists, and we
have yet to meet it.

Over the weekend, in welcome isolation from the intrusions
of the outside world, we had frank and far-ranging discussions
that resulted in a number of projects that would increase our
cooperation and communication. As an outgrowth of this meeting, for example, Joyce Miller, the national president of the
Coalition of Labor Union Women, decided to convene the first
meeting of what came to be known officially as the Women's

Roundtable. Leaders of some twenty major women's organizations, including WOMEN USA, met on September 9, 1982, to explore ways of developing a public relations campaign to stimulate the women's vote in 1982. At that time, only a few activist groups, like WOMEN USA, the National Association of Social Workers, and the League of Women Voters, were working in the field on women's voter registration, issue education, and getting out the vote. The roundtable believed it could reinforce these efforts by a media campaign urging women to vote and giving them a sense of purpose and unity with other women who would be casting their ballots around the country. The National Education Association put up the money for billboards carrying the banner, "It's a Man's World — Unless Women Vote." The public service women's vote announcements that WOMEN USA had used extensively in its program were made available without charge to all groups participating in the coalition for distribution through their state and local affiliates for placement on radio and TV stations across the country. Although it is, of course, impossible to measure the impact of our last-minute media campaign in turning out the women's vote in 1982, we naturally like to believe that the roundtable's effort made a contribution.

After the 1982 election, the roundtable set up a national Women's Vote Project specifically to provide technical assistance to participating organizations to help them maximize the impact of any women's voter-registration programs they plan to conduct among their own memberships. The project intends to use the media again in 1984 to stress the need for women to register and vote. The organizations participating in this project — numbering some thirty-eight groups with memberships totaling more than 6 million women — are those with whom WOMEN USA is working at both the national and local levels to provide a focus, direction, and specific plan of action for many organizations whose crowded agendas might otherwise squeeze out women's voter-registration, issue-education, and get-out-the-vote projects.

In addition to WOMEN USA, other women's organizations and groups, which target specific populations that include large numbers of women, are working in different ways to expand the voting electorate. The best known is the League of Women Voters. Since its founding in 1920, the league has been encouraging women to exercise their political rights and responsibilities through many activities. With 1245 local chapters in fifty states, the District of Columbia, Puerto Rico, and the Virgin Islands, the league is the largest and oldest organized women's voter group. In addition to its nonpartisan voter-registration activities, the league engages in legislative lobbying and monitoring, educational efforts to explain to citizens how the government works, and promoting candidate forums, most notably through its sponsorship of the 1976 and 1980 nationally televised debates between the major party presidential candidates. More recently, the league held a Conference on the Women's Vote that brought experts together to discuss the gender gap.

Another activist group that works in the women's vote field is the National Association of Social Workers. In the 1982 election the social workers endorsed candidates and conducted voter-registration campaigns in a total of seven congressional districts in Florida, Connecticut, Iowa, Massachusetts, Ohio, and Pennsylvania. Recruiting their own members as volunteers, they registered twenty thousand low-income and minority-group members — about 62 percent of them women — in public housing projects, poor neighborhoods, unemployment lines, cheese distribution sites, and on college campuses. Unlike WOMEN USA's nonpartisan approach, the social workers followed up on their get-out-the-vote campaign with activities directed at voters who would support the candidates the association had endorsed in these races. Similar efforts in even more states and areas are now under way as more and more of their members have joined in these political activities.

The National Organization for Women is focusing its political activity around the defeat of Ronald Reagan and the drive for passage of the ERA. As in the past, NOW has targeted for defeat incumbent U.S. Senators, Representatives, and state legislators who oppose the ERA and is supporting candidates — many of them women — who are pro-ERA with direct financial contributions and the membership's involvement in their campaigns. It is working for the election of more women at every level, and is encouraging women to seek office.

The National Abortion Rights Action League is intensifying its efforts to organize pro-choice women through meetings at local homes, training the women in political activities while registering them to vote on the spot.

The National Women's Political Caucus is emphasizing female voter registration as an integral component of its overall political strategy designed to move the women's political agenda forward in this election year and is continuing its efforts to elect women candidates.

The American Nurses' Association has identified members who will serve as vote coordinators in more than half the congressional districts around the country. These coordinators are responsible for ensuring that all nurses in their area are registered to vote, know the candidates' positions on the nurses' platform, and actually vote on Election Day.

The Wider Opportunities for Women's Workforce Network, the Displaced Homemakers Network, and the National Coalition Against Domestic Violence have joined together to register women to vote and poll them about their policy preferences at some five hundred service centers throughout the country.

Women's groups are not the only ones involved in voter-contact programs to reach women. For example, Project Vote, a group formed in June 1982 — and on whose board I serve as a result of WOMEN USA's and its joint activities in Ohio during the last election — has targeted low-income voters for extensive nonpartisan voter-registration drives in the industrial states of Illinois, Maryland, and New Jersey and in other areas around the country. By their estimates, more than 27 million Americans live in families whose annual income is less than $10,000, and only one person out of every four poor people actually votes. Project Vote is also seeking out new registrants in unemployment and cheese lines and in other locations where high concentrations of the poor and unregistered are apt to be found.

As the impact of the Reagan budget cuts and economic policies has trickled down to states and individuals, more groups are recognizing the need to enfranchise the powerless in our society. In New York, a broad coalition called the New

York Voter Project is at work, and a human SERVE (Service Employees' Registration, Voting, and Education)Fund also has been established to encourage workers in health and welfare agencies to register the beneficiaries of the social programs they administer. Their New York model has been exported to other states, where college students planning careers in the social services are being recruited as volunteer registrars in poor communities.

Civil rights organizations were conducting voter-registration drives aimed at racial minorities long before most women's groups began to direct their energies to such projects. The Atlanta-based Voter Education Project, the National Association for the Advancement of Colored People, and the Joint Center for Political Studies' Project Big Vote all work to increase blacks' political participation, while the Southwest Voter Education Project and its new midwestern affiliate have been directing similar outreach efforts in Hispanic communities. Their most recent success stories include the 1983 elections of Mayor Harold Washington in Chicago, where 66 percent of all eligible blacks voted, and of Federico Pena in Denver, Colorado, where an estimated 20 percent of the population is Hispanic. These examples give credence to our assertion that every vote counts, and if we mobilize the women's constituency as effectively as blacks and Hispanics have motivated their own, we'll prove again in 1984 that a voting woman can make a difference.

This upsurge in attention to voter-registration campaigns aimed at women in minority and low-income groups — and women compose the majority in these categories — comes partly as a reaction to the Reagan administration's policies, which have the effect, if not the intention, of further disadvantaging people whose position in society was never secure. Long after the Reagan presidency has faded from the scene — and I hope that won't be too long in coming — I expect our efforts to continue and intensify until we have a government that represents what people really want. In the meantime, the Reagan administration serves as a catalyzing force, giving us an even greater incentive for working together in the coming campaign and beyond.

The Women's Presidential Project

The women who had met in Vermont in 1982 continued to get together with other women in Frances Lear's New York apartment through the fall and winter of 1982–1983. As the time passed, our talks centered increasingly on the presidential race. In addition to discussing the possibility of running a woman for the presidency or vice presidency, I also proposed that we put pressure on the announced Democratic presidential candidates to be sure they were prodded along the proper course. We were convinced that raising women's issues to public prominence early in the campaign offered the Democratic Party and its eventual nominee the best chance for defeating Reagan or any Republican who won the nod. In February 1983 we agreed to issue an alarm and elicit answers from the current crop of presidential hopefuls. We drafted a six-page statement, noting that the Reagan administration had "worsened the twin problems of the victimization of women and the feminization of poverty in our nation." We called on the candidates to respond to a series of questions in twelve major issue areas. We included employment and pay equity, the nuclear freeze, the military budget and disarmament, programs for children and families, health, education, foreign policy, reproductive rights, the ERA, minority rights, the environment, and Social Security and related issues to show the breadth of our concerns and the depth of our conviction that these subjects had to be addressed if Democrats were to triumph in 1984. "Whether women turn out, turn off, or turn elsewhere in the political spectrum," we warned, "depends on the choices and programs offered us." We clearly stated our belief that "the majority of women can be attracted to the Democratic Party and its candidates if — and only if — the party demonstrates through immediate action its commitment to the women's issues and concerns outlined in this statement. Otherwise, women may stay home on Election Day or be very selective in deciding where to direct our political energies."

Our Women's Presidential Project statement was released in April 1983; it was signed by 225 women activists from forty-six states, including present and former members of Congress, state officeholders, members of the Democratic National Committee, leaders of women's, civil rights, and labor organizations, academics, writers, artists, and actresses.

We scored our first victory when the candidates took us seriously, as well they should have. We received the kind of detailed responses we had sought — more than forty pages in some instances — and were able to share the candidates' views with women throughout the country. Our statement served as the basis for questioning candidate positions in political forums scattered all across the campaign trail. The candidates began to compete for our support, and in their appearances before the NWPC and NOW conventions submitted to public questioning on issues raised by our project. These events and the women's response to the individual candidates became major news in the press and TV. We know, from inside accounts, that we forced the candidates to take an early and long look at their voting records, campaign strategies, and staffing policies and at the programs they were proposing to attract the women's vote. Our interviews with their campaign staff members and periodic evaluations of the candidates' performances and responses helped to raise their political and public consciousness about the gender-gap issues early in the presidential campaign.

We also paid attention to developments within the Democratic Party, particularly moves that might affect equal division at the 1984 convention. After the 1980 election, the Hunt Commission was established to write the rules for the next convention. Harking back to the good old days of managed conventions, it allotted 561 delegate positions to Democratic governors, members of the U.S. Senate and House, state party chairs and vice chairs, and other elected party officials. It also set aside an additional 303 delegate slots to be filled by the state parties' appointments of local leaders and elected officials. Delegates chosen in these categories do not have to consist of equal numbers of men and women, an indirect way of undermining the equal-division principle. However, the states are required to correct any imbalance between the sexes when they select their at-large delegates. Because Democratic officeholders and party officials are predominantly white males, women and minorities will be forced to compete with one another for the limited number of at-large slots, which may create unnecessary antagonisms.

There was also an attempt to cancel the 1982 Democratic Party midterm issues conference, but it was finally held, at Philadelphia. The Democratic Congresswomen presented the women's Economic Equity package, a floor demonstration in support of the ERA was carefully staged, and the Democratic National Committee staff joined a NOW picket line outside the conference site to show solidarity with the ERA cause.

Clearly, we women must remain very strong in our determination to keep the party reforms we have won. I believe that will happen. One indication that our tactics are working has been the increasing number of women placed in important positions within the party. When Charles Manatt was elected chair of the Democratic National Committee in 1981, Lynn Cutler of Iowa and Polly Baca Barragan of Colorado were elected vice chairs; they have played prominent roles in public and in the day-to-day operations of the committee. Manatt also hired highly qualified women for top staff positions, including Ann Lewis as political director, Angie Martin as director of campaign services, and Dotty Lynch as survey director. Cutler heads the Women's Division, which is encouraging the inclusion of women's views and women leaders in the platform drafting process and formulation of party policy. (Perhaps because she was viewed as being too much of a national figure, Cutler lost a congressional race in 1982, which was unfortunate for Iowa as well as for the women's cause.) Lewis chairs the National Women's Vote '84 Task Force, which will ensure that there is a women's component in every political program offered by the DNC. The task force has commissioned special reports and analyses of the women's vote, held workshops to train state parties in techniques for building women's vote coalitions, and developed model materials to reach women voters.

A leadership conference for Democratic women was held in late 1983 to highlight women's issues and provide a public forum for elected women officials and candidates, and the recently established Democratic Women's Council is seeking to build a new financial network of women contributors. The DNC Women's Caucus continues to press for greater party support of women candidates and promotion of women's issues.

Moving into the 1984 presidential election year, the Democratic and Republican task forces of the National Women's Political Caucus have been gearing up for the nominating conventions. The Democratic task force is distributing information on the delegate selection process to encourage caucus members to run for delegate positions. The Republican task force has drafted a Republican feminist platform, hoping to build delegate support for a women's agenda at the 1984 convention that will include support for the ERA, abortion rights, rigorous enforcement of affirmative action statutes, measures to achieve economic equity for women, and restoration of funding for the maternal and infant nutritional and health care programs that have been undermined by the Reagan administration.

One Woman, One Vote, One Voice, One Volunteer . . .

My emphasis to this point has been on what organizations and women in leadership positions have been doing to advance the women's agenda. While our role is important, our success will be assured only if women — one by one, and in groups of twos and threes and in tens and hundreds — throughout the country join with us, recognizing that our votes will make our voices heard. Now I want to address each woman directly.

Whether you are rich or poor, young or old, white, black, Hispanic, Native American or Asian / Pacific American, working or unemployed, a homemaker or in the marketplace, you have a resource vital to our victory: your vote. If you don't do anything else, make a pledge today to register and vote in 1984. Call your local board of elections right now and find out where, when, and how you can register. If you can't find the number in the phone book, just call City Hall, where someone can refer you to the proper office. You may be able to register by mail. If you can, ask for enough registration forms for other family members or roommates who are not registered either. If you have to send in a written request for a registration form, don't postpone writing that letter. Persuade other members of your household to do the same.

If you have to register in person, put it on your schedule now.

Plan to go during your lunch hour or make it the first stop on your next shopping trip. Ask your unregistered friends or family members to join you. If you don't know for sure whether you're registered — if you've moved recently or haven't voted in a long time — don't leave it to chance. Call the board of elections or drop by in person to confirm that your name is on the voter checklist. Don't wait until the last few days before an election — you may miss the deadline or just let it slip your mind. Take the initiative today, rather than presuming that sometime between now and Election Day someone else will make sure you register to vote.

Registering to vote isn't the only thing you can do. Many avenues of political participation beyond the simple act of voting — vital as that is — are open to you. Let me describe some of them to you, in the hope that they will stimulate your interest in becoming politically active.

When you register to vote you may have the option of joining a political party. In most states, choosing a party, rather than being an independent, permits you to vote in primaries and at party meetings. Your vote can be crucial in a primary. For example, most women candidates must face a primary contest before they can go on to win a general election. Because fewer people vote in primaries than in November, your vote has even more value. If you live in a city or state where one political party usually wins the general election, the vote in the primary is where the real decisions are made. If you want to be part of that decision-making process — and you should want to — be sure to join the political party of your choice when you register to vote.

Your most important party vote this year may be the choice of who will win the presidential nomination. In many states your opportunity to vote will come in a presidential primary. If your state does not have a presidential preference primary, you can participate in the presidential nominating process by going to the party caucus in your precinct, town, or county, depending on where you live. At that meeting you can vote for a presidential candidate and for delegates who will carry that preference forward to higher levels of the process until the national convention delegates are ultimately chosen. Going to the meeting is also an excellent way of getting in touch with the active party members in your community, hearing about candidates for other offices, learning about local issues, and finding out what your party is planning to do in the coming election. It's a good place to bring up your concerns, question your candidates and party leaders, and make your own suggestions about what should be done. For example, if you are concerned about the quality of education in your community, you might raise that issue and find that a member of the school board is present and can provide the information you need. If you think the present board is inadequate, you can find out when and how the board members are elected. You may want to suggest that the party hold a forum on educational issues with school board members or candidates. You may decide that you want to run for the school board yourself and you can begin lining up support for your candidacy at the caucus. Take part and take action. Don't be afraid to speak up, and be sure to take some responsibility for implementing the suggestions you put forward. You'll win respect through your willingness to work.

You may want to consider playing an ongoing role in your party organization. Many people think that parties are run solely by insiders and old-timers, but most local groups are searching for new blood and volunteers who are willing to assume responsibility. As your party precinct chair or committee member, you would have a great deal of flexibility and an opportunity to exercise your creativity and political judgment in building your party organization. You could plan a voter-registration drive, perhaps linking it to a social event, like a picnic or potluck supper, to attract new registrants. You might make a telephone survey of voters in your precinct to find out what issues are on their minds, passing that information along to your party's candidates so they can address those concerns.

You could put a priority on recruiting women candidates for elective and appointive positions that will be opening up, developing your own talent bank of persons to recommend to your party's officeholders. You could form an informal citywide or countywide network with other party officials to coordinate larger-scale projects. You will find little opposition to your ideas as long as you are prepared to take charge and provide a realistic plan for accomplishing your goals. The political process can work for you if you are willing to work in and through it.

If you do not have a strong party preference, you may want to concentrate your energies on a particular issue, organization, or activity that more closely suits your interests. Most problems have a political solution, and most issues have been raised, or need to be, in the political process. Local issues often have national implications. For example, if the lack of day-care facilities is a problem for working women and men in your community, you can take up the issue with your mayor or city council. Like the women in our Kansas City, Missouri, WOMEN USA project, you could build your own coalition around this issue, start a petition drive to bring it to the attention of your local officials, and organize a call-in campaign to local radio stations and a write-in campaign to your local newspaper editors to get media attention and support for your position. Contact business executives, labor leaders, school personnel, and church officials to assess the facilities that might be available to meet community needs. Plan a community survey to determine how many people in what specific areas of the city need day-care arrangements for their children. With publicity, a plan of action, and public support, you have a good chance of accomplishing your goal.

The day-care issue goes beyond the local level. Raise your sights and talk to state legislators from your community to find out if any legislation is pending or whether they would be willing to sponsor a day-care bill for the whole state. Contact the governor's office and your state commission on the status of women to interest them in your cause. Your Senators and Representative in Congress should also be urged to support national legislation on this issue. In an election year, question all candidates for public office on the day-care issue and get commitments to take action from them.

Whether your issue is day care, ending pollution, providing shelters for victims of domestic violence, or furthering the cause of world peace, you can begin to have an impact by using these strategies to achieve your goals at the local level. If you take the initiative, you just might be successful.

If you have multifaceted interests, you may want to join an organization concerned with many issues. (See directory in Appendix.)

Write letters expressing your views to your elected officials. Attend political meetings and question your candidates. Think about running for office yourself or becoming involved in another candidate's campaign. If you don't choose to run, mobilize support for another candidate — female or male — whom you regard as an advocate of your issues. Talk with the candidate. Offer to hold a coffee hour, organize a door-to-door canvass, distribute campaign literature at your office or in your neighborhood, or make phone calls from your home. There are thousands of campaign jobs to be done. Match your skills with the candidate's need to maximize the effectiveness of your contribution to winning this election.

Whatever you choose to do this year, be sure, at a minimum, to register and vote. Plan your own political agenda today, whether it be meeting the simple goal of getting ten of your friends and family members to vote or joining in an issue or candidate's campaign.

These are just a few ideas for becoming more active and effective in the political process. Remember, if we want equal rights, we must take equal responsibility for making sure the government works for all of us. Right now, you may feel that you don't have the time to get deeply involved, but think about your priorities. Try to squeeze out a few hours a week or a month — whatever you can spare — to help improve our society for yourself and all of us. Be part of that process. Contribute your ideas, energies, time, and money, or whatever you can, to the women's movement for mobilizing the majority.

12

"The Bella Abzug Agenda"

BY THE FALL of 1983, White House officials had concluded that the gender gap was not just Ronald Reagan's problem but largely a Republican Party problem, according to a September 19 story in the *Washington Post.*

An unidentified senior White House adviser attributed the gap to intransigent opposition to all Republican candidates from "the Jewish, the black, and radical women." Another unidentified White House official was quoted as saying, "These women are talking ERA, but they are really committed to more social spending, cutting defense spending, making concessions to the Soviets in the arms talks. It's exactly contrary to the Reagan philosophy. It's contrary to the Republican philosophy . . . I call it the Bella Abzug agenda. It's the liberal agenda."

That is how White House conservatives define liberalism in 1984, a word that, with my name attached, is supposed to make voters gasp in horror. In fact, the so-called Bella Abzug agenda is the agenda of a majority of American women, and the word *liberal* doesn't scare them or me. Why should it?

Here's one dictionary's definition of that nasty word: "Favorable to progress or reform, as in religious or political affairs; of or pertaining to representational forms of government rather than aristocracies and monarchies . . . favorable or in accord with concepts of maximum individual freedom possible, especially; as guaranteed by law and secured by governmental protection of civil liberties; favoring or permitting freedom of action, esp. with respect to matters of personal belief or expression; characterized by generosity and willingness to give in large amounts; . . . of, pertaining to, or befitting a freeman."

Another dictionary defines *liberal* this way: "Free from narrow prejudice; open-minded . . . open to the reception of new ideas or proposals of reform; favorable to changes and reforms tending in the direction of democracy."

I'll buy those, with one addition: add to *befitting a freeman* the words *and a freewoman.*

Reagan Republicans, abetted by conservative Democrats, identify liberals with allegedly lavish and wasteful spending on social programs which, not by coincidence, affect women, children, minorities, the elderly, the poor, and the sick. What do all these groups have in common? Until recently, they have been considered to be politically powerless. When choices have to be made — and that is what government is about, choices and priorities — the powerless lose out.

In its first year in office, the Reagan administration set the tone by proposing $11 billion in cuts in disease-prevention programs for children and women and life-line support programs for needy families. Congress "compromised" by enacting $9 billion in cuts. The same alliance liberally authorized $750 billion in tax cuts that benefit corporations and upper-income Americans the most. For the military industrial power bloc, the liberality of the White House and Congress is unbounded, and that has been true since World War II, under Republican *and* Democratic administrations.

One audit showed that the Pentagon pays $17.95 for a three-inch steel bolt whose list price is sixty-seven cents. Why not, when the Reagan administration has successfully pushed its plan to give the Pentagon $2 trillion over a seven-year period for the largest arms build-up in peacetime history?

In a passionate speech about our nation's priorities, Marian

Wright Edelman, head of the Children's Defense Fund, noted that the President was proposing to spend $28 million *an hour* on the Pentagon, while "the House Democratic leadership wants to spend only $27 million an hour, and they are being labeled soft on defense." Then she described some of the choices we can make.

If we gave up just one hour's worth of that increase in military spending, we could pay for nineteen thousand free school lunches for a year; a day's worth would provide almost a half million children free school lunches for a year.

If we built one less of the planned 226 MX missiles that cost $110 million each, and are militarily unnecessary, we could use the money saved to eliminate poverty in one hundred and one thousand female-headed households a year.

If we passed up spending $100 million a year on a hundred military bands, we could put that money into teaching two hundred thousand educationally deprived children to read and write and provide work for more teachers.

The choices are endless. Less money for the arms race, which a majority of American women and men say they want halted, could mean more money for jobs, housing, public transportation, health, rebuilding our nation's infrastructure, cleaning up our polluted air and water, and helping to meet the needs of women and the poor.

Through the phenomenon of the gender gap, American women are telling our male rulers that they are making the wrong choices. It is a message meant not only for the present occupants of the White House and the Congress, but for both major parties and all those who hope to lead this nation in the years to come.

I have reported the results of electoral and public opinion polls that show the state of mind of a majority of American women. But I didn't need the polls to tell me how many women feel. For the past decade or more, I have traveled to all parts of our country, speaking to women of every kind, in groups and individually, and listening to them. What I have been hearing is an instinctive outcry against social injustice, against discrimination based on sex or race, against leaders who speak of peace, but reflexively plan for war. There is a sense among these women that something is deeply wrong and lopsided in our country. Some worry about themselves and their families, others have a larger sense of community and issues, and almost all fear for the fate of the earth in this nuclear age.

Although much of what I have written here has been directed at Reagan Republicanism, the Democratic Party, too, must share the responsibility for the state of our nation. It has allowed the boundaries of national debate to move to the right, while millions of Americans who provide the base of support for the Democrats are moving in the other direction. Its leaders and policies have lagged far behind what large numbers of the American people are ready to support, and time after time, Democratic leaders and far too many of its members of Congress show a collapse of courage when the key votes come — whether on budget cuts in social programs, funding the MX missile, upholding the rights of women and minorities, flagrantly unfair tax benefits, or authorizing the President to keep our marines in Lebanon for eighteen months. They are more ready to compromise with Reagan Republicanism than to mobilize their constituencies, except during rhetoric time in election campaigns. Yet, for all the limitations and frustrations of working in it, the Democratic Party remains the major vehicle of reform politics and continues to attract the elements of the old New Deal coalition as well as a majority of the new political women and minority activists. Some women's rights advocates will continue to work in the Republican Party, but for most of us the Democratic Party is our arena of action.

As I indicated earlier, the organized women's movement has won some important victories in party politics, but these have been largely internal victories, a way of getting women's strength recognized and respected. This is only the first move in the developing political maturation of the women's movement. The gender-gap woman, in all her phases and aspects, represents a huge constituency in search of effective leadership. That must come from an independent, highly organized, well-financed women's political force with its own political platform, leaders, goals, and priorities. With that independent base, it can operate in coalition with other groups inside and outside the

Democratic Party, exert pressure on the Republicans, and command the attention and influence our numbers merit.

A rainbow coalition, as Jesse Jackson calls it, borrowing from our rainbow of women theme at the Houston National Women's Conference, could work together as a powerful, continuing bloc, organizing people around its priorities, picking and promoting the candidacies of both women and men, targeting elections, and involving more people in the early stages of the electoral process. This is the democratic approach we must take, stressing participation, pressure, and leadership at every level, not just sitting back and waiting for candidates to be thrust on us every two or four years.

Our women's political movement has so far underestimated our strength. That failure is a legacy of the past and of traditions that have taught women to speak softly and carry a lipstick, rather than to assert our needs and make demands. The movement, hampered by fear of being considered strident or imitation males if we speak up, has struggled so hard to get so little. Our tactics have too often been marked by timidity and self-deprecation; few women put themselves forward as candidates, and even while discussing possible women candidates for the vice presidency, most women leaders feel that only superwomen can be proposed as leaders of our country. We still act as though we have to work twice as hard as men and be three times as smart and competent just to qualify for consideration.

Women are still regarded by many male politicians and the media as a special-interest group, as if we were peanut or chicken-feed lobbyists. That description makes me angry. Let us remember who we are.

We are a majority of this nation. From its founding, we have worked in its fields, homes, shops, and factories. We have borne and raised its generations. We have nursed the sick and cared for the old; we have taught the children. We have cooked, cleaned, done all the household chores, and worked without pay as family chauffeurs, seamstresses, laundresses, hostesses, and all-purpose nurturers. We have given millions of hours in volunteer work to countless organizations and institutions that provide human services. We have served in the armed forces and given our lives for our country. We have paid taxes and created wealth by our labor. We have enriched our national culture and been the most public-minded citizens and do-gooders. We have done all this in the face of discrimination and wage exploitation, yet when we sought to get a guarantee of equal rights into our Constitution, the men who hold effective power would not give it to us.

As in other nations, the United States, throughout its history, has been marked by conflict between classes and social groups, between male rule and female subordination, between those who would reserve power only for a moneyed elite and those who say democracy must be shared by all the people. Today, those of us who place humane, predominantly female values and democratic rights in the foreground are being attacked by Reagan Republicans for offering what they ridicule as "old ideas." But eating every day, having work, shelter, clothing, education, and health care are ideas that will never go out of style, no matter how much heads of corporations hope that robots will replace human beings and that women will meekly continue to accept lower wages and inferior status.

So, without shame or apology, I say that the Bella Abzug agenda calls for equal rights and opportunities for women and minorities, full employment, a national health-care system, preservation of Social Security, a national housing program, federally subsidized child-care centers, government planning to revitalize industry and develop new technologies with full participation by the people who labor in them, welfare programs for those who are unable to work and for their children; tax reform; restoration of Medicaid funding for abortion; a clean, safe environment in our neighborhoods and workplaces; decent public transportation, and much more. And if anyone wants to know where the money will come from, it will come from the benefits of full employment, reforming the tax structure, and cutting the Pentagon budget, with the serendipitous side effect of enhancing the prospects for peace.

Those prospects will really improve only when there is a united effort by the United States and the Soviet Union to return to a policy of détente. As strongly as most Americans disapprove of the Soviet government and its denial of democratic rights to its citizens, it is dangerously simplistic, as former diplomat George Kennan has pointed out, to adopt Ronald Reagan's "evil empire" cartoon view of the Russians and to blame them for every incident around the world in which oppressed people rebel against their own governments. It is shameful that American foreign policy almost invariably aligns our military and economic power with the interests of repressive right-wing regimes; it is foolish to promote cold war confrontations and a costly, futile nuclear competition with the Soviet Union instead of trying to defuse the arms race and expand trade, scientific, cultural, and educational exchanges with the Soviet bloc. These are the essential ingredients of a watchful but peaceable policy of détente, which is the only sane alternative to our present perilous course.

Women who believe in some or all of the Bella Abzug agenda can help work for it by joining the large numbers of women who are waking up to their potential power. In the last years of the ERA campaign, women began to realize that pressure from the outside was not enough. They recognized what I have been preaching for years: we had to get into big-league politics, make demands on the parties, and use our strength to change the outcomes of elections and the composition of legislatures.

That is what is happening now. The gender-gap vote is evidence of the growing political awareness and experience of American women. The more active we become, the better it will be for society as a whole. I am not claiming that women's political power is a magic cure for what ails our nation and the rest of the world. First, winning political power is a long process that will continue into the indefinite future. Second, international economic problems are too severe, the contrasts between rich and poor nations too sharp, the momentum of conflict and the possibility of a nuclear holocaust too threatening for any of us to pretend that simply by getting more women to be politically active, we are going to save the earth. Much more is urgently required, with men and women acting together to stop the madness of the arms race.

The gender gap is not an unresolvable war between the sexes and it may very well reflect the different ways in which men and women have been acculturated. According to all national polls, men support our quest for equality on the more narrowly defined women's issues but seem much less willing to examine critically the premises of society and governmental decisions in the same way that women are unafraid to do.

As long as male voters continue to accept and defend the status quo, there will continue to be a gender gap. That voting and opinion gap does not reflect the views of all women, but its breadth and depth is unquestionable, and it will continue to grow until the majority views of women prevail. I believe that eventually the different thinking of women will register in the consciousness of men as well, and then the gap will narrow. I look forward to that day.

In the meantime, participating in politics, registering, and voting are the minimum that we can do. It is an opportunity that millions of women and men in many other nations do not have. Some have died for this basic democratic right. You don't have to die for it. You just have to walk into a voting booth in your neighborhood and pull the lever.

That is only the first and easiest step toward making possible our dream of equality for women in a more peaceful world. Today, in our vaunted democracy, we have government that does not represent us and that actually works against policies favored by a majority of Americans. We women must get used to thinking of ourselves as a mighty multitude, with important allies among men and underrepresented groups. Although women are a majority of that coalition-in-the-making, we are not even now being recognized as such. We can change that. We can learn to become political leaders and activists, or we can sit back and let a minority of men in government, backed by powerful money and military interests, run our country and try to run the whole world.

It's up to us.

Appendix

Directory of Organizations Active in Gender-Gap Politics

For more information on how to become involved in pursuing women's equality and peace goals through the political process, write to WOMEN USA Fund, 11 Hanover Square, New York, NY 10005 (telephone: 212-422-1492).

Other Organizations

American Association of University Women
2401 Virginia Avenue, N.W.
Washington, DC 20037
202-785-7711

The AAUW is a membership organization open to all women with college degrees. Its goal is to advance the status of women, especially in the fields of education and employment, and to eliminate sex discrimination. It has adopted a specific legislative program, including support for ERA ratification, and is lobbying for its enactment.

American Nurses' Association
1101 14th Street, N.W.
Washington, DC 20005
202-789-1800

The ANA is a membership organization for nurses concerned about increasing access to health care, improved education and training programs for nurses, women's economic equality, and other issues. Its national Political Action Committee expected to spend $250,000 in 1984 in support of candidates for the U.S. Senate and House of Representatives — many of them women — who support nurses' concerns. It also is registering nurses to vote.

Asian/Pacific Women's Network
c/o Irene Hirano
6720 Sherbourne Drive
Los Angeles, CA 90056
213-295-6571

The network seeks to promote the involvement of Asian-American women in all aspects of national life.

B'nai B'rith Women
1640 Rhode Island Avenue, N.W.
Washington, DC 20036
202-857-6655

This national organization of Jewish women works in Washington and locally on women's issues and cooperates with other major women's groups.

Center for the American Woman and Politics
Eagleton Institute of Politics
Rutgers University
New Brunswick, NJ 08901
201-932-9384

The center conducts research, holds conferences, and provides public information about women's political participation and tracks the numbers and activities of women in public office.

Center for Women Policy Studies
2000 P Street, N.W., Suite 508
Washington, DC 20036
202-872-1770

The center was established to educate the public and policy makers about the need for changes in the legal and economic status of women. Persons associated with the center testify before congressional committees and government agencies on many issues related to sex discrimination.

Children's Defense Fund
122 C Street, N.W.
Washington, DC 20001
202-628-8787

The fund is involved in research, public education, litigation, drafting legislation, and other activities intended to promote and protect children's rights in public policy.

Church Women United
475 Riverside Drive
New York, NY 10015
212-870-2347

This group seeks to promote world peace and the attainment of women's rights through active participation in the electoral process.

Comision Feminil Mexicana Nacional
379 S. Loma Drive
Los Angeles, CA 90017
213-484-1515

The comission is an advocacy group that was formed to promote the rights of Mexican women.

Coalition of Labor Union Women
15 Union Square
New York, NY 10003
212-242-0700

CLUW works to promote equal job opportunities for women, affirmative action in the workplace, and greater involvement of union women in the political and legislative process.

Congressional Black Caucus
344 House Annex
Washington, DC 20515
202-226-7790

The caucus seeks to promote the interests of black Americans through the legislative process, working to advance full employment, education, health care, welfare reform, and other issues of particular concern to minorities.

Congressional Caucus for Women's Issues
2471 Rayburn Building
Washington, DC 20515
202-225-6740

The caucus works to promote women's issues through the legislative process, especially in areas concerning women's equality.

Congressional Hispanic Caucus
557 House Annex
Washington, DC 20515
202-226-3430

The caucus works to promote the interests of Hispanics, including civil rights, employment programs, immigration policy, and other matters, through the legislative process.

Displaced Homemakers Network
1531 Pennsylvania Avenue, S.E.
Washington, DC 20003
202-547-6606

The network provides technical assistance and public information about programs and services available to displaced homemakers and serves as an advocacy group for their concerns.

Federally Employed Women
481 National Press Building
Washington, DC 20045
202-638-4404

This organization represents women employed by the U.S. government, working on sex equity issues and greater employment opportunities for women.

Girls Clubs of America
1725 K Street, N.W.
Washington, DC 20006
202-659-0516

The Girls Clubs, serving more than 200,000 girls between the ages of 6 and 18 years of age at 250 centers throughout the country, are seeking to promote women's equality issues and greater participation in voting by young women.

Gray Panthers
3635 Chestnut Street
Philadelphia, PA 19104
215-382-3300

The group, open to women and men, works to combat discrimination based on age wherever it occurs.

Indian Rights Association
1505 Race Street
Philadelphia, PA 19102
215-563-8349

The association seeks to promote and protect the legal and human rights of Native Americans of both sexes.

League of United Latin American Citizens
400 First Street, N.W., Suite 716
Washington, DC 20001
202-628-8516

Through voter-registration programs and other methods, LULAC's goal is to heighten the political awareness and participation of Latin Americans.

League of Women Voters
1730 M Street, N.W.
Washington, DC 20006
202-429-1965

The league is a nonpartisan organization designed to promote political responsibility and active, informed political participation by all citizens. The league conducts voter-registration drives, initiates candidate forums, sponsors the presidential debates, and lobbies on such issues as ERA ratification, equal access to education and employment, world peace, and environmental protection.

Mexican-American Women's National Association
1201 16th Street, N.W., Suite 420
Washington, DC 20036
202-223-3440

The association promotes the leadership role of Chicanas in professional, family, and community organizations, participates in legislative hearings as spokespersons for Chicanas, and engages in public education activities.

National Abortion Rights Action League
1424 K Street, N.W.
Washington, DC 20005
202-347-7774

NARAL engages in direct political action, organizing and training women who support the pro-choice position on reproductive rights. It directly supports, through financial contributions and campaign services, candidates identified as pro-choice, represents the pro-choice position in legislative hearings, and educates the public.

National Association for the Advancement of Colored People
1025 Vermont Avenue, N.W., Suite 820
Washington, DC 20005
202-628-2269

Committed to the achievement of equal rights and the elimination of racial prejudice and discrimination in all aspects of American life, the NAACP is conducting a massive voter-registration drive in 1984 to stimulate minority registration and voting in the next election.

National Association of Asian-American Women
12 Beekman Place
New York, NY 10022

This group holds meetings and organizes and represents the interests of Asian-American women.

National Association of Social Workers
7981 Eastern Avenue
Silver Spring, MD 20910
301-565-0333

This professional membership organization engages in partisan activities, including the endorsement of, and making political contributions to, candidates who support its human services platform. NASW is conducting voter-registration drives, primarily aimed at low-income persons, in 20 states. The association has published a 40-page pamphlet entitled *Power at the Polls,* which provides a "how to" guide for beginning a voter-registration program.

National Board YWCA of the USA
135 West 50th Street
New York, NY 10020
212-621-5234

The YWCA has adopted a legislative action agenda that includes the goals of eliminating racism and promoting peace, economic equality, and social justice. In addition to its programs of counseling, providing technical assistance, and sponsoring educational activities for young women, it is also involved in promoting voter registration and political participation by its constituency.

National Coalition of 100 Black Women
60 East 86th Street
New York, NY 10028
212-560-2840

This leadership group of nationally active black women seeks to promote the political involvement of other black women at the local, state, and national levels.

National Commission on Working Women
2000 P Street, N.W., Suite 508
Washington, DC 20036
202-872-1782

This nonmembership group, composed of individuals and representatives of business, labor, the media, and education, seeks to focus public and government attention on the needs of working women, especially those concentrated in low-paying and low-status jobs.

National Council of Jewish Women
15 East 26th Street
New York, NY 10010
212-532-1740

This group seeks to promote the civil liberties and equal rights of all American women through public education and social activism.

National Conference of Puerto Rican Women
927 15th Street, N.W., Suite 910
Washington, DC 20005
202-522-3360

The conference works to achieve the equal rights of Puerto Rican and other Hispanic women, educates and orients Puerto Rican women about their rights, and stimulates their political participation.

National Congress of Neighborhood Women
249 Manhattan Avenue
Brooklyn, NY 11211
212-388-6666

The congress lobbies before Congress and government agencies for programs that address the needs of working-class and poor women, organizes community groups of low- and moderate-income women, and provides technical and financial support for community programs designed to benefit these constituencies.

National Council of Negro Women
815 Second Avenue
New York, NY 10017
212-687-5870

A coalition of 27 national organizations representing more than 4 million members, the council seeks to develop the leadership skills of women in black communities.

National Education Association
1201 16th Street, N.W.
Washington, DC 20036
202-833-4000

A professional membership association of educators, the NEA engages in direct political activities, including the endorsement of and financial support for candidates who support its action plan for better education, sex equity, and other issues.

National Federation of Business and Professional Women's
   Clubs, Inc.
2012 Massachusetts Avenue N.W.
Washington, DC 20036
202-293-1100

A membership organization for working women, the BPW seeks to promote the interests of and opportunities for women in employment, advocates legislative changes to secure the equal rights of women in all areas, and works through its regional and local affiliates to encourage greater political participation by its members.

National Gay Task Force
80 Fifth Avenue
New York, NY 10011
212-741-5800

The task force lobbies for the enactment of legislation to secure the civil rights of gays, engages in public education and political activities to end discrimination based on sexual orientation, and encourages gays to become more politically active and effective in the electoral arena.

National Organization for Women
425 13th Street, N.W.
Washington, DC 20004
202-347-2279

NOW participates in political, legislative, and public educational activities designed to promote women's equality. For 1984, it has set specific goals of defeating President Reagan, doubling the number of women serving in Congress, and providing direct financial and other forms of support to women candidates. It will be lobbying for passage of the Equal Rights Amendment in Congress and by the state legislatures.

National Urban League
500 East 62nd Street
New York, NY 10021
212-310-9000

As part of its program to end racial segregation and discrimination, the league is conducting non-partisan voter-registration drives in black communities to stimulate greater political participation.

National Women's Conference Committee
6717 Loring Court
Bethesda, MD 20817
301-365-0339

This national women's network, formed to promote the implementation of the National Plan of Action adopted by the 1977 National Women's Conference in Houston, works to secure the legal, economic, and social changes necessary to ensure women's equality.

National Women's Education Fund
1410 Q Street, N.W.
Washington, DC 20009
202-462-8606

This nonpartisan resource organization provides training, technical assistance, and public information programs for the purpose of increasing the numbers and influence of women in public life.

National Women's Political Caucus
1411 K Street, N.W.
Washington, DC 20005
202-347-4456

Committed to the goal of achieving an equal voice and role for women in the political process, this multipartisan organization has developed a Win with Women 1984 campaign designed to boost the number of women serving in state legislative positions across the country. Through its Republican and Democratic task forces, the NWPC is focusing on the election of caucus women as delegates to the major party national conventions.

Network: A Catholic Social Justice Lobby
806 Rhode Island Avenue N.E.
Washington, DC 20018
202-526-4070

The network lobbies on behalf of the poor and powerless on a variety of economic and social issues, including ERA adoption, equal employment opportunities, and world peace.

New York Human SERVE Fund
622 West 113th Street
New York, NY 10025
212-280-4053

Students and persons employed in the social services are conducting a nonpartisan voter-registration program, enrolling low-income persons at social service agencies, welfare centers, unemployment lines, day-care facilities, settlement houses, family planning clinics, and other sites in the New York metropolitan area.

9 to 5 — National Association of Working Women
1224 Huron Road
Cleveland, OH 44115
216-566-9308

A national membership organization with local chapters, 9 to 5 provides public information on the status of working women, engages in lobbying and political activities to promote the interests of working women, and develops the political skills and participation of its members.

North American Indian Women's Association
1420 Mt. Paran Road, N.W.
Atlanta, GA 30327

The association seeks to improve the health, education, and social status of Indian women through the development of programs that focus on their needs.

Older Women's League
1325 G Street, N.W.
Washington, DC 20005
202-783-6686

A membership organization with 73 local chapters, the league is an advocacy group for promoting quality in health care, Social Security, pensions, and other programs for older women.

Operation Big Vote
Joint Center for Political Studies
1001 Pennsylvania Avenue N.W., Suite 400
Washington, DC 20004
202-626-3552

The center provides technical assistance and other support services for voter-registration programs in black communities and collects data on black political participation and voting patterns.

Peace Links
723½ 8th Street, S.E.
Washington, DC 20003
202-544-0805

Founded by Betty Bumpers, wife of Senator Dale Bumpers of Arkansas, Peace Links sends members from its national Peace Panel to PTA meetings, church groups, garden clubs, and other nonpolitical organizations to brief women on the issues of nuclear war, the arms race, and alternative proposals for peace. The organization stresses extensive networking at the local level. Among its volunteer speakers are 40 congressional and gubernatorial wives.

Planned Parenthood Federation of America
810 Seventh Avenue
New York, NY 10019
212-541-7800

In cooperation with other groups and individuals concerned with protecting and expanding social service programs, the federation is engaging in voter-registration drives at family planning centers and other locations where social services are provided.

Project Vote
1200 15th Street, N.W., Suite 201
Washington, DC 20005
202-299-3933

This informal coalition of labor, civil rights, women's, church, environmental, and community groups conducts nonpartisan voter-registration programs aimed at recruiting low-income, unemployed, and minority-group political participation.

Rural American Women, Inc.
1522 K Street, N.W., Suite 700
Washington, DC 20005
202-785-4700

The organization seeks to promote public knowledge about the contribution of rural American women to our society, and to promote their interests in the public policy arena.

Southern Christian Leadership Conference
334 Auburn Avenue, S.E.
Atlanta, GA 30312
404-522-1420

A nonpartisan organization committed to the general goal of ending racial discrimination in America, the SCLC is conducting voter-registration and citizen-education programs in black communities located primarily in the 16 southern and border states.

Southwest Voter Registration Education Project
201 N. St. Mary's Street, Suite 501
San Antonio, TX 78205
512-222-0224

The project conducts nonpartisan voter-registration and education programs in selected Hispanic communities in the Southwest, and compiles data on Hispanic political participation.

Voter Education Project
52 Fairlie Street, N.W.
Atlanta, GA 30303
404-522-7495

The project is conducting voter-registration drives among blacks in the 11 southern states, develops citizen-education programs to stimulate black voter turnout, maintains liaison with black elected officials, and conducts election studies on black political participation.

Voters for Choice
2000 P Street, N.W., Suite 236
Washington, DC 20036
202-659-2550

This nonpartisan Political Action Committee has the goal of electing pro-choice legislators to Congress and provides financial support to candidates who defend a woman's right to abortion.

Women's Action for Nuclear Disarmament
691 Massachusetts Avenue
Arlington, MA 02174
617-643-4880

WAND was founded in 1980 by Dr. Helen Caldicott, a pediatrician and leader of the antinuclear movement. It provides educational material, sponsors meetings and forums, and has a congressional PAC that mobilizes women to work for the election of peace candidates and the defeat of those who favor continuation of the arms race.

Women's Campaign Fund
1725 I Street, N.W.
Washington, DC 20009
202-296-5346

The fund promotes and supports the election of progressive women to office at the national, state, and local levels. It provides direct financial contributions, campaign services, and other forms of assistance to women candidates.

Women's Equity Action League
805 15th Street, N.W., Suite 822
Washington, DC 20005
202-638-1961

WEAL engages in research, public education, litigation, and legislative activity to secure women's legal and economic rights.

Women's International League for Peace and Freedom,
    U.S. Section
1213 Race Street
Philadelphia, PA 19107
215-563-7110

Founded by Jane Addams after World War I, WILPF has chapters in 26 countries. Its U.S. section works for disarmament and women's issues, provides educational resources, holds meetings, and sponsors public campaigns, such as its Stop the Arms Race (STAR) campaign. Its publications include analyses of the economic impact of military spending on women.

Women's Legal Defense Fund
2000 P Street, N.W.
Washington, DC 20036
202-887-0364

The fund engages in education and public information activities and provides volunteer legal representatives to promote women's rights in employment, education, and other areas through court action.

Women's Research and Education Institute
204 4th Street, S.E.
Washington, DC 20003
202-546-1093

The institute, the research arm of the Congressional Caucus for Women's Issues, provides public information and technical assistance for the development of women's rights legislation and other programs, and monitors the impact of legislation designed to enhance women's rights and roles.

Women Strike for Peace
145 South 13th Street
Philadelphia, PA 19107
215-923-0861

WSP started in 1961, when 100,000 women came together to protest the resumption of nuclear testing by the Soviet Union and the United States. The group, among the leaders in the anti–nuclear arms race and disarmament movements, was also involved in the campaign to end the war in Vietnam. Its Washington office monitors White House and congressional activities on war and peace issues, and its branches in major cities conduct petition campaigns, lobby, and perform other activities in behalf of peace.

Women's Vote Project
1410 Q Street N.W.
Washington, D.C. 20009
202-462-8606

This coalition of about forty women's organizations is working to provide technical assistance for women's voter registration and get-out-the-vote drives and plans to conduct a national media campaign on the importance of women registering and voting.